Decoding WALL STREET

Contents

Dedication

To Kunarig Claire Powell, who never discouraged me from pursuing my dreams and aspirations, who never set limits on my imagination, who always believed in me and led me to believe in myself.

—Bob Powell

Preface

It's fun to have fun, but you have to know how.
—Dr. Suess,
The Cat in the Hat

The date isn't clear, but it was sometime in the fall of 2000 when Dave Caruso called Bob Powell to ask about co-authoring a book that would explain the terms and concepts of Wall Street in plain and sometimes funny English.

Bob said, for better or worse, "Sure, I'd be happy to." After all, he had been a financial journalist working in a variety of mediums (media), including print, radio, television, and the Internet, since the early 1980s. But Bob had never written a book. His journalist and other friends had always asked him, "When are you going to write a book?" Well, like most writers, he thought he had one in him but could never find the right topic. So, when Dave called, well, Bob got intrigued. And thus he found himself without a social life for the next several months, turning down the opportunities to go to parties and spend time with friends to sit instead in front of a computer monitor and a qwerty keyboard.

Almost everyone to a person said they couldn't wait to read such a book (and they were serious). Most, if not all, people, including long-time and seemingly sophisticated friends and family, expressed a desire to learn, not complicated asset allocation strategies nor the five best mutual funds to buy right now, but simply the terms and concepts of Wall Street and how it all works. They wanted to read a book that would speak to them in a language that was not condescending and definitely not academic.

And it was they who we thought about as we labored over the table of contents, the chapters, and, ultimately, the words. First, we thought, our friends and family need to understand the economy and basic economic principles. After all, much of what goes on today in the stock markets and supermarkets, on Wall Street and Main Street, is affected by what goes on in the economy. Then, our friends and family need to understand the major types of investments, stock, bonds, and money markets, as well as the places where those investments get bought and sold. And then our friends and family also need to understand the companies behind those investments, the investment bankers that create securities, the analysts who tell people what to buy and sell, and the investment management firms that buy and sell those securities.

Our friends and family also need to understand the investment that made investing what it is today—mutual funds. And they need to understand the entire supporting Wall Street cast—the new media and Internet sites that spread the investment word, as well as the federal and other agencies that make sure the right words get spread.

Finally, we always thought that a book that helped someone better understand Wall Street, but not help them apply their new-found knowledge, was a bit like kissing a poster of Bo Derek (more on that later). It's a kiss, but it's not the real deal. So, we decided to include a few chapters that would help people become better investors, not in the traditional personal finance how-to book fashion, but in keeping with the tone and tenor and bass and alto of this book.

So that's our story. Call it a labor of love, a labor of hate. Call it like you see it. We tried to and we hope you enjoy two guys' effort to help you, our family and our friends understand that fleece is a fabric used to keep people warm in the winter and not something that happens to unsuspecting investors.

Acknowledgments (Dave Caruso)

With my 40-plus years on this earth there are a whole lot of people that I should thank, but not all of them had anything to do with financial planner and currently a senior vice-president at a major Wall Street firm. His practice is in Manchester-by-the-Sea, just north of Boston. He is a frequent guest for financial matters on MSNBC, CNN Money, Bloomberg, Fox News, New England Cable News, and is called upon for answers to financial questions by publications as diverse as *Medical Economics, Parenting,* the *Boston Globe,* the *Boston Herald* and a number of local newspapers and radio stations throughout the USA. He is the co-author of the personal finance guide *Let's Talk Money.* He is also the Financial Editor of WBZ Radio and a financial analyst for WBZ-TV in Boston. Dave has been married to his wife Diane for 17 years and has two children, Alex and Laura.

Robert J. Powell, III (Bob) is the president of E_3, a Boston-based communication company. Bob is a former investment adviser and a financial journalist with more than 20 years of experience in the financial services industry, serving in a wide variety of roles with a wide number of publications and investment firms. He is currently serving as executive producer of *Make Me Rich,* a new personal finance public television series co-produced with Connecticut Public Television and Radio. He is also a strategic planning consultant for Acadient, Inc. a Boston-based distance learning company serving the financial services industry. Bob was also instrumental in the launch of the Mutual Fund Industry Specialist℠ Certificate Program.

Postscript

We wrote this book before the tragic attack by terrorists on the United States of America on September 11, 2001. And it goes to press in the wake of that sad and unimaginable event. Clearly that attack has affected the financial markets profoundly. As we write this, it's clear that these are not the "nowhere but up" times that the '90s were. Many people are deeply affected by the downturn the stock market is taking as this book finds its way to bookstores. Still, the concepts in this book remain valid.

Since the attack, we want to note that Wall Street and Main Street are likely to change in ways that no one could have predicted or anticipated. Products will change, firms will change, and there will be new concepts emerging. But even so, this book will still give you the grounding you need to understand these changes.

We intentionally wrote this book in a light hearted, tongue-in-cheek fashion. But in this post-attack era America is entering, we certainly understand that Wall Street's and Main Street's sense of humor may be forever changed, and that some people might be slightly put off by our style. To them we say, we meant no harm. We hope, rather, that this makes the reading go a little easier and that you accept it in the spirit in which it is offered, to help our readers figure out what Wall Street is all about and how it affects our lives.

—Dave Caruso and Bob Powell
September 26, 2001

1

The Essence of Wall Street

There's a place on this earth called Wall Street. It's a street like most streets in America. It's got sidewalks and streetlamps, people walking to and fro, and drivers honking their horns. Unlike most streets in America, however, it's a street that represents the financial hopes and dreams of millions of people who are saving for college or retirement. And, unlike most streets in America, it's a street that has become larger than life.

Yes, just say the words "Wall Street" and watch people's reactions: love, hate, fear, greed, and—of course—hope. But the most common reaction by far, at least for average Americans, is confusion.

Wall Street is a place that simply confounds most people. Few people know how it works. Few people know how those who work there make money and lose money there. Most important, and most unfortunate, even fewer still know how they can make money there and avoid losing money.

Why All the Confusion?

Why are most people so confused about Wall Street? We believe there are two reasons. One, the history of Wall Street, which developed a language as it developed a financial world and a unique culture. And two, the people who invest and advise on Wall Street. They're in it for a profit. You can understand that it's not exactly in the best interests of the sellers of stock to inform the buyers why they're getting rid of it. So, before you dip your toes into the water, it's a pretty good idea to know what's down there.

First the history. Wall Street traces its name back to 1653, when it was a place of defense, not commerce. Dutch settlers, seeking to protect themselves from attacks by the British and Native Americans, built a 12-foot stockade fence on what is today the hub of financial activity for the world. The wall was down by 1685, when the British laid out a street in its place and called it Wall Street.

Now, the real wall is gone, but a figurative wall remains, one that prevents "intrusions" by harmless and mostly unarmed investors who merely want to understand the terms and language of Wall Street, so that they too can enjoy some of the riches available on Wall Street. Today we have a verbal wall of numbers and wacky jargon that requires decoding.

Yes, Wall Street—as represented by the people, the brokerage firms, and the financial media, among others—has created a language that has made it virtually inaccessible to the average investor who's just trying to turn his or her 401(k) molehill into a modest mountain. Sadly, it's become hard for the average investor to talk the talk and walk the walk of Wall Street. Terms like "short squeeze," "triple witching hour," and "M1," "M2," and "MTV" (whoops! I mean "M3") are enough to stop all but the most brazen and foolhardy from scaling the "wall." (We'll tackle some of those terms later in the book.)

Through the three centuries since the stockade wall became two stock exchanges and a world of its own, Wall Street has created its own special jargon so that the people who eat, sleep, and breathe the markets—whether stocks, bonds, or commodities—can communicate with each other. But, to be fair, in this respect Wall Street is not unlike most industries.

Take the medical profession as an example. Doctors and pharmacists refer to the number of times a patient should take medicine as "bid," "tid," and "qid." Huh? Well, those are abbreviations for Latin terms that mean twice a day *(bis in die)*, three times a day (*ter in die*), and four times a day (*quater in die*), respectively. And "qid" is not to be confused with "qd" or "qod," which mean every day (*quaque die*) and every other day (*quaque* other *die,* although Latin purists would insist on "qad," for *quaque altera die*). Talk about an obscure language to communicate key concepts!

Anyway, the problem as we see it is that investors have been forced to deal with the lingo of Wall Street professionals, which is a bit much for most people. While it may be OK for us not to understand the language of an architect to live in our houses or the vocabulary of a mechanic to drive our cars, we think it's pretty vital for Americans who need to save and invest to understand the products and services offered by Wall Street firms, in terms Americans can understand, not the terms of some managing director of corporate finance. Unfortunately, Wall Street doesn't come with an owner's manual—at least not until now.

What You're Reading

Decoding Wall Street is a book that will explain in plain—and, we hope, at times funny—English the terms used by the people who work on Wall Street.

We'll explain in Chapter 2 some basic economic concepts that are mentioned on the nightly news, such as **leading economic indicators**, **consumer confidence**, and **inflation**. Then, in Chapters 3 and 4, we'll discuss **equities** (more commonly called **stocks**) and **fixed-income securities** (more commonly called **bonds**). In Chapters 5 and 6 we'll provide some insight into what we believe is America's most popular, but least understood investment of all, established by the 1940 Investment Company Act—the **mutual fund**. In Chapter 7, we'll take a glimpse at those Wall Street institutions called the **New York Stock Exchange**, the **American Stock Exchange**, and the **Nasdaq**, where people buy **stocks**, **bonds**, and **options**.

But wait, there's more! The people who create and buy and sell stocks and bonds work for companies in what is broadly called the **financial services industry**—**brokerage firms**, **insurance companies**, **mutual fund firms**, and **banks**. We'll explain the differences and similarities among those types of companies in Chapter 8.

In Chapter 9, we'll help you navigate the process by which a company goes public. No, that's not the process by which a company comes out of the closet. "Going public" refers to what has become a household term in America—the **IPO (initial public offering)**. It's the process by which a company raises money by working with an investment banker to sell pieces of the company to people hoping to make money, too. (Of course, desire and reality can be miles apart. A doorman at a Boston hotel told Bob about the stock he'd bought on a tip, a pharmaceutical company that was expecting to get the OK from the Food and Drug Administration to start selling its new drug. The approval didn't come and the stock went into the toilet—a technical term used on Wall Street, meaning **capital loss**.)

There's a lot of excitement and glamour in selling new securities, but most of the action on Wall Street is to persuade people—investors big and small—to keep on buying and selling securities. It has to keep generating **transactions**. To make sure this happens, Wall Street has created something called a **research department**. Once the investment banker sells a new stock to someone, the research department—the "sell side" analyst—has to follow the stock and issue reports that advise people whether to sell the stock, buy more of it, or just keep holding on to it. In Chapter 10, we'll tell you about those documents that are commonly and collectively called **research reports**.

The people who read those reports, the people who buy and sell securities from Wall Street, run the gamut from that hotel doorman to multi-gazillion dollar investment firms. Because money talks and big money shouts, it's those multi-gazillion dollar investment firms that control what happens in the market. But who are those people? In Chapter 11, we'll look at the big mutual fund firms and the big pension plans (the firms that manage lots of money on behalf of us working slugs).

Wall Street moneymakers, if left to their own devices and avarice, would certainly pick clean a chicken, if given the opportunity. Fortunately, there are some watchdogs on Wall Street that are looking out for your best interests. In Chapter 12 we'll talk a bit about the press, those news and information organizations that—

like us—are trying to help investors make sense of Wall Street. And in Chapter 13, we'll address some of the federal, state, and other regulatory and enforcement agencies and organizations that are trying to protect and educate investors.

More and more people are today investing on their own, often via their computer, transmitting buy and sell orders over a modem, reading research reports on the Web, and—sadly—often losing money—sometimes lots of it. We'll talk about investing online in Chapter 14.

Now, this book is intended to help you better understand the terms and language of Wall Street. If you learn how to be a better investor, well, that's a great bonus. Then, we added Chapters 15 and 16.

Chapter 15 starts by revealing some investment myths that Wall Street and others would have you believe. Then, it goes beyond, to discuss the importance of being earnest and planning. And we'll talk about taking care of your things and about personal issues, including the virtues of patience and faith. And then finally, in Chapter 16, we'll talk about all the paper and paperwork associated with Wall Street and the importance of keeping good records, should you decide to join the investing crowd once you read this book.

Start Big and Basic

So, with Chapter 2, we start with the big picture. We believe it's important to know some basic economic principles, the elements of a business cycle, the factors that influence inflation and deflation, for starters. It's important to know the difference between **federal fiscal policy** and **monetary policy**. Why? Because these things influence stock prices and understanding them can help you determine when to buy and when to sell.

On any given day (such as when we're writing this book in spring and summer 2001), you're likely to read a story such as the following:

> *Concerned about the gross domestic product, after two major and conflicting economic reports, the Fed is considering lowering interest rates to counter a potential recession.*

There! How's that for Wall Street Speak (WSS)? What the heck is "gross domestic product"? And what's "the Fed"? And what's a "recession"? You've probably heard and read those words, but do you really understand how the gross domestic product, the Fed, and a recession influence what happens to you and your investments? Well, they're just a few of the WSS terms that we'll decode in this book, terms that you should understand in order to make the most out of your money.

Nice segue, David.

Thanks! I couldn't have done it better myself, Bob.

2 Your Economy

Any book worth its salt about Wall Street requires a primer on economics—or what some call "the dismal science." We have our reasons as to why it's called dismal, but first, we're obliged to provide you with this disclaimer. Some people spend a lot of time studying the economy in order to make investment decisions. Those folks are often referred to on Wall Street as **top-down** or **macro** analysts. Others worry less about the big picture and more about the details, a specific company's management and new product line. These folks are referred to as **bottom-up** analysts. We tend to be in the latter camp, along with our hero Peter Lynch. Lynch summed up our feelings about studying the economy when he said, "If you spend 14 minutes a year on the economy, you've probably wasted 12."

So, let's not waste time. Let's spend a little of it as wisely as possible on the economy.

What's Happening?

Everyone—from accountants to zookeepers—are participants in and observers of the economy. Everybody is always trying to get a handle on whether the economy is growing or falling. Think of it this way: Bob's mother-in-law is inclined to look at the thermometer, the barometer, and the sky, as well as watch The Weather Channel before traveling north to visit her daughter and grandchildren (and Bob). Well, buyers and sellers of stocks and bonds and other types of securities look at their economic equivalent of weather instruments to get a sense of whether the economy is hot or cold or will become hot or cold. Economists—who are a lot like meteorologists since they have to forecast the future and need only be right half the time to keep their jobs—are also checking the instruments, hundreds upon hundreds, thousands upon thousands of data points, government reports, and other minutiae. And the more you know about these instruments, the better informed you'll be—as an investor or just as a cocktail party host.

The Business Cycle

The big thing to remember is this thing called the **business cycle**. The business cycle is a reflection of the economy. In essence there are four phases to the cycle:

1. **Expansion.** The economy, as measured by the gross domestic product (more on that in a second), is growing. Consumers are spending and companies are building and selling lots of stuff.
2. **Peak.** The economy is topping off.
3. **Recession.** The economy is heading south. Consumers are postponing purchases of durable goods—stuff that lasts a long time.
4. **Trough.** We've hit rock bottom.

Business cycles are a constant in life, like death, taxes, and in-law problems. Each cycle has a predictable pattern. Up and down, up and down ....

But no two cycles are the same: no one can predict the amplitude (top and bottom) and duration (length) of each business cycle. That's why economists try to figure out what's going to happen, a pursuit keeps some of those dismal scientists gainfully employed and others looking for work. (By the way, there are some experts who subscribe to the broken clock theory. Just as a broken clock that shows the same time 24/7 is correct twice a day, an economist who makes the same prediction over and over is bound to be right sometimes.)

Now as we write this book, lots of people are watching two figures:

1. **Gross domestic product (GDP).** The GDP measures the economy's overall growth. If it grows too fast, the demand for goods and services can be greater than the supply. This causes prices to rise, raising the fear of inflation. If the GDP is flat or declines, it may indicate a period of sluggish economic activity, maybe even a recession. Of note: consumer spending today represents about two-thirds of our GDP. (We'll talk more about this in a bit.)
2. **Unemployment rate.** The Bureau of Labor Statistics of the U.S. Department of Labor (not to be confused with the Misuse of Muggle Artifacts Office in the Ministry of Magic of Harry Potter fame) conducts a monthly sample survey of 60,000 representative (whatever that means!) households to measure the rate of unemployment in the U.S. As of this writing (July 2001), the unemployment rate had risen to 4.5%, up from a low of 3.9% in October 2000. That's a sign of potential bad times ahead.

In general, there are two main types of price changes associated with the phases of the business cycle:

1. **Inflation.** Put simply, inflation is the steady rise of the prices for the goods and services that we buy. People on Wall Street refer to inflation as "too much money chasing too few goods and services." In other words, there's more demand than supply. That naturally makes prices go up. Inflation usually occurs during periods of expansion and high employment: when times are good, people have money and spend it. (We'll talk more about inflation in a bit.)
2. **Deflation.** This is the opposite of inflation: it's the steady fall of prices for goods and services. This happens when supply is greater than demand. That imbalance tends to make prices go down. Deflation usually occurs during recessions or when unemployment is rising.

Economic Indicators

With all the economic figures floating around out there, let's focus on the economic version of Charles Dickens' *Christmas Carol*. The three ghosts who visit Ebenezer Scrooge as Christmas Past, Christmas Present, and Christmas Future become known, in our story of the economic strategists, as the **lagging** indicators, the **coincident** indicators, and the **leading** indicators. These indices represent what's happened, what's happening now, and—most important—what we think will happen:

- **Lagging indicators:** measurable economic factors that change after the economy has already begun to follow a particular pattern or trend
- **Coincident indicators:** measurable economic factors that vary directly and simultaneously with the business cycle, thus indicating the current state of the economy
- **Leading indicators:** measurable economic factors that change before the economy starts a pattern or trend, used to predict changes in the economy

Lagging Indicators

No one—save a game show host—cares much about the lagging indicators. They're history. Although they might be a nice subject for reflection with a glass of brandy on a cold winter night in a paneled den, as those dismal scientists reflect on the good old economic days, they do nothing to line Scrooge's coffer or put a turkey on the Cratchit table. Sure, the past can give us some sense of the future as history tends to repeat itself, yet I assure you that Wall Street traders are not putting any of their long weekends into getting the data on this stuff.

There are seven lagging indicators here, playing the ghost who tells you whether you've had a wonderful day or been run over by a train.

1. **Average duration of unemployment:** how long John and Joan Doe have been "between jobs"
2. **Inventories to sales ratio, manufacturing and trade:** what's sitting on the shelves and what's going out the door

3. **Labor cost per unit of output:** the cost of making a product, usually a "widget" (whatever a widget may be)
4. **Average prime rate:** the interest rate charged to the highest-quality creditor (which the average consumer will never be)
5. **Commercial and industrial loans:** how much money businesses have borrowed from banks and not yet paid back
6. **Consumer installment credit to personal income ratio:** the relationship between the balance on our charge cards and the figures on our paychecks
7. **Change in consumer price index for services:** rates of change in the services that we use

Coincident Indicators

Coincident indicators are the little ghosts of the here and now that keep our economic Scrooges awake. There are only four of these guys who are the news of the hour:

1. **Employees on nonagricultural payrolls:** whether full-time or part-time, permanent or temporary, all workers not involved in farming
2. **Personal income less transfer payments:** how much we're earning, minus retirement and disability insurance benefit payments, medical payments, income maintenance benefit payments, unemployment insurance benefit payments, veterans' benefit payments, and other such payments
3. **Industrial production:** how much stuff we're making in the factories
4. **Manufacturing and trade sales:** how much we're selling of the stuff we make

Leading Indicators

Here's the crystal ball, the ghosts that play Christmas Future: the leading economic indicators (LEI). Wall Streeters will wait for the LEI and see the world flash before their eyes as it comes rolling off the government press release. It's what Wall Street economists get paid to do, to try and figure out tomorrow's economic temperature so that other analysts in specific stocks and industries can get a better take on how to make money (or at least avoid losing any) as the cyclical economic world moves by.

There are 10 jewels in this grouping:

1. **Average weekly hours, manufacturing:** how much time people are putting into cranking out those widgets
   Employers usually adjust work hours before hiring or laying off workers. So, according to Charles R. Nelson, author of *The Investor's Guide to Economic Indicators,* hours should rise or fall ahead of major moves in the economy.

2. **Average weekly initial claims for unemployment insurance:** how many people went from little pink slips to small checks
   This number, released weekly, is based on the claims filed at state unemployment offices. If the number rises, it means more people have been laid off or are having trouble finding a job. Some believe this number rises prior to the start of a certifiable recession.

3. **Manufacturers' new orders, consumer goods and materials:** the demands for stuff that we buy as individuals
   The volume of new orders received by manufacturers should give a clue about production in the months ahead. More orders, better economy. Fewer orders, worse economy. Unfortunately, stuff happens and orders can be cancelled, which is why economists don't depend solely on this indicator.

4. **Manufacturers' new orders, non-defense capital goods:** the demand for stuff that organizations buy with their capital expenditures, like equipment, machinery, engines, trains, boats, planes, and so on
   Like manufacturers' orders for consumer goods, this number can help Wall Streeters predict whether production will rise or fall in the future.

5. **Vendor performance component of the National Association of Purchasing Management index:** how fast manufacturers get what they need from suppliers
   Delivery time reflects the strength of demand. When deliveries are slow, it indicates that demand is brisk and orders are

backlogged, the sign of a strong economy. When deliveries become faster, it indicates that demand is weak, a signal that the economy is cooling off.

6. **Building permits, new private housing units:** a measure of our belief in the old saying, "As construction goes, so does the economy"
   If permits for new housing rise, we're likely headed for good economic times. Not only is a house a big investment, but people tend to buy lots of stuff to furnish their new homes.

7. **Stock prices, 500 common stocks:** the Standard and Poor 500 index, which is just Wall Street's bet on where the economy is headed
   Many economists believe the stock market leads the economy by some six to nine months, since investors tend to buy stocks based not on past performance, but on future performance. That's why they call it investing and not gambling. So, if companies are expected to earn more money, then stock prices rise and the economy will improve. If companies are expected to lose money or grow profits more slowly, then stock prices fall and so the economy declines.

8. **Money supply:** known affectionately as "M2," the value of cash, most bank accounts and CDs, travelers' checks, and money market funds
   Wall Streeters watch the money supply and how fast it's growing to predict inflation. The faster the growth, the more likely inflation. The slower the growth, the more likely a recession.

9. **Interest rate spread:** the difference between rates for longer-term bonds (10-year Treasury bonds) and rates for short-term bonds (federal funds), often called the **yield curve**, which is how the bond market is betting on the economy
   Usually, the spread is around 2 to 3 percentage points or what Wall Streeters call 200 to 300 **basis points**. If the spread grows larger, it means that Wall Streeters are expecting inflation and long-term interest rates to rise. If it grows smaller, Wall Streeters are expecting inflation and interest rates to fall.

10. **Index of consumer expectations:** what we're thinking and feeling or expecting to do, not actually doing, as determined by a monthly survey by the University of Michigan
    This indicator gives Wall Streeters a sense of consumer spending plans for the next half year.

Index of Leading Economic Indicators

The U.S. Index of Leading Economic Indicators, which is released on the first few business days of the month by The Conference Board, a non-profit, non-advocacy research firm, is a composite of those 10 economic statistics. The index is constructed as a weighted average of the indicators, designed to predict economic conditions in the near term.

All things considered, the index has been a fairly good predictor of recessions; it has successfully predicted, for instance, each of the eight recessions that have occurred since 1950. Unfortunately, it often gives false signals and the lead time between a turn in the index and the economy can vary greatly, which makes predictions more difficult. That's why the financial markets don't pay as much attention to the index as they do to the various components.

Now before we talk more about the indicators that comprise the index, let's talk more about the index in general.

The way the index works is simple. If the index declines for three consecutive months, that's a sign that the economy will fall into a recession, which it almost did in the early part of 2001. If the index rises, that means the economy is growing.

If history can be our guide, the index typically grows at about the same rate as the overall economy (the GDP) or 3%. If it grows faster, that's a signal for rapid growth. If it grows slower, that's a signal for a sluggish economy. Now, if you look at the various components and then look at the whole, things should fall in place. Many of these indicators—such as contracts and orders for plants (not green but involving lots of green) and equipment, permits for new houses, new business incorporations, and new orders—will typically rise prior to the actual event. So, if many of these indicators rise, it's likely that the economy will follow.

How Do You Feel? The Consumer Confidence Index

The most important economic indicator, according to Brian Nottage, a senior economist with www.economy.com, the parent organization of *The Dismal Scientist,* is **consumer confidence.**

The Consumer Confidence Index (CCI), released monthly by The Conference Board, measures how optimistic or pessimistic consumers are about the economy in the near future, based on a survey of consumer attitudes on business conditions, jobs, family income, and spending plans. The survey uses a representative sample of 5,000 U.S. households, of which some 3,500 typically respond to questions about the following:

1. current business conditions
2. expectations regarding business conditions six months from the time of the survey
3. current employment conditions
4. expectations regarding employment conditions six months from the times of the survey
5. expectations regarding total family income six months from the time of the survey.

Respondents indicate whether they feel positively, negatively, or neutral. The Conference Board divides the number of positive answers by the sum of the positive and negative responses and comes up with a benchmark number, which was set at 100 in 1985. During good times, the number has ranged between 120 and 130. As of this writing (June 2001), consumer confidence was at 117.9. OK. Why does the CCI matter? The thinking behind the CCI is simple. If consumers are optimistic, they'll tend to purchase more goods and services, which means an increase in spending that will stimulate the whole economy. On the other hand, if consumers are neutral or pessimistic, they'll probably spend less and the economy will go stagnant or decline.

So, confidence, both consumer and business (economists measure business confidence, too), is viewed—along with inflation and productivity—as one of the most important indicators of the

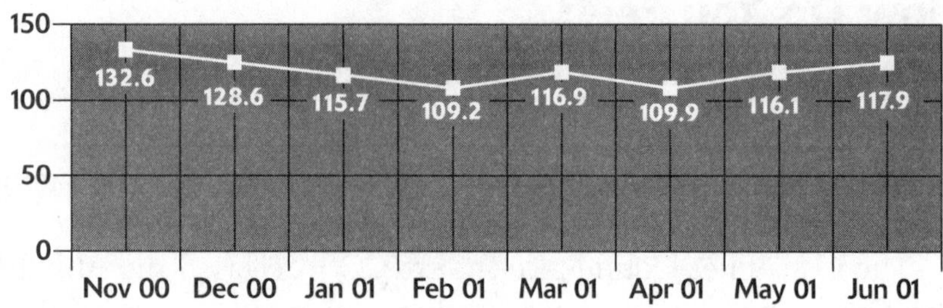

Figure 2-1. Consumer confidence

direction of the U.S. economy. Economists can use the number to forecast the direction of the economy several months ahead—and now so can you!

Inflation and the Consumer Price Index

Besides the leading economic indicators, the second most important bit of economic data, at least according to Nottage, a senior economist with www.economy.com, is inflation, measured by the Consumer Price Index. The CPI, which is released monthly by the Bureau of Labor Statistics, reveals how fast the prices of goods and services purchased by people like you are rising or falling—historically, a rise of about 3% a year. The CPI tracks prices of such items as food, clothing, housing, transportation, energy, health care, and entertainment. Most Wall Street types, however, prefer to look at the **core CPI**, which is the CPI excluding food and energy. The prices of the other types of goods and services rise or fall more steadily than food and energy prices, which are subject to spikes that skew the index, so Wall Streeters consider core consumer prices a far better indicator of inflation (see Figure 2-2).

But the CPI is more than just a reflection of current economic conditions. It's important because it's used to adjust Social Security payments and cost of living increases in pensions and wages. That's why in areas of the U.S. where lots of retired people live, more of them read the business section of the local newspaper when the CPI is released than the obituaries.

Consumer Price Index (Seasonally Adjusted)							% Change	
	Jun 01	May 01	Apr 01	Mar 01	Feb 01	Jan 01	Mn Ago	Yr Ago
All Items	177.9	177.5	176.8	176.3	176.2	175.7	0.2	3.3
Except								
Food	186.3	185.7	185.5	185.1	184.7	184.1	0.3	2.8
Health Care	272.7	271.7	270.9	269.8	268.8	267.4	0.4	4.6
Energy	136.5	137.8	133.7	134.1	134.1	134.4	-0.9	8.5
Gasoline, Unleaded Regular	135.8	139.8	131.7	124.9	130.5	129.4	-2.9	1.9

Figure 2-2. The CPI and changes from month to month

Supply and Demand—The Law of the Land

So what else is important to understand? Well, let's look at supply and demand and all else should fall into place.

As we said earlier, the best measure of our economic health, of the goods and services we're producing and buying is the gross domestic product (GDP). The GDP is the official measure of the total production (supply) and consumption (demand) of goods and services in the U.S. It's made up of personal consumption, government spending, and gross investment, otherwise known as **capital formation** (the money businesses spend to buy machinery and plants and to produce goods to sell), and exports minus imports.

According to *The Dismal Scientist* (www.dismal.com):

> *Total GDP growth of between 2.0% and 2.5% is generally considered to be optimal when the economy is at full employment (unemployment between 5.5% and 6.0%). Higher growth than this leads to accelerating inflation, while lower growth indicates a weak economy.*

If prices rise steadily, that's good for the economy. However, if they rise faster than 3%, that's bad, since most incomes do not grow quickly enough to keep up.

Three components of the personal consumption factor in the GDP equation are most important to watch, because they serve as indicators of the relative health of the economy:

- **durable goods** (stuff that's supposed to last more than three years, like cars and washing machines)

- **nondurable items** (stuff that lasts less than three years, like food and clothing)
- **services** (like your plumber, landscaper, or auto mechanic)

An important element of GDP is **disposable income**. That's what people have left of their incomes to spend or to save after paying their bills, taxes, and other obligations. If disposable income rises, consumption and spending will likely rise, so the economy will grow.

By the way, the best place to get economic data such as disposable income is the Bureau of Economic Analysis (BEA), an agency of the Department of Commerce. The mission of the BEA (www.bea.doc.gov) is "to strengthen the understanding of the U.S. economy and its competitive position by providing the most accurate and relevant GDP and economic accounts data in a timely and cost-effective manner." And nothing is ever in equilibrium. And that's where the government comes into the picture.

The Government

To recap this mega economy, about two-thirds is what we consumers spend every year. The remainder is about evenly split up between government spending and corporate America, with a little sprinkle of imports and exports added in to keep us honest.

There isn't a whole lot anybody can do to control the consumer or corporate portion of our economy, because it's ultimately dictated by supply and demand. It's all about how we feel and what we're in the mood to buy.

On the other hand, the government's job is to fix things when they're broken. The government takes taxes out of our pocket, then spends these tax dollars (or overspends them) on what it thinks is best for the United States in terms of our economy and freedom from our enemies. We call this spending of our taxes **fiscal policy**. This is what the government does to tweak the economy, by either cutting or raising spending and by either cutting or raising taxes. Its unofficial partner in this process of tweaking the economy is the Federal Reserve Bank, through what is called **monetary policy**.

The Fed—as Wall Street calls it—is an independent entity that's supposed to be free from political influence. (Just bear in mind that the members of the system are appointed by the President of the United States and they hang out in Washington, not far from 1600 Pennsylvania Avenue.) It has a long history, going back to 1913 and the Federal Reserve Act.

The Federal Reserve Bank, which is the nation's banker, tries to keep the economy growing steadily at a rate of 2% to 3%. It uses a variety of tools, most of which are far too complicated to explain here. In 25 words or less, the Fed borrows or sells government securities, increases or decreases the money in circulation, and raises or lowers interest rates. The result is either **easy money** or **tight money**.

Of course, not everybody agrees on how to keep the economy strong. A **monetarist** says that the Fed should be calling the shots. (Monetarism advocates control of our money supply to keep it in step with the our ability to produce goods, in order to curb inflation. It also advocates cutting government spending and returning as much of the economy as possible to the private sector. Monetarism was first advocated by the economist Milton Friedman and the Chicago school of economists.) A **Keynesian** thinks that government spending is more important. (The name comes from British economist John Maynard Keynes, who wrote *General Theory of Employment, Interest and Money,* published in 1936.) The federal government plays a major role. It promotes stable prices and full employment through taxation and government spending.

Not Things, but People

In this whirlwind chapter, we've discussed business cycles, lagging and coincident and leading economic indicators, the Consumer Confidence Index, the gross domestic product, the law of supply and demand, the Consumer Price Index, inflation and deflation, the Federal Reserve Bank, and other fundamentals of economics. Whew! But we've tried to keep things simple. There are many concepts and terms used in "the dismal science" that we haven't covered, but now at least you know the essentials. And maybe you understand better the words of Ludwig von Mises, one of the most influential capitalist economists of the 20th century: "Economics is not about things and tangible material objects; it is about men, their meanings and actions." So, let's move on to what David and Bob call "the jovial art"—stocks.

WALL ST

3

Stocks

As a child David tried to play the drums. He realized that by playing the drums he could make a lot of noise (it's hardwired into a boy's genes) and he could imitate some of the sounds in those groovy songs of the '60s just by ear. He figured he had a lock on the Beatles when Ringo Starr retired. All was well until his dad said he had to take music lessons.

Then it became work; he was just figuring out this reading stuff—and the last thing a cool kid needed in his life was to learn to read music as well. He wasn't willing to work hard and thus cast away his drumming stardom. (Bob, by contrast, had no choice once his parents bought the really expensive drum set but to read music. Eventually he had a cameo role—clanging cymbals and tinkling triangles—in the Rhode Island Junior Philharmonic Orchestra.)

As with music, you'll need to learn the basic investment notes if you have designs on decoding Wall Street. The main notes are **stocks**, **bonds**, and **cash**.

Stocks are the sharps of the investing world. They represent the actual ownership of a company, be it IBM (International Business Machines, one of the world's largest technology companies) or QSound Labs (Bob's barber's favorite stock). Stocks are often the foundation of an investor's portfolio. You can hold stocks for however long you like, so they're good for all types of investment objectives." Investors can buy stocks for income, for capital appreciation, or for speculation.

Bonds, meanwhile, are the flats of investing. Bonds represent debt: you're lending money to a company for a specified period of time and the company pays you some interest and, with hope, returns your principal (and we don't mean Sister Mary Elephant) at **maturity**. (That's the date upon which the company or entity that borrowed your money will return it.) It's the same principle as with a certificate of deposit. The only difference is that if you buy a CD, you're lending money to a bank rather than to a corporation, a city or state, or even our friends in Washington. Most of us think of the bank as the lender—if we get down on our knees long enough—but when we buy a CD we reverse the roles.

We'll talk more about bonds in the next chapter.

Now, the price of a stock, which normally reflects a company's profitability, rises and falls by the second. Thus, stocks are viewed as volatile investments. (**Volatility** is the relative rate at which the price of an investment goes up or down.) In return for that risk, however, there's the potential for a greater return than from other investments. As in life, investing comes with a tradeoff: the greater the risk (as in volatility), the greater the potential return.

At this juncture, it's important to note that there are many types of risk associated with investing. Most people think about risk as volatility, but the loss of what Wall Street calls **purchasing power** is an equally important risk you must consider. That's the risk that a dollar won't buy as much tomorrow as it does today. Inflation—rising prices—is the major culprit when it comes to the risk of losing purchase power. In simple terms, it's the risk that the buck you spend to buy a cup of coffee today (maybe not the grande at Starbuck's) will buy you only a half-cup some 10 years hence. Of note, inflation averaged 3.1% from 1926 through 1999, which means $1 in 1926 is now worth about one thin dime.

Inflation is an important aspect of investing. As rule, you want your investments to outperform inflation by about 3% per year over the long term. (If we use the historic rate of inflation of 3%, that suggests that you might want your investment portfolio to rise 6% per year.) Over the short term, however, you may want an investment that provides an adequate return and safety of principal, which is when you get 100% of your money back—$1 in and $1 out.

Bonds happen to be that safer note; they have less risk (as in volatility) and offer you a stated return. Bonds aren't subject to **market risk**, but they're subject to something called **interest rate risk**. That means the price of the bond (or bond fund) you own will fluctuate in value in the opposite direction from interest rates. If interest rates rise, the price of your bond will fall in value. And if interest rates fall, the price of your bond will rise in value. That shouldn't be important, so long as you plan to hold the bond to maturity. It's worth noting that bonds are subject to inflation: the value of the dollar you loan XYZ Company will be worth less when XYZ returns it. The bottom line is this: as with all investments, there are risks associated with investing bonds. It's just a different risk with a different return.

So what's the big takeaway, as Wall Streeters are apt to say? The essence of the markets is this: you can be an owner or a lender and there are different risks and returns associated with those investments.

Now that we've outlined the three major instruments—stocks, bonds, and cash—let's get on to the subject of the chapter, stocks.

Anything but Common

In the vernacular, **common** stocks are anything but. Each and every one, whether it's International Business Machines or QSound Labs, marches to the beat of its own drum. But the common denominator is that if you own a common stock, you own a piece of a corporation.

A **corporation** is one of three ways a business can be formed. (The other two are **sole proprietorship** and **partnership**.) If you walk down Main Street in your home town, you're likely to see all sorts of businesses—the office supply store, the grocery store, the mom-and-pop drug store, and so on. Some of those businesses have been formed as sole proprietorships, which means one person owns them. Some are partnerships, which means they consist of several owners. Some of those businesses on Main Street are corporations.

That means that anybody can become a part owner, just by buying stock. If your local hardware store is a corporation, there's little difference—in structure, at least—between it and Home Depot, the country's largest home improvement retailer and a member of the much-esteemed *Fortune* 500 list.

Each corporation has issued common stock and, in some cases, **preferred** stock. (We'll get to the differences in a moment.) Each offers the owners or stockholders what Wall Street calls **limited liability**. That means if the company goes belly up (not a technical Wall Street term), the stockholders can't lose any more money than they've invested. $1 in, $1 lost. Nothing more. Unlike the owners of sole proprietorships and partnerships, the owners of a corporation are not liable for any debts of the business.

The big differences between your local hardware store and Home Depot relate to the type of stock issued and something called **market capitalization**.

Private and Public

In the case of the local hardware store, the stock is likely **privately** held. That means the owners want you to mind your own business, not theirs. Think of it this way: it's like a private club, not open to outsiders. There's no market where privately held stock can bought and sold and no readily available market price associated with the stock.

In the case of Home Depot, the stock—be it common or preferred—is **publicly** held. That means there's a market (like the New York Stock Exchange) where the stock is bought and sold. And there's a readily available market price for such stock. You can usually find the market price of a stock in—you guessed it—the stock tables of your local newspaper. You can also find the prices of publicly held securities on your favorite Web site.

Those tables, by the way, list corporations by combinations of letters that Wall Streeters call **symbols** (not drum cymbals). A symbol is usually an abbreviated version of the company's name. So, Home Depot is HD, International Business Machines is IBM, and QSound Labs is QSND.

Size Counts

Market Value. Besides the type of stock, the major difference between Home Depot and your local hardware store is size or value. Often called **market capitalization**, it reflects the total value of the company. A privately held company like the local hardware store probably isn't worth that much, a couple hundred thousand dollars or so, while the publicly held company like Home Depot is worth $116 billion.

To calculate the market capitalization, Wall Streeters multiply the total number of shares **outstanding** (that is, issued and in the hands of stockholders) by the market price of a share. Our example, Home Depot, had as of May 2001 about 2.3 billion shares outstanding and a share price of $50, which means market capitalization of $116 billion.

Market cap, short for capitalization, is important because Wall Streeters tend to categorize stocks as large-cap, mid-cap, small-cap, and micro-cap. **Large-cap** stocks are those that have a large market capitalization, usually $5 billion or more. **Mid-cap** stocks are those that have a mid-sized market capitalization, usually $1 billion to $5 billion. **Small-cap** means capitalization between $250 million and $1 billion. Finally, **micro-cap**, as you might logically deduce, is for anything smaller, under $250 million. Small-cap and micro-cap stocks have historically produced greater investment returns, but—as you might imagine—with greater risk. Market cap is also important in corporate board rooms, where corporate executive types often play the "Bigger is better" game.

Book Value. There's another type of value associated with corporations—**book value**. To get a company's book value, Wall Streeters subtract a company's liabilities from its assets and then divide the result by the number of outstanding shares. Often people who refer to themselves as **value investors** use book value when evaluating whether or not to buy a stock.

Par Value. The last type of value you might encounter on Wall Street or while cruising financial Web sites is **par** or **stated value**. Ultimately, it's a value that you need not worry about. It's number pulled out of thin air when a stock is issued. It has no bearing on reality and you will be hard pressed to find anyone on Wall Street, save some actuary or attorney, who can explain its use and value.

The Stockholder's Bill of Rights

Now, owning a piece, even if it's only—as they say on Wall Street—a fractional piece, entitles you to certain rights. You have the right to vote on the big issues of the company, including the board of directors, mergers, and stock splits.

The board of directors is composed of the people who presumably represent your interests as a shareholder. What are your interests? Well, typically your bottom-line interest is either **capital appreciation** or **dividend income**. That means that either you'll want the value of your stake in the company to grow in value faster than other types of investments or you'll want the company to pay at least a stable dividend. After all, as they say on Wall Street, investing is about wealth accumulation or wealth preservation. Or, as they say on my street, it's all getting and keeping.

Now the board of directors presumably makes sure this happens by overseeing the company's officers and management and their ability to deliver results. If the company's brass doesn't deliver, then it's the board's responsibility to replace the management. On paper, that's how it's supposed to happen. But in reality, management is often part of the board of directors and management often stacks the board with directors who are sympathetic to management. Sadly, boards become nothing more than rubber stamps for management.

Here's another dose of reality associated with your right to vote for a board of directors. Your vote and the votes of your fellow average shareholders don't count for much in the scheme of things. Ultimately, it's hard for the average shareholder to oust board members and overthrow management. Let's take, for example, Toys 'R' Us, a company in which Bob's children (Alex, Jacob, and Scott) each own 100 shares of stock. The company had outstanding (stocks don't sit) 197,522,040 shares of common stock as of April 30, 2001, the date of its **proxy statement**. (That's a document that the Securities and Exchange Commission requires a corporation to send to its shareholders. It provides information about matters on which the shareholders will vote.)

That means Alex, Jacob, and Scott each own a whopping 0.00005% of Toys 'R' Us. For those of you who aren't good with numbers, those stakes are infinitesimal. By contrast, most of Toys 'R' Us stock, as for most publicly traded companies, is held by management or institutional investors. For Toys 'R' Us, those big investors would include Legg Mason, a Baltimore-based brokerage and mutual fund firm, with 27 million shares (or 13.95%), Harris Associates, a Chicago-based investment firm, with 21 million shares (or 10.82%), and Brandes Investment Partners, a San Diego money manager, with 14 million shares (or 7.5%). Those institutions have the ability to influence the course of corporate events. Average shareholders like Alex, Jacob, and Scott don't—unless they can convince several hundred thousand similarly small investors to join forces.

To be sure, an average shareholder can try to nominate and elect his or her own directors or even put before the board certain initiatives. Sometimes the "little people" can make trouble and even effect change.

As a reporter for *The Boston Herald*, Bob covered numerous annual meetings, but his favorite was that of Gillette Corp. Each year, some concerned shareholders would protest the company's use of animals to test cosmetics and shaving cream and they would propose, against management's recommendations, that the company ban animal testing. As expected, the proposal never passed, but it always made for a good picture, if not story.

By contrast, Warren Buffett, one of this nation's greatest investors and the man who happens to be the largest shareholder in Gillette Corp., recently spearheaded an effort to remove the company's CEO and install in his place—you guessed it—his personal choice.

Owning a piece of a company comes with some other shareholder rights. It entitles you to a bunch of financial statements and a pretty annual report telling you how the company is doing and any dividends that may be paid out.

A Type for Every Face

Beside market cap, Wall Streeters refer to common stocks using

Wall St Extra

He's Not My Type

There are two types of voting: statutory and cumulative.

Statutory permits a shareholder to cast one vote per share owned for each director. It's like the voting system that we have in the United States. Each registered voter has one share in the United States and, under normal circumstances, can cast one vote for president. (The Electoral College, meanwhile, is a whole 'nother story, best told in another book.)

Now, let's look at a real-life example of statutory voting, using Bob's children. Alex, Jacob, and Scott each own—for reasons that should be obvious—100 shares of Toys 'R' Us. There were nine people nominated to serve on the Toys 'R' Us board of directors, according to the company's proxy statement issued April 30, 2001. Under the statutory type of voting system, Alex, Jacob, and Scott could each cast 100 votes for each person nominated. Alex, Jacob, and Scott can't, however, cast more votes for any one director than the total number of shares owned. So, for instance, Alex can't cast 150 votes for Arthur B. Newman because he likes the name or likes his pedigree.

With **cumulative** voting, a shareholder would multiply the number of shares owned by the number of directors to be elected. The result would be the total number of votes that the shareholder could cast for one director or divide in any way.

Using the above example, if Toys 'R' Us voting were cumulative, not statutory, Alex would have 900 votes (100 shares times nine nominees) to cast any way he pleased. He could cast all 900 votes for Arthur B. Newman or split his votes among the nine nominees.

For the record, the more common type of voting is statutory, although some states require cumulative voting.

other codes. The most common are income, growth, value, defen-

sive, blue chip, and special situation.

Income Stocks. These stocks are those that pay good dividends (about 3% to 10% or more). Typically, the dividend is usually paid quarterly out of a company's earnings and is a fixed dollar amount, like $2.10. That's called a **cash** dividend. The other kind of dividend is called a **stock** dividend. In that case, the company gives out more stock so that it can retain its earnings, presumably to keep growing.

Wall Streeters translate the dividend into something called a **dividend yield** to determine whether the stock is a good buy or not. The dividend yield is calculated by dividing the dividend by the stock price. For example, if the dividend was $2.10 and the stock price was $42.00, the dividend yield would be 5%. Usually, the buyer of an income stock wants income (that makes sense!) or what Wall Streeters call **total return**—capital appreciation (or growth) plus dividends.

On the whole, **income stocks** are less volatile than **growth stocks** and are sometimes referred to as **value stocks**. Usually, companies with a long history of profits, like banks or utility companies, have dividend-paying stocks.

Figure 3-1 from *The Research Driven Investor* by Timothy Hayes (McGraw-Hill, 2000) shows the dividend payout ratios for the years 1932-1993. The average for the 49.2-year period charted was 51%. Right now the ratio is at a historic low, because investors don't want dividends, they want growth, so the few dollars left in corporate coffers are being plowed back into the companies, not given as dividend trinkets.

The ratios are for the **S&P 500**. That's the **Standard & Poor 500** stock index, which tracks the performance—the rising and falling stock values—of the nation's 500 largest and best-known companies.

The rule of thumb for valuing the dividend yield on the S&P 500 was to sell your stocks when it ducked below 3% and buy when it was over 6%. Considering that the average blew below 3% in 1990, following that rule would have meant being out of the market for the greatest stock decade in history—which would not have been a very good decision. The post-WW II average of the S&P 500 yield was under 4%. It's currently at 1.2%. So for now on this indicator, it's best to remember the words of Emily Litella on *Saturday Night Live:* "Never mind."

Growth Stocks. These stocks, meanwhile, pay zilch for dividends but have the potential for price appreciation. That's because the company's sales and earnings are growing faster than average. One meas-

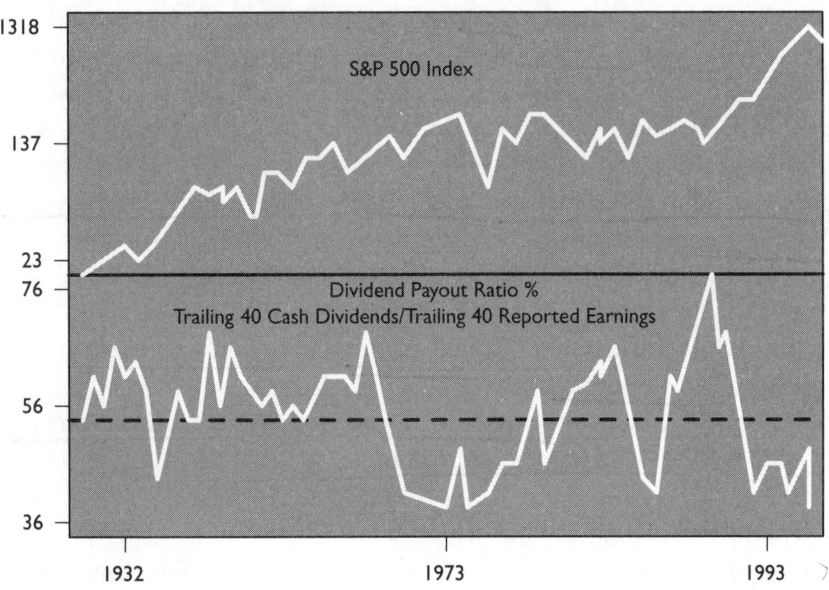

Figure 3-1. Historical performance of the S&P 500

ure of how fast a company is growing is something Wall Streeters call the **price/earnings ratio**, or **P/E**. Analysts use the P/E to determine whether a growth stock is a good buy or a goodbye. The P/E ratio is simply the stock price divided by the company's earnings per share. Companies typically issue thousands upon thousands of shares of stock, but Wall Streeters prefer to calculate revenue and other data on a per-share basis. So if a company earns $1 per share and its stock price is $20, then the P/E would be 20. If the company earns $2 and its stock price is $20, then the P/E would be 10. Presumably, a company with a higher P/E would be growing its profits faster than the company with a lower P/E. It would also be a more volatile stock.

Blue Chips. Not to be confused with cow chip or potato chip, a **blue chip** is any of the highest-quality companies, those with solid earnings and management. The name of this type of stock comes from the gambling tables, where blue chips were always the most expensive. **Red chips**, by the way, are stocks that trade in China on the Honk Kong exchange. Red chips are more of a gamble.

Defensive. These stocks are those that are typically unaffected by the business cycle, such as utility stocks.

Special Situation. These are stocks that are expected to rise for some particular reason, perhaps some unusual event. (For example, Bob's good friend is always pushing a stock called Apache Corp., which is sitting on a gazillion barrels of oil in Poland. As gasoline prices rise precipitously across the U.S., Apache becomes a special situation—at least for Bob's friend.)

Now that you have the basic notes, we can move on to some more Wall Street jargon you'll need to add to your repertory.

Preferred Stock

Preferred stocks are a hybrid security, offering the best of common stocks and bonds. Like common stocks, preferred stocks provide investors with ownership in a corporation and the chance for capital appreciation. Like bonds, preferred stocks don't give you a chance to vote on corporate matters but they pay a guaranteed, fixed amount of money on a quarterly basis, before dividends go out to common stockholders. (Preferred stocks are also a lot like convertible bonds, which we'll discuss in the next chapter.)

Another important aspect of preferred stocks is relative security: if the company gets into financial trouble, you won't be the last to get paid. The first ones to get paid are the IRS, employees, lawyers, lenders (bondholders), and then preferred stockholders. The last one to get paid anything if a company tanks (not a technical term) is the common stockholder.

So what's it like to own a preferred stock? Well, imagine driving a car with the parking brake on. Preferred stocks don't fall and rise in value as do common stocks and they don't pay as high a rate of interest as bonds. They are somewhere in between. (Call 'em "tweeners," if you dare, at your next cocktail party.)

Yes, preferred stocks are special securities purchased for specific reasons. Think of it this way. Sometimes you go to the grocery store and buy meat from the deli counter to make your sandwiches. Other times, perhaps you forget your lunch, so you go to the local submarine sandwich shop. Well, it's the same with preferred stocks. They satisfy a very specific need for some income with the chance for some capital appreciation.

No, the truth of the matter is this. In all his years in the business, Dave can't recall using preferred stocks in his client's portfolios. So the likelihood of a preferred stock ending up in your portfolio is zero to none. Most of the time these securities are purchased by large institutional investors to produce income or reduce volatility.

Terms and Definitions

Stock proxy is the near equivalent of a ballot without the chads. It's basically an absentee ballot. When you become a stockholder, you'll get a chance to vote on important issues, like the board of directors, stock splits, a company buyout, or any big-time change that could affect the price of the stock. The company will send you a proxy, just in case you don't want to attend the meeting in person. If you don't send in that proxy, then you don't get a say in the management of your company.

A **stock split** is just a mechanical function that reduces the price of a stock and gives you more shares of it. For example, if you own 100 shares of General Electric (GE) and it's trading for $150 a share and then it splits 2-for-1, the shares will be trading at $75 and you will own 200 of them. Don't get excited and go crazy over the split, because you still own the same dollar amount—$15,000. Yet stocks with a history of splits, like GE, are usually good to own because splits occur only if the stock price goes up. Wall Streeters also like to split stocks (not logs) for psychological reasons. Average investors like to buy in what are called **round lots**, or in increments of 100 shares. Time was when it was easier to buy 100 shares at $75 than 50 shares (**odd lot**) at $150. But, there's really no difference in whether you own 100 shares of a $75 stock or 50 shares of a $150 stock.

There's another kind of split that Wall Street will make as well. It's called a **reverse split**. (No, that's not putting the banana slices on top of the scoops of ice cream on top of the chocolate syrup.) Let's say you own 1,000 shares of a $2 stock and it has a reverse 10-to-1 split. After the split, you'll have 100 shares of a $20 stock. That may sound good on the surface, but reverse stocks have a dubious history. A reverse split is usually declared to make a low-priced stock appear more mainstream or to disguise a falling price. So a word to the wise: don't let Wall Street try to sell you on buying a company that's gone through a reverse stock split.

Another term to know is **street name**. Time was when everyone knew what a **stock certificate** was and looked like. People kept their certificates in safe deposit box or in the top drawer of their dresser under lock and key. After all, a stock certificate is the written evidence of ownership in a corporation. Way back when, certificates were works of art. They had pretty pictures depicting a famous scene from Greek mythology or some such thing. Today, however, investors are unlikely to know whether a certificate has a pretty picture or not. That's because most people own stocks in what is called street name. (That's not to be confused with "street person name," which is used to describe investors who've lost all their money in the market.) Rather, street name is the term used when a brokerage firm holds your securities in its name on your behalf. Few people want to deal with the hassle of lost or stolen securities, so instead they opt for the security of street name. There's another advantage: once your certificates are held in street name, your brokerage firm will generate a monthly or at least quarterly statement, complete with performance and other reports. Finally, it's definitely more convenient to leave a stock in street name: if you choose to buy or sell a stock, you've only got three days to deliver the money or the shares. That's called **settlement day**, otherwise known as T+3 or transaction plus three days. (Of note, the world is fast moving toward a T+1 settlement day, in which case it becomes even more necessary to put your stock in street name.)

Public means that a stock is traded on any of the major exchanges, such as the New York Stock Exchange, the American Stock Exchange, or Nasdaq. The prices of publicly traded stocks are published in most major daily newspapers (in really small print that requires anyone over age 50 to search for the bifocals or grow longer arms). Increasingly, software programs like Quicken or Money or Web sites like Morningstar or Financial Engines will track the price of your stocks.

A **private** company, by contrast, can issue common stock but typically there's no market for such stock. Usually, it's a closely held concern, as in just a few family members or senior people own the company. What's more, it's tougher to put a price on such stock because the company is not required to open its financial books to the public.

IPO and **tombstone** sound like a Western gang. IPO just stands for **Initial Public Offering**. That's when a company goes from private to public, usually to raise cash and provide "liquidity" for the owners to sell their stock. (**Liquidity** is one of those Wall Street terms; it means cash, easy access to cash. When you have a liquid investment, it doesn't mean beer or wine unless you have a well-stocked bar or cellar.) Rather it's how quickly and easily the investment can be converted into cash. As for tombstone, that's just the ad in the newspaper that looks like a tombstone, with the name of the company and all the brokerage firms that are getting paid to sell the stock.

Prospectus is the legal mumbo-jumbo that's required when a company sells securities to the public. These reports many times run in the hundreds of pages; a read of these will surely set your pillow calling unless you truly know what you're looking for.

Employee Stock Options

This can turn into the home run category if you work for the right company. If it's the wrong one, then—like the cops say—"You're busted." There were 386 companies that averaged 25% a year returns or better for the decade ending in the year 2000, according to the Morningstar stock universe (and yes, that includes the year 2000 whupping!). They include companies like Microsoft, General Electric, Amgen, and Dell Computer. At a 25% a year growth rate, you would have made nine times your money invested over a 10-year period. An article in *The Wall Street Journal*, June 16, 1999, estimated that about a third of Microsoft permanent employees were millionaires because of the thousands of low-priced shares they received through incentive options, profit sharing, or stock investment plans. On the other hand, we had gobs of dot-com millionaires in March 2000 who ended up in the dot-com trash heap after the AMEX Internet index dropped over 80% from its peak, not to mention those companies that closed their doors altogether.

When it comes to options, there are two basic types: incentive stock options (ISOs) and non-qualified employee stock options (NQSOs). You can also own a piece of the company store by buying the stock at your local broker or signing up for employee stock purchase plans (ESPPs) if your company offers them. They all have different uses and tax ramifications.

Incentive stock options (ISOs) are usually the best of the bunch. A company gives these to key people as incentives for turning around an ailing company, getting a company started, or just making the company run more efficiently and profitably. The key elements are the price you can buy the shares at (**exercise price**) and the period of time after which the shares are truly yours (**vesting**).

When you exercise the option, you pay your exercise price for the stock, say $1. When you sell the stock, that $1 becomes your **cost**. When you sell the stock, the difference between your cost and the sale price is a taxable gain. So if you sold it for $100 you have a $99-a-share gain. If you sell the stock within one year of exercising your option, then that's considered a short-term capital gain and you pay your taxes at your incremental tax bracket of up to 39.6%. If you sell the stock a year or more after exercising your option, then your maximum long-term gain is 20% of the $99. So, unless you like paying taxes, it's best to wait at least a year—unless you think the stock is going to take a dive.

Just beware of the nasty tax animal called **AMT—alternative minimum tax**. This can cause the difference between the exercise price and the current price to be taxed in the year that the stock option is exercised, not the year that the stock is sold. This can be a big ouch, so get hold of your tax person before you exercise any ISOs. Even if you don't have the cash to exercise the options, most companies will provide something called a **cashless transaction** that allows you to borrow the money to pay for the stock. Of course, you still have to pay the interest on the loan or sell enough stock to cover the loan.

Non-qualified employee stock options (NQSOs) are incentives for new hires or just rewards for those employees who help the company do well but may not be the heavy hitters in the corporation. What usually happens here is that each year a number of employees are awarded stock at that year's current price or **grant**

price. You may be given 200 shares at $10 a share and you must exercise that option in, say, five to 10 years. When you exercise the option, you are taxed fully on the difference between the current price of that stock and your original offer. So if your original grant was $10 and it's now $30, then $20 per share—or $4,000—is taxed as ordinary income and that becomes your new cost basis for the stock. At that time your employer will put it right on your W-2 wages and you have to pay the taxes right then and there. If you're short on cash, most companies will provide a cashless transaction for exercising these shares as well.

Employee stock purchase plans (ESPPs) are not options, but they're an option for everyone in the company to own a piece of the corporate rock. Then, when your boss gives you a lashing on your job skills, you can tell him or her to be careful because you're a shareholder of the company.

The employer sets up a plan to buy company stock, after tax and usually at some discounted amount, like 15% of the current price. So if the stock is at $10 a share, you can buy it for $8.50. It's sort of a forced savings program in which you buy company stock on sale. There are limits to the amount of stock that you can buy, usually between 5% and 15% of your salary. When you sell any of your shares, you're taxed in two ways: you have to count the discounted amount (in our example, $1.50 a share) as ordinary income and the remainder gain or loss as either short-term (maximum 39.6% tax) or long-term (maximum 20% tax), depending on how long you've held the shares.

Coda

We started this chapter talking music, so let's leave that way as well. We've spent a little time here talking about the music of Wall Street. The three major themes are stocks, bonds, and money markets. That's very much like classical, folk, or rock music in that there are different strokes for different folks.

When it comes to the music of stocks, you can do it three ways. The first is to just buy the CD (that's compact disc, not Certificate of Deposit) easy listening version through mutual funds and let the musicians do the work. (But you should be able to appreciate what those mutual fund musicians do with your investment, so we'll see you in Chapters 5 and 6 for some mutual appreciation lessons.) The second way is to hire an advisor or money manager and watch the concert live, with interaction between you and the manager. (The musician does the work, but you request what you want and you react to the results. Just don't hold up your lighter in your advisor's office: the sprinkling systems may be very sensitive!) Last, you can take on the task of playing the instrument of individual stock picking yourself—but you need to take the time to learn the music properly before you take on that task.

Each instrument has its own characteristics, like the growth stock horn, the value git-fiddle, the harping of income, or the drum of a special situation. All of them can be sweet music if you like their sounds. Sometimes the greatest music of all can be just dumb luck, like a corporate musical family you work for that happens to have a great band. Taking stock in your own employer can make a whole lot of sense, especially if that company grows at 25% a year; you get the free lesson of options and it forces you to save. So now that you're learning how to name that stock tune, let's move on to the next musical chorus—bonds.

4

Bonds

If you walk down Main Street in your hometown, you'll further witness what Wall Street is all about. Look at the Home Depot in your town. It's likely that the company borrowed money from investors to build the building. Look at your town's water and sewer system. It's likely that your elected officials borrowed money from investors to build that system. Look at the interstate highway that you drive on to work. It's likely that the U.S. government borrowed money from investors to build that road.

Well, that's what bonds are all about. Corporations, municipalities (state, city, or local governments), and the U.S. government all borrow money from investors like you for stuff that usually takes a long time to pay back. The company issues or sells bonds to investors with the promise to pay the buyer:

- the principal or **face amount** or what is sometimes called the **par value**, at a specific date in the future, often called the **maturity date**, and
- interest, otherwise known as a **fixed rate of return** (which is why bonds are sometimes referred to as **fixed-income securities**).

Think of it this way: when you or your parents bought your house, you borrowed money from a bank and promised to back the principal (face amount) at a certain point in the future (maturity date) plus interest. Well, your mortgage is a bond.

Investment Building Blocks

Stocks and bonds are similar in one way. Behind stocks, bonds are the second most important part of an investor's portfolio. In fact, many money managers will often advise investors to put 60% of their money in stocks and 40% in bonds, or some variation of that mix. That's because bonds are presumed to be less risky than stocks, that is, not as volatile. Bonds also are presumed to provide a lower rate of return than stocks, too. In fact, bonds have generated about 5% per year—just half of what stocks have generated since people began tracking such things. Lower risk, lower return.

So owning bonds provides an investor with the chance to reduce the risk that's often associated with stocks; usually, unfortunately, bonds also reduce the potential return of a portfolio. Wall Streeters often refer to the mixing of stocks and bonds as **asset allocation and diversification**. In plain English, asset allocation and diversification just means putting your eggs in lots of different baskets so that you don't lose all your eggs (nest egg included) if any basket goes the way of Humpty Dumpty.

Equity Versus Debt

On the whole, though, stocks and bonds are more different than similar. Indeed, stocks and bonds can be as different as night and day. Stocks are **equity** securities, representing ownership in a company, while bonds, which are also called loans or IOUs, are **debt** securities. The owner or holder of a bond, which is often called a **senior security**, is a creditor—not an owner. If the issuer goes belly up (not a Wall Street term that requires decoding), the bondholder stands to collect some of the proceeds of the sale of the company's assets before anyone else.

Maturity and Denominations

The other important characteristics of bonds are the **maturity dates** and **denominations**. Bonds are normally issued with maturity dates ranging from 10 to 40 years. But Wall Street sells bonds with shorter maturity dates and longer maturity dates. Treasury bills are often issued for a 90-day period and there are some bonds that mature in 100 years (not something that would interest the average person!).

Bonds are often referred to by the **term** or life of the bond. There are three major terms: short, intermediate, and long term. Usually, though not always, a short-term bond pays a lower interest rate than an intermediate-term bond and an intermediate-term bond pays a lower interest rate than a long-term bond. Usually, though not always, the shorter the term, the less volatile or risky a bond will be.

The **yield curve** is a term Wall Streeters use to describe the various interest rates associated with different maturities. Usually, though not always, the yield curve slopes upward from left to right, as seen below. That's called a **normal yield curve**. Other yield curves are described as **flat** or **inverted**, although some might view the latter as abnormal.

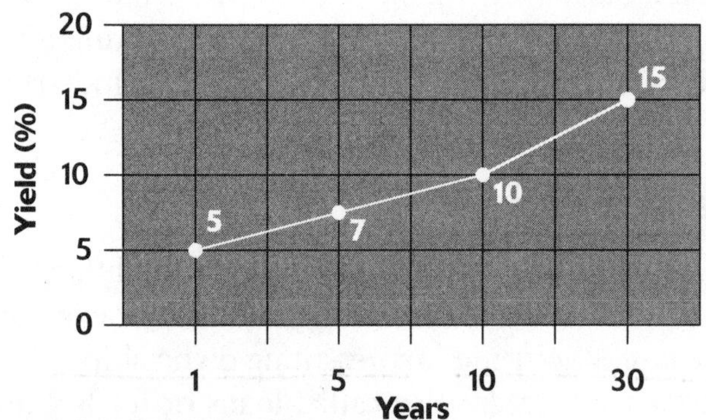

Figure 4-1. Normal yield curve

A Basis Point for Your Thoughts

One other point (no pun intended) to make about bonds. Wall Street types often refer to the difference between yields as **basis points**. A basis point is 1/100th of 1%. Thus, the difference between a bond with a yield of 10.20% and a bond with a yield of 10.35% would be 15 basis points.

Denominations also come in wide variety of flavors. Corporations usually issue bonds in $1,000 denominations. The U.S. government usually issues Treasury bonds (Treasury notes and Treasury bills) in denominations from $1,000 to $10,000. Municipalities usually issue bonds in $5,000 denominations.

Loan

Bonds, as we've just stated, are loans. You let someone borrow your money in return for interest payments—and your principal, of course. It's just that simple. And, as with most loans, there are some inherent risks with bonds. There's the risk that the entity might not pay the interest, the principal, or both. Think of it this way. When you borrow money for your house, there's a risk—and we don't mean to insult you personally—that you might miss one of your mortgage payments, maybe even default on your loan, maybe even have the bank reclaim your house and put it on the auction block.

So, when you buy a bond, there are risks, just as there are risks for banks or credit unions whenever somebody takes out a mortgage.

Thankfully, there are companies that rate the ability of an entity to pay interest in a timely fashion and pay back the principal. These companies, which logically enough are called **rating agencies**, assign a grade to a particular entity and the bond it is trying to "float." (**Float**, by the way, is a Wall Street term people use to describe the sale of a bond.)

Rules of Thumb

Wall Street has many rules of thumb. (Why there are no rules of index fingers is beyond us, especially since Wall Street is so fond of indexes—consumer price index, composite indexes, Standard & Poor's 500 stock index ....) There are three of those rules of thumb worth memorizing about bonds.

Rule #1

The higher the grade or bond rating, the lower the amount of interest an entity has to pay to investors. The lower the grade, the higher amount of interest an entity has to pay to get investors to buy the bond.

Bonds that have really bad grades are not held back like children in school. Rather, those bonds, which are called **junk bonds**, must pay a really high interest rate, because chances are good that the entity might not make good on its promise to pay back the people who loaned the money.

For example, a company with the highest possible bond rating would pay investors just 8% to borrow money, while a firm with a lower bond rating might have to pay 10%. If a company is trying to borrow $10 million to build a new widget factory in Ireland, the difference between 10% and 8% could be substantial. (That's one reason why corporate types are always trying to wine and dine the people who rate bonds. A higher bond rating could save a company or municipality a lot of money.)

Rule #2

The longer the maturity (the date on which the principal is due), the higher the interest rate. The shorter the maturity, the lower the interest rate.

Watch the financial news and you'll notice that the U.S. Government issues various types of bonds, called **bills**, **notes**, and **bonds**. We'll get to those later. The point here is that the bonds referred to as **Treasury bills**, which mature in 90 days, have a low interest rate and the bonds referred to as **Treasury bonds**, with maturities ranging from 10 years to 30 years, pay a higher interest rate.

There are three reasons for this. One has to do with the time value of money. Usually, though not always, money that's borrowed over a short term costs less than money borrowed over a long term. Think of it this way. If you let someone borrow money from you for 30 years, there are a few things you need to consider before you set the interest rate. You have to consider the possibility that the person might not pay you back. On Wall Street that's called **credit risk**. You also have to consider how much less one dollar will be worth 30 years hence. That's called **purchasing power risk**. Finally, you have to consider how else you can invest your money once you get it back some 30 years from now. That's called **reinvestment risk**.

Rule #3

After bonds start trading in the bond market (more on that later), the price of the bond moves in the opposite direction of interest rates. So, if interest rates rise, the price of the bond falls. If interest rates fall, the price of the bond rises.

For example, if a bond is trading at $980 and rates rise, the bond might start trading at $970. This, by the way, is perhaps the most difficult concept on Wall Street. As a columnist for *The Boston Herald*, Bob would often be asked on deadline what happens to bond prices when interest rates. His stock answer: "It's that inverse correlation thing."

Calling All Bonds ...

One other feature of bonds is the **call**. Most bonds will be paid back at maturity. There are, however, some exceptions. Some entities issue bonds with the right to redeem the bond prior to maturity. That's a "call." The entity issuing the bond may do this because it's come into some cash and it wants to get rid of the obligation. Or maybe interest rates have fallen and it wants to refinance, just as you do with your mortgage.

What's in It for Them?

The big up side for companies or entities issuing debt securities is that they get the money they need to finance long-term projects. The other big up side, at least for corporations, is—as they say on Wall Street—there's no dilution of equity or ownership in the company. In other words, the owners of the company get the money, but don't have to give up their stake in the business.

The big down side, however, is the obligation. Equity has no obligation; debt, on the other hand, requires that a company make interest payments, typically semiannually, and the principal payment. If the company fails to make the interest payment and defaults on the loan, the creditor gets to take pieces of what's left of the company after it declares bankruptcy. Many a used office furniture store is stocked with the cubicles from companies that have gone belly up.

What's in It for You?

For investors, the big up side to bonds is income and safety of principal. Those are the terms that describe the common investment goals of people who buy or invest in bonds. The big down side, as we've mentioned, is credit risk and purchasing power risk.

Ye Olde Yield

We've discussed the fact that bonds pay interest. The amount paid is often referred to as a **yield**. There are three major types of yield—coupon yield, current yield, yield to maturity.

The **coupon yield**, sometimes called the **nominal yield**, is the interest rate stated on the face of the bond. If you owned a $1,000 bond with 5% coupon, it would pay interest of $50 per year.

Once a bond is issued, starts trading in the open market, as Wall Streeters are wont to say, the value of the bond will fluctuate. If interest rates rise, the price of the bond will fall. And if interest rates fall, the price of the bond will rise. The **current yield** of the bond is simply the coupon rate divided by the current market price. If the 5% $1,000 bond you bought in the open market is trading at $900, then the current yield would be 5.5%. That's because the current yield reflects how much money you earn on invested capital: $50/$900.

Got that? Good, because here's the curveball—**yield to maturity** (YTM). In some circles, that term means that you should give up your seat on the subway or bus to your elders. But on Wall Street, the term refers to how much money you'll really make over the course of time when you buy a bond. Most, if not all, big-time investors use yield to maturity to compare and contrast potential investments. The formula is a little tricky, based on the specific type of bond and particularly when we get that funky February 29 day.

So most experts let the computers do the standard calculating for them. That way the bond guys and gals can blame Intel for a bad chip if the numbers are off.

Taxing Questions

There's one more important aspect of interest from a bond. How it gets taxed depends on who's doing the issuing. The interest paid on corporate bonds is taxed by the federal and state governments as interest income. The interest paid on municipal bonds is exempt from state and federal taxes, provided you're a resident of the municipality issuing the bonds. And the interest paid on government bonds is usually exempt from state and local taxes.

Trading Places

Like stocks, bonds can be bought when they first go on sale or bought and sold at any time prior to maturity. Most bonds are traded, that is bought and sold, on the New York Stock Exchange as well as in the over-the-counter market. (**Over the counter**, by the way, is a term that refers to how bonds and other securities are traded, by negotiation as opposed to auction.) The price of the bond will vary depending on market conditions. Bonds can trade at:

- **par**, the face amount,
- a **premium**, more than the face amount, or
- a **discount**, less than the face amount

When bonds are bought and sold, the buyer and seller have to contend with **accrued** interest—the interest due to the seller but not yet paid. Bonds usually pay interest every six months but interest accrues every day. So, when the bondholder sells, the buyer pays the market price plus the accrued interest, then gets reimbursed at the end of the six-month period.

Understanding Prices

One more difference between bonds and stocks is how they're priced. Like stocks, bonds have **bid** and **ask** prices. Unlike stocks, however, bid and ask prices are quoted as a percent of the par value.

Thus, a bond trading at par would be quoted as 100 and cost $1,000 to buy. A bond trading at 98 would mean 98% of $1,000 and cost $980 to buy. Usually there's no commission to buy and sell a bond. Typically the cost of buying and selling is priced into the bond.

From Overview to Details

So, now you know the basics of bonds. That's a great start: you're ready to get into some particulars. As we noted at the start of this chapter, bonds are issued by several types of entities: corporations, municipalities, and the U.S. government. And so, as you might well expect, there are some differences among the bonds issued.

We've already mentioned differences in denominations: corporations usually issue bonds in $1,000 denominations, the U.S. government usually issues Treasury bonds (Treasury notes and Treasury bills) in denominations from $1,000 to $10,000, and municipalities usually issue bonds in $5,000 denominations.

So, you're dying to know, what other differences are there? Well, let's take the three entities one at a time.

Corporate Bonds

Corporations usually issue debt securities as a way of raising money (sometimes called **long-term capital**) to fund big projects—such as building a manufacturing plant or for a merger or acquisition—and in some cases to cover operating expenses. The buyer or investor of these bonds makes a loan to the company and thus becomes a creditor of the corporation. The bond pays a fixed rate of interest, usually semi-annually.

As we discussed earlier, the company promises to repay the loan (principal amount) on a specified date in the future, called the maturity date. Wall Streeters call bonds **senior securities** because in the event of liquidation or bankruptcy, the claims of bondholders are settled before everyone else. Corporate bonds are usually issued in $1,000 denominations, with maturities ranging from 10 to 40 years, and in one or both of two forms—registered or bearer.

A **registered bond** is issued with the name of the owner printed on the face of the certificate. You can transfer your bond to someone else only by signing a transfer. That makes this type of bond very safe against loss or theft.

A **bearer bond**, also known as a **coupon bond**, is not registered: the interest and principal are payable to whoever is holding the certificates. (Think of those movies or TV shows where someone steals bearer bonds—as good as cash.) Bearer or coupon bonds are being phased out in favor of registered bonds.

Corporate bonds are riskier and pay a higher rate of interest than municipal and government bonds. The higher rate of interest presumably pays for the higher risk associated with the loan. Also, the interest is taxable.

Within corporate bonds, however, rates of interest vary greatly. The companies with the highest credit rating pay a lower interest rate; those with the worst credit rating pay a higher interest rate. That just makes sense.

This difference between high yield and high quality (low risk) relative to government bonds is called a **spread**. (OK, technically it's **"yield spread,"** but the bond people never use that term because it's assumed when you mention the word "spread" and "bonds" in the same sentence.) Professional bond buyers watch the spread very closely to see where they can get the best return versus the risk. A junk bond can pay some very high yields, like 10% to 15%. They're sometimes called "stocks in drag."

Of note, most bonds are issued under a **trust indenture**, an agreement between the company selling the bond and the investors buying the bond, the creditors. This written agreement establishes the terms of the issue (including interest rate, maturity date, and convertibility—which we'll discuss shortly) and protects and enforces the bondholder's rights. This document is a bit like the document that comes with a stock's IPO.

Now that you know the basics of corporate bonds, we should add that there are many types of corporate bonds. The most common are called **debentures**. Debentures are bonds that are backed only by "the full faith" of the corporation, not by any collateral. If you're guessing that debentures are among the riskiest of corporate bonds, you're right. Some bonds are backed by specific assets or guarantees, which make them safer than debentures.

Convertible Bonds

One last mention on corporate bonds is a hybrid security known as **convertible bonds**. These are bonds that can be converted into stocks of the issuing company. In many ways, convertibles are kissing cousins of preferred stocks. Like regular bonds, convertibles pay a fixed rate of return and have a maturity date. Unfortunately, the interest rate paid by these bonds isn't as high as for regular bonds. Like stocks, these bonds offer the potential for appreciation and—as you might imagine—tend to fluctuate in value more than regular bonds.

Usually, corporations issue convertibles during a bull market. That's because most investors are interested in buying equities (stocks), which offer a better chance of making money than debt (bonds). Convertibles presumably give investors the best of both worlds—safety of principal, some income, and some growth potential.

On Wall Street, the important concepts with convertible bonds are parity and conversion. **Parity** refers to the point as which the value of the bond and the value of the underlying stock are equal. **Conversion** is the process of switching from one religion to another or, on Wall Street, the point at which you would exchange your convertible for a hard top. Just kidding. (But you knew that, we hope!) It's the point at which you would convert your convertible bond into the underlying stock.

U.S. Government Bonds

Overview

Government bonds, also called **governments** or **govies**, work the same way as corporate bonds—with two exceptions:

Safety They are backed by the "full faith and credit of the U.S. government." In essence, that means there's a pretty good chance that you'll get your money back. For starters, it's unlikely that the U.S. government will go out of business anytime soon. And two, the U.S. government can do whatever it must to pay off its obligations. Specifically it has unlimited powers to tax the rich and poor—as you're probably painfully aware. Thus, the government's credit rating, as you might imagine, is not a problem.

Tax-advantaged investment The interest income investors receive from government bonds is not taxed by any state—although it's subject to federal tax as ordinary income. (To be sure, this deal isn't as good as you get with municipal bonds: interest from those bonds is not taxed at either state or federal level.)

Down Side

With the exception of credit risk, government bonds are subject to the types of risk associated with other bonds:

Purchasing power risk, the risk that your money will be worth less than today when the bond matures. This is a big risk when cost of living is greater than normal and less of a risk when inflation is normal or when the cost of living is falling. It's also more of a problem with long-term bonds.

Reinvestment risk, the risk that you won't be able to reinvest your money at the same rate of interest as today. In short, this is the risk that you won't be able to earn the same level of interest income when your bond matures. In practical terms, let's say you need to generate 10% or $100 per year in interest income from a $1,000 investment to tip the kid who delivers your paper. Five years hence, when the bond matures, the best deal you can find comes with just an 8% yield. So, you have to either come up with the $20 shortage out of pocket or stiff the kid.

Interest rate risk, the risk that the value of a bond trading in the open market will decline in value (that is, it's adjusted to reflect the current market conditions) if interest rates rise. In Wall Street speak, the yield on the outstanding bonds has to remain competitive with other bonds, so the price of the bond is adjusted to reflect the current market conditions. Thus, if you have to sell the bond to make bail or deal with some other unfortunate event, you could be in for big surprise. Of course, if interest rates fall, the value of the bond would rise and you could afford bail on additional charges.

The bottom line on which risk is real and significant and which is unreal and insignificant is what happens to interest rates. And no one, not even Alan Greenspan, can tell you what's going to happen to interest rates tomorrow.

Choices, Choices ...

The U.S. Treasury Department issues two types of debt to pay for the expense side of the federal budget:

Marketable securities, which include Treasury bills, Treasury notes, and Treasury bonds, among others, and

Nonmarketable securities, which include Series EE and Series HH bonds.

(A marketable security is one that could be converted into cash quickly and easily. A nonmarketable security is, well, you figure it out!)

Most marketable government bonds are traded in the over-the-counter market. However, if you follow the price of such securities in the newspaper, you'll notice that the quotes are different from those of corporate bonds. Instead of trading in 1/16 or 1/8 fractions like corporate bonds, they trade in fractions of 1/32s. So when you look in the paper and see a quote of 99.23, that's not a decimal, it's 23/32 or .71875. When you see the quotes in a paper, you have to dust off your 3rd-grade fraction tables: 1/32 = .03125, 2/32 = .0625, 3/32 = ... Fun, eh? That's pretty much what you would expect from the government, I guess: they just want you to use the education they provided for you years ago.

Treasury Bills

T-bills, which are not to be confused with T-bones or T-Rex, are short-term securities, with maturities ranging from three months to one year. These bills are issued in denominations of $10,000 to $1 million.

Unlike most bonds, T-bills do not pay a specific rate of interest; rather, the government sells the bills at a discount and the interest income is the difference between the purchase price and the amount received at maturity. Let's say you buy the T-bill for $9,843.50 and redeem it at maturity for $10,000; the difference, $156.50, is the interest income. There is no **coupon** (Wall Street speak for interest rate or interest payment). The interest rate is simply how much the bill earned over the time period you held it. T-bills, which are issued every four weeks and traded continuously, are not quoted in the newspaper in dollars. Rather, they are quoted as in yields, like "bid 3.25%" and "ask 3.20%."

Treasury Notes

Treasury notes, which are not to be confused with love notes, are intermediate-term securities, with maturities ranging from one year to 10 years. Like most bonds, these notes, which are issued in denominations of $1,000 up to $1 million, pay interest every six months. Like most bonds, the notes are issued, quoted, and traded as a percentage of face value. The quotes are usually expressed as 1/32 of 1% of par value.

Treasury Bonds

Treasury bonds are long-term securities, with maturities ranging from 10 years to 30 years. These bonds, which are issued in denominations of $1,000 to $1 million, with $10,000 being the more common amount, pay interest every six months.

The bonds are liquid and marketable, as Wall Street likes to say. That is, they're easily and readily sold and bought, both when issued and in the open market. The bonds are priced at a percentage of par.

Agencies

In addition to the Treasury Department, there are also agencies of the U.S. government that sell bonds. Although these bonds don't carry the full-faith-and-credit guarantee of government-issued bonds like U.S. Treasuries, they're considered secure because they're issued by a government agency.

Here are some federal agencies that issue bonds:

- Federal Home Loan Bank (FHLB)
- Federal Farm Credit Bank (FFCB)
- Federal Housing Agency (FHA)
- Tennessee Valley Authority (TVA)
- Federal National Mortgage Association (Fannie Mae)
- Federal Home Loan Mortgage Corporation (Freddie Mac)
- Farm Credit System Financial Assistance Corporation
- Federal Agricultural Mortgage Corporation (Farmer Mac)

- Student Loan Marketing Association (Sallie Mae)
- College Construction Loan Insurance Association (Connie Lee)
- Small Business Administration (SBA)

These agency issue bonds to help support projects relevant to public policy, such as small business, farms, loans to first-time homebuyers, or electricity. It might appear as if every government agency is issuing bonds, but we're sure that there are exceptions. It's a big sector of the investment world: according to the Bond Market Association, agency bonds now outstanding in the market are worth some $845 billion.

Nonmarketable Securities

Whatever you do, don't confuse Treasury bonds with U.S. savings bonds. **Savings bonds** are a whole 'nother animal.

There are two primary kinds. Series EE Bonds mature generally in eight years and are offered in denominations of $50 to $10,000. Those bonds, like T-Bills, are issued at a discount. That is, you would buy a $50 bond for $25 and it would reach a value of $50 over time. Series EE Bonds are a lot like zero-coupon bonds, which are bonds that are sold without the coupon (fixed rate of return). Series HH Bonds, on the other hand, mature generally in 10 years and are offered in denominations of $500 to $10,000. These bonds, like T-notes and T-bonds, are issued at par. A good place on the Internet to learn more about savings bonds is www.savingsbonds.com.

Asset-Backed Securities

Somewhere over the years, you've seen a movie where the greedy banker wanted to get a piece of someone's hide before they would loan any money. They wanted collateral—the assurance that if the borrower doesn't pay up they get the goods. Usually that would be a house. That's what most of the **asset-backed securities** are—mortgages.

Did you ever wonder who owns your mortgage, that debt that you sweat out each month to make the payment on? Maybe you, in small part.

If you own a government bond mutual fund or mortgage-based security, you might actually own a piece of your own home. That's because there are three major organizations that pull all the U.S. mortgages together: the Government National Mortgage Association (GNMA), the Federal Home Loan Mortgage Corporation (Freddie Mac), and the Federal National Mortgage Association (Fannie Mae). These organizations buy the mortgages from the finance companies and banks, even though the banks still service the loans—and hunt you down like a dog if you're late on payments.

The twist to these bonds is that you never know when you're going to get your original principal dumped back into your lap. Imagine that you're a homeowner and every month you pay back a whole lot of principal and a little interest. Well, if you own any of these bonds, you put out a whole lot of money ($25,000 is the minimum purchase of a GNMA) and you get back a bunch of interest but also a little principal payment. If everyone owned their home for 30 years and interest rates were relatively stable, then you could count on a gradual stream of interest and principal. But few people stay in a house for 30 years and fewer still keep the same mortgage, especially if the rates come down. When that happens, homeowners refinance and send a big chunk of money back to the bondholder. Unfortunately, the bond owner then has to reinvest that big chunk of money at a time when rates are lower. Ouch!

So, when interest rates go down, it's a good news, bad news scenario. For homeowners, it's good news since they can refinance their houses in a very competitive marketplace. For investors, though, it can be bad news. If you buy mortgage bonds, you better know what you're doing and not just buy the highest rate out there. That highest rate is most likely to be the first one to refinance and dump the money back in your lap. So this is a great place to consider a mutual fund, so you can leave it to the fund managers to try and figure this principal payment game out for you.

CMOs

Collateralized Mortgage Obligations (CMOs) are bonds guaranteed by some type of asset, such as real estate, credit card balances, and automobile loans. They tend to pay higher yields and are a bit more regular in principal payments than loans that are purely backed by real estate, which are subject to big swings when rates go down and property owners refinance.

How does that work? Well, a CMO is a bond backed directly or indirectly by mortgages. It allows cash flows to be split, creating different classes of securities with different maturities, called **tranches** (French for portion or series). Each tranche is characterized by its interest rate, average maturity, risk level, and sensitivity to mortgage prepayments. This structure increases the consistency of the return, but there's no guarantee on either the rate of return or the maturity date of a CMO tranche.

Municipal Bonds

State and local governments also issue bonds to underwrite the construction or maintenance of streets, water and sewer systems, and other such programs. Wall Street calls these **municipal tax-free bonds**, or **munis**. When states and local municipalities need money for schools, roads, bridges, community centers, or ballparks, they tap investors. The advantage they have is that they can pay much lower rates and still attract the bondholders, because the interest is tax-exempt at the federal level and—if you live in the same state as the issuer of the bonds—state level, too. If you're in the 28% federal tax bracket and have a 5% state tax, that boosts you to 33% total, so a 5% tax-free bond is like getting the equivalent of a 7.4% fully taxable bond. You can figure out the taxable equivalent by dividing your tax-free rate by the reciprocal of your tax bracket. In our example, that's .05 divided by (1 - 0.33) = 0.0746.

Municipal bonds have another big advantage—safety. When it comes to safety of principal, munis are second only to U.S. government bonds. Rare is the city or state that goes belly up. Even rarer still is the town that won't tax its citizens to meet its obligations.

But munis are unlike government bonds in one respect—credit ratings. Like corporate bonds, munis come with a credit report or, more correctly, a credit rating. It's the same rating system as used for corporate bonds. As with corporate bonds, a municipality's credit rating is a reflection of its ability to meet its obligations. The towns, cities, and states that pay their bills on time and have cash in the bank have a good credit rating and those that don't have a bad credit rating. Those with good credit ratings get to pay investors a lower interest rate when they borrow money and those that don't pay a higher interest rate.

So, as you might imagine, many a municipal treasurer spends plenty of time talking to the analysts at the credit reporting firms trying to improve the municipal credit rating, sort of like lobbyists schmoozing with legislators to get favorable treatment.

Figure 4-2 illustrates the grades the rating agencies give out.

Grade	Moody's	Standard & Poor's
Prime	Aaa	AAA
Excellent	Aa	AA
Good	A	A
Average	Baa	BBB
Fair	Ba	BB
Poor	B	B
Marginal	Caa	–

Figure 4-2. Bond grading, Moody's and Standard & Poor's

The top four grades are referred to as **investment-grade bonds**. Those are bonds that most investment managers can buy without any questions from their bosses. The **non-investment grade bonds** are often referred to as **junk bonds**. These are bonds, either municipal or corporate, that are included in what are called **high-yield bond mutual funds**. On the whole, those are risky mutual funds made less risky because they contain a large number of bonds. So even if the bond from one entity goes belly up, the entire portfolio is largely unaffected.

In some cases, municipal governments have bought insurance to make the bonds even safer. So corporations like Municipal Bond Insurance Association (MBIA) or American Municipal Bond Assurance Corp. (AMBAC) have contracted with local governments and security brokers to add another element of comfort. You might get a little less interest on an insured bond, but most folks would be glad to give up a little bit to have the word behind their bonds insured.

Muni bonds are like most bonds. They have coupons, they trade in the open market, they can be sold for a profit or a loss, and they have all sorts of denominations and maturities.

The Long and Short of It

Although most of the Wall Street talk is about stocks and bonds, there's a whole 'nother class of assets, as people on Wall Street are wont to call them, that we should discuss at least briefly—**money market securities**.

Wall Streeters like to distinguish the **capital market** from the **money market** in this way. The capital market deals with debt and equity securities with maturities of more than one year, while the money market deals with short-term debt securities, with maturities of less than one year—and sometimes as short as one night.

Money market securities, as you know if you have your savings in a money market deposit account at your bank or a money market mutual fund with your investment company, are a lot like bonds, especially U.S. Treasury bills (which, by the way, are technically a money market instrument). Money market instruments are IOUs issued by a wide variety of institutions, including banks and big *Fortune* 500 companies. They're offered at a discount and they pay interest at maturity. So, instead of paying a coupon or fixed rate of return, a money market instrument is issued or sold at 90 cents, for example, and at maturity it's worth $1.00—the principal plus 10 cents interest.

In most cases, the average investor doesn't buy these securities directly. Rather, your mutual fund manager buys the securities and you follow the interest rate on your fund in the newspaper. By the way, money market funds all have the same net asset value or $1.00 (we'll talk more about funds in Chapters 5 and 6), but usually pay different rates of interest. That's because all of the money market mutual fund managers are buying and selling different securities in the market, hoping to outperform the other money market mutual fund managers. Usually, money market funds are safe. But investors should beware of funds that pay an interest rate that's extremely higher than average.

Money market instruments, since they're usually issued by large banks and stable companies, usually have a high credit rating and are highly liquid, which means they're easy to buy and sell. But most people, save the CFO (chief financial officer) of a company, know little about these things that have such odd-sounding names as the following:

- federal funds
- repurchase agreements
- bankers' acceptance
- commercial paper
- brokers' and dealers' loans
- negotiable certificates of deposit

So, let's decode these money market terms so you can understand what's happening with this class of assets—and impress your friends and neighbors at parties.

Federal Funds

The Federal Reserve requires banks to keep a certain amount of money in reserve. When a bank doesn't have enough in reserve, it borrows money from another bank that might have more money in reserve than it needs. The interest rate the bank with the excess money charges the bank with the shortfall is called the **federal funds rate**. Usually, the bank that's short a few bucks needs a loan for only one night. (Honest! It's just like you or me hitting up a friend for a little cash just before payday.)

Now, the federal funds rate is important because it usually helps economists and other Wall Street types get a handle on the demand and supply of money in the economy. In fact, many believe it's the leading indicator of short-term interest rates in the future. In short, if the FF rate is high and rising, it's a sign that money is tight. If the FF rate is low and falling, it means that lots of banks have money in excess of the reserve requirement.

Repurchase Agreements

Repurchase agreements, or what Wall Street calls **repos** or **RPs**, are a crazy sort of instrument. Here's the situation. A Wall Street firm, often called a dealer, buys more securities than it can afford and, in effect, borrows money to finance its purchases. Usually, the dealers promise to repurchase the security at a specified date and price.

Bankers' Acceptances

Bankers' acceptances, or **BAs** in Wall Street Speak, are IOUs used to finance merchandise sold in the international import-export market. In essence, a BA is a check or time draft drawn on a bank by an importer or exporters of goods. BAs have maturities ranging from one day to 270 days

Commercial Paper

Commercial paper, or **CP** for short, is an unsecured short-term IOU with a maturity ranging from a few days to 270 days. Big businesses issue CP to finance their short-term credit needs, usually accounts receivable (the money owed to them) and seasonal and large inventories.

Brokers' Loans

If you're already an investor, you may be familiar with something called a **margin account**. That's an account that allows you to borrow up to one-half of the amount in your account to buy more securities. Well, the firm that loans you the money to buy more securities borrows the money to finance your margin purchase. That loan is often called a **call loan**. It has no maturity date, may be terminated at any time, and has interest rates that change daily. The loan is payable on demand the day after it's contracted. If the loan is not called, it's automatically renewed for another day. The call loan interest rate—which is published daily in *The Wall Street Journal*—is used to determine the rate of interest a brokerage firm will charge its margin investors.

Negotiable Certificates of Deposit

Banks issue something called **certificates of deposit** or **CDs**, as evidence of **time deposits**. You probably know about time deposits. They're like the traditional deposit in a savings account—except that you promise to leave your money with the bank for a specified period of time, such as one year or six months, and the bank, in return, gives you a better rate of return than you would receive for a savings deposit. If you need to get your money back from the bank, you pay an "early withdrawal penalty" to compensate the bank for the financial inconvenience.

Most of us are familiar with that kind of CD, which is non-negotiable. But big banks also issue big CDs that are negotiable. That means they can be bought and sold, without a penalty. Usually, the negotiable CD is issued in units of $1 million. For that reason, they're also known as **jumbo CDs**. You're not likely to buy one of those CDs, at least not directly. They're of interest primarily to institutional investors.

In Closing ...

On Wall Street, few people talk with the same passion about bonds and money market instruments as they do about stocks. But at the end of the day, or chapter, bonds have paid for much of what you see in the world—the roads you drive on, the schools you attend, the building you work in. And money market instruments keep the Wall Street machines operating, from the biggest banks and investment firms down to your corner bank and your brokerage firm. So, although stocks may get most of the headlines, our economy also depends on bonds and money market instruments.

WALL ST

5

The Feeling Is Mutual:

An Overview of America's Investment of Choice—Mutual Funds

A mutual fund, according to the trade group that represents the industry, is an investment company that pools money from shareholders and invests in a diversified portfolio of securities run by a professional money manager.

Think of it this way. You and some of your neighbors give the person down the street some money to manage. You toss in $20, four of your neighbors chip in $10 each, and one neighbor checks in with $50. Your money manager invests the $110 in a handful of stocks and all of the investing neighbors get to share in the profits and losses on a prorated basis, each according to his or her investment. The beauty of mutual funds is that it gives people diversification and professional money management.

Diversification

Diversification is a Wall Street word that traces its roots back to the saying, "Don't put all your eggs into one basket." If you put all your money into one stock and it goes south for the winter, you're out of luck. But if you have your money in two stocks or three stocks or 10 stocks and one goes south for the winter, you're probably still in the game.

Typically, average investors don't have enough money to buy enough stocks to reduce the risk. In times gone by, if you had $10 and wanted to spread it out among 10 companies, the transaction costs of buying $1 worth of one stock and $1 of another would have been greater than the value of the investment. In other words, even if you could afford the eggs, the cost of buying the baskets would keep any sane person out of the game.

And that's where mutual funds come in. The manager of a fund is able to buy lots and lots of different types of securities with the money that you and other investors put into the investing pool. That buying power gives each of you ample diversification relatively cheap.

Professional Money Management

The next important element of mutual funds is professional money management. In truth and reality, when you invest in a mutual fund, you really aren't handing your money over to the guy down the street—unless you live on Marblehead Neck, a lovely town on the coast of Massachusetts that's home to Peter Lynch. No, you hand it over to a professional money manager or a team. Most of these folks have MBAs and many of them are CFAs (Chartered Financial Analysts), a designation that's a bit like a mini-MBA for analysts.

We'll talk more about those concepts later in the chapter.

Big Bucks from the Little People

In a way, a mutual fund is America's investment. In a way, a mutual fund is the mass transportation system of the investment business. If Americans are in love with investing, the feeling is ... mutual.

Back in 1980, there were 564 funds; today there are more than 7,800. If you include the different classes of shares, there are more than 12,081 funds, according to Morningstar, the Chicago-based tracker of mutual funds. Back in 1980, there was $100 billion in mutual fund assets; today that figure is up to $7 trillion. Today, there are also 228 million shareholder accounts and 83 million individual shareholders.

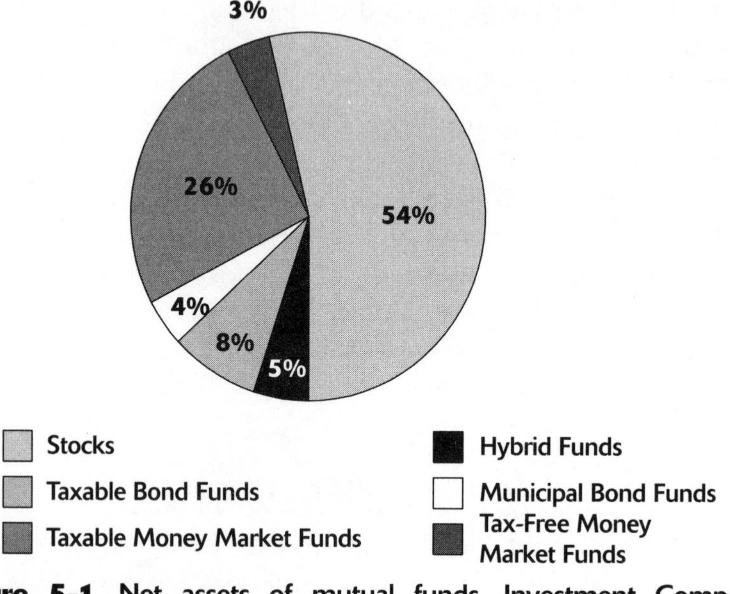

Figure 5-1. Net assets of mutual funds, Investment Company Institute, May 30, 2001

Instead of talking in terms of huge dollar figures, let's think in terms of a pie (just like grandma's apple pie). This chart shows how the mutual fund companies are holding our pie, nicely sliced out.

Now there are three basic types of mutual funds: stock, bond and income, and money market. As the chart (Figure 5-1) depicts, stock funds account for some 54% of the industry's $7 trillion in assets, money market funds account for some 29% of assets, and bond funds make up 12%. Stocks and bonds you know all about from Chapters 3 and 4. Money market funds? That's where investors typically put their money as a place to park it, especially when interest rates are high or the market is low.

There are four main types of mutual funds.

- **Open-end mutual funds.** An open-end fund is, as we've said, an investment company that pools money from shareholders and invests in lots of securities. These are the most common and are priced daily at the net asset value (NAV). Every single day the manager will use their discretion to buy whatever they want within the portfolio guidelines.

- **Closed-end funds.** A closed-end fund is a type of investment company whose shares are listed on a stock exchange or are traded in the over-the-counter market. They have stock symbols and, strangely enough, the actual price of the shares will sell at a premium or a discount to the actual value of the underlying securities, or NAV. When that basket of goods is hot in the market, it trades at a premium; when it's not, it sells at a discount.
- **Unit investment trusts.** Another type of investment company worth noting is something called a unit investment trust (UIT). A UIT is an investment company that buys and holds a fixed portfolio of stock, bonds, or other securities. These securities trade every day and can be sold at their NAV, but it's harder to get quotes on these funds from the major servers. Also there's very little activity in these funds, as the investments are bought in a single basket of stocks (much like an index) or bonds and will be sold only if allowed by prospectus. Many of them have a limited life as well.
- **Exchange traded funds.** ETFs are the latest version of a mutual fund. They have easily available symbols and trade like stocks. Yet they trade very close to their true intrinsic value (NAV) at all times during the day. They're usually an index of a particular style, classes, industry, or foreign country. These funds offer the best of mutual funds, diversification, without the big downside, unwanted tax bills. (Yes, open-end mutual funds are required by law to distribute gains once per year and, in some cases, it's possible that an investor could watch the value of his or her investment decline and still have to pay taxes on the gains in the portfolio.)

We should point out here that open-end funds don't trade like regular stocks. According to the Investment Company Institute (ICI), mutual funds are required by law to determine the price of their shares once each business day, based on the value of the investments in their portfolios. When an investor buys or sells fund shares, he or she receives the next share price the fund calculates. So in the paper today you'll find the price you would have paid or received the day before to buy or sell a particular fund. Tomorrow's paper will contain the price that investors are paying to buy or receiving to sell that fund today.

According to the ICI, each mutual fund determines its net asset value every business day by dividing the market value of its total assets, minus any liabilities, by the number of shares outstanding. On any given day, an investor can determine the value of his or her holdings by multiplying the NAV by the number of shares owned.

Expert Management

People like mutual funds for a variety of reason, chief among them—as we've said—professional management. Most people have neither the time nor the desire to manage their money. So they choose to pay a fee to a mutual fund manager. The fees pay for their expertise. These portfolio managers eat, sleep, and dream the stock market, so it probably makes sense to let them handle your stash of cash. So you climb on the mutual bus with other investors and you leave the driving to them.

That doesn't mean you'll always make money or even beat the averages; the managers may be smart professionals, but they're still human. However, you're probably human, too, so it makes sense to trust in a professional, to take advantage of the greater knowledge and dedicated attention to the market. If you look at all the mutual funds, you'll find the average manager tenure is about 4.1 years, which may not reassure you, but the average number of years that these professionals spend in the business is much longer, because they tend to change jobs and portfolios a lot.

Who's Doing What with My Money?

Now, when it comes to professional management, there are at least five types worth knowing.

Investment advisor/management companies. They call the shots on what to buy and sell and to match the objectives of the mutual fund. According to Morningstar, there are 433 advisor complexes, compared with 123 in 1980. So there are plenty to chose from. We'll talk more about those folks later in the book. (**Advisor complexes**, also known as **fund families**, are the organizations that create the various mutual funds, such as Fidelity Magellan, Janus Twenty, and so forth. Those advisor complexes make the buy and sell decisions.)

Distributor. These are the salespeople who try to make sure that the world knows this is a good fund and you need to put your money in it.

Custodian. They hold the money and the securities and protect it for the shareholders.

Accountants. They make sure no one cooks the books regarding performance and that the tax and financial reporting get done properly. (Just in case you're unfamiliar with the term, we should point out that "cooking the books" is a fraudulent activity by some corporations to falsify their financial statements. And although a good example of cooking the books is "cookie jar accounting," the term "cooking" here has nothing to do with chefs and gastronomy. By the way, that "cookie jar" stuff is a corporate accounting practice of setting aside a reserve to reduce profits in good years and then using that reserve to boost profits in bad years.)

Transfer agents. They make sure all the buys and sells and orders are done properly.

Diversification

We've all been told at least once in our lives not to put all our eggs in one basket (although some think one basket is enough to hold all their eggs). The mutual fund business was based on this fundamental idea to spread your risk around.

The average stock mutual holds 143 stocks in 10 sectors. The top 10 holdings account for 35% of the whole portfolio. Diversified mutual funds can't put more than 25% of the portfolio in more than one stock and only 5% maximum in any other stock. Non-diversified funds can put up to 50% in any one company. So non-diversified funds may give investors some big performance numbers, if they're right, and some equally bad performance numbers if they're wrong. Thus, non-diversified funds are a bit more volatile—read herky-jerky—than diversified funds.

Now, lots of mutual fund investors own lots of different mutual funds. And it's especially important that investors diversify by style as well as security. An investor who owned five funds, all of which bought the same stocks, wouldn't be a very diversified. When that happens, it's called **overlap**.

The Prospectus and Pretty Pictures

If the devil is in the details, then Satan has arrived in the form of a **prospectus**. Every mutual fund has to print one of these and keep it updated. In today's world you get them online if you just go to the Web site of your mutual fund company. The one we used for this illustration took us less than 10 minutes to grab. Prospectuses are not easy to read or even understand, but they're sure getting easier since the SEC tried to force the industry to make them user-friendly. Here are the basics of a prospectus:

Investment Objective and Strategy. This tells you what the fund is trying to do with your money. It tends to leave the door wide open for most investments, but it will tell a bit about the size of the companies it wants to buy or what investment discipline it will use.

Past Performance. It will give you at least an annual return summary of the net return after fees for the past 10 years or however long the fund has been around. The prospectus should include some sort of benchmark that's a fair comparison for the fund's objectives.

Fees and Expenses. This is what a prospectus does best, by explaining who gets paid and for what. It will include the various classes of shares and how much it will cost you to buy and own them. One section is the sales charges. That's what goes to the person selling you the fund. No-load funds don't have this sales charge. Then come the asset management fees, in percentage terms per year. On top of that come distribution or 12b-1 fees, other expenses, and a final total operation expense. There will also be a chart that tells you how much money you will pay over one-, three-, five-, and 10-year periods, assuming a $10,000 investment and a 5% return.

Financial Highlights. In this section of the prospectus, they tell you total returns over the last five years in more specific detail.

Major Players. Here the prospectus lists the credits: who manages the fund and their experience, who sells it (distributor), the board of directors, who processes the trade (transfer agent), and who holds the money (custodian).

Other Stuff. They will tell you specifically how to open an account, account minimums, how dividends and capital gains are handled, exchange privileges, the risks of the fund, and other materials you can get.

In addition to the prospectus, there are Statements of Additional Information, the Annual Report, and the Semi-Annual Report. And don't forget the sales literature—pretty charts, colorful numbers, beautiful pictures, and carefully drafted text telling you all the reasons you need to own this fund. The prospectus is like the instructions on one of those "partial assembly required" toys; the sales literature is the pretty box with the cool-looking toy surrounded by smiling kids that caused you to buy the toy.

Although there are a lot of details here in the prospectus, it's not the best source for making a decision. That's because it tells you just the facts, not the "how to" and the comparisons necessary to make a good decision relative to all the other funds out there. It's a good read, though. It helps you understand the mechanics of the fund you're considering buying.

Fees and Expenses

Shareholder Transaction Expenses: Paying the Advisor

Dave is forever amazed at how many people will slap down $10,000 or even $100,000 into a fund and not even ask what it costs. Can you imagine going to the mall and buying something without a price tag on it?

So the best rule of mutual funds is to spend at least as much time researching your buy as you would when buying a microwave or a car. Be sure to always know what you're paying for every investment you make and what you're going to get for service on that cost.

The main dividing line is whether you want help and, if so,

how much. If you've got it pretty well put together and you need to talk to a service representative only to buy a fund, then no-load (no sales charge) funds are for you. If you need the help of a financial planner or stockbroker, then you'll have to shell out some more cash for their ongoing advice and service. Sales charges, contingent deferred sales charges (CDSC), or 12b-1 fees are the compensation to the advisors. Also be aware that there are programs called **wrap fees**, where a fee is tacked on your account of usually 1% to 2% to pay for their service as well. Just be sure you're aware of both sales charges and ongoing fees. Even though no-load funds don't charge a sales fee, you're still paying management fees.

Fees, Charges, and Loads

You should know that funds are generally sold in one of three ways:

- direct to the public, sometimes called a **no-load fund**
- through an advisor, usually called a **load fund**
- through an institution, like a **defined contribution plan**.

In general, if you buy a no-load fund, you don't pay a sales charge; if you buy a load fund, you pay a sales charge; and if your defined contribution plan buys funds, you typically don't pay a charge.

A load fund usually collects a sales charge in one of four ways:

- front-end or up-front: you pay a percentage fee that's deducted from your initial investment
- back-end: you pay a redemption fee when you sell
- level-load: you pay a percentage fee as long as you hold the fund
- contingent deferred sales charge (CDSC): you pay more to sell out of the fund in year one and less in year five.

Let's get into a little more detail, so you can understand the alphabet soup of share classes.

Front-end sales charge or load funds are the pay-now funds. These are usually called **A class shares**. You pay a sales charge, usually between 1% and 8.5% and you can leave the funds whenever you want, without restrictions. Funds in this class usually have a lower 12b-1 fee. If you stay in the same family of funds, you'll never ever pay a sales charge again because of the unlimited switching privileges. There are over 3,300 funds in the Morningstar universe that charge loads.

Back-end funds are where you get whacked with charges if you pull out of the fund family. These are called **B class shares** and there's usually a magic period of five to seven years. The charges drop over that time. After that period, you can sell without incurring back-end charges. The 12b-1 fee usually goes away after seven years. Also after a seven-year period, the shares usually become A shares. There are over 2,200 of these funds in the Morningstar lineup.

Level-load funds impose an asset-based charge—the annual 12b-1 fee is the sales charge. These are usually called **C or D class shares**. You don't have to lock up your money for a long time, although the funds tend to have a 1% charge if you move out within a year. The 12b-1 fee is 1% for as long as you own the shares. There are about 1,500 of these funds.

The **contingent deferred sales charge (CDSC)** is a type of back-end load. The difference is that the charge declines over time, usually on a sliding scale. For instance, if you sell mutual fund shares that have a CDSC after one year, you may owe a 4% charge, but if you hold for three years, the charge may decline to 2%.

Institutional shares are called T, I, M, Y, or Z class or some other letter way down in the alphabet. These have lower management fees and no sales charges, but you usually need $1,000,000 or more to buy the shares. (Yeah, me neither!) There are less than 2,400 of these funds around.

Now, some of the terms associated with fund sales charges can be a bit misleading. A no-load fund purchased through a fund supermarket like Charles Schwab often has what's called a **12b-1 fee** attached to the fund. A 12b-1 fee isn't a load, but it's an extra expense associated with purchase and sale of the fund. Usually, it's not much, say 30 basis points, or 30/100ths of 1%, but it's still an expense.

Each fund has **annual fund operating expenses,** which include:

- The management fee, charged by the fund's investment advisor for managing the fund's portfolio.
- The distribution (12b-1) fee, charged to pay for marketing and advertising expenses and compensate sales professionals. (The fund can't pay out more than 25 basis points to the salesperson or more than 1% of assets in total 12b-1 fees.)
- Other expenses, fees paid to the fund's transfer agent for shareholder services, like Web sites and toll-free telephone numbers.

After all the expenses are tallied, the fund typically reports its expense ratio, or the total annual fund operating expenses. The number is usually expressed as percentage of average net assets, such as 0.97%.

Fund firms typically offer some services for the fees they charge. The standard model usually comes with toll-free telephone service, 24-hour access to account information and transaction processing, consolidated account statements, and—as marketers are wont to add—much, much more.

Paying the Money Manager

Fee one is the **shareholder transaction expense**, the fee charged directly to your account for specific transactions—purchase, redemption, or exchange. Fee two is for the **annual operating expenses**. These expenses reflect the normal costs of operating the fund. These fees are not charged to directly to your account, but are deducted from fund assets before earnings are distributed to you and your fellow shareholders.

The **management fees** are ongoing fees (we'll talk more about these later) charged by the fund's investment advisor for managing the fund, for buying and selling securities. They get paid whether they do well or poorly. And when they do poorly, they usually don't get fired. Yes, there are some provisions in certain funds that cut the fees if a portfolio doesn't meet its benchmark. For instance, when the Fidelity Magellan fund was struggling a few years back, the fund cut expenses when it didn't beat the S&P 500.

The tell-all number of management fees is the **expense ratio**, also known as the **management expense ratio**. This includes operating expenses, management fees, organizational costs, 12b-1 fees, and administrative fees. However, it doesn't include commission costs within the fund or sales costs going to the advisor.

Management fees vary based on the type and style of the fund. Money market mutual funds are the cheapest, followed (in order) by bond funds, big stock funds, smaller companies, and international funds. The average bond fund has a 1.1% expense ratio, so $11.10 of every $1,000 invested goes toward paying the mutual fund manager to run the fund. The average stock mutual fund expense ratio is 1.55%. But the percentage can vary significantly. A Morningstar study in 1998 showed that 78% of shareholder accounts paid less than this 1.55% average, which means that 22% paid more, as high as 2% to 3%.

Fund Type	Percentage
10B+ Stock Fund (stock mutual funds with more than $10 billion in assets)	.74%
1B-10B Stock Only (stock mutual funds with between $1 and $10 billion in assets)	1.04%
International	1.87%
All Bonds	1.11%
Small-Cap Style	1.61%
Institutional All	.94%
Institutional Bond	.70%
Institutional, Stock	1.06%
Index Funds	.67%
True No-Loads	.93%
Average B Share	1.95%
Average A Share	1.28%
Average C Share	1.95%
Average All Funds	1.37%

Figure 5-2. Types of funds and management fees

The Other Half of the Equation—Performance

Fees are easy things to deal with, because you can count them up and make a quick decision on which fund is best—assuming the funds give the same rate of return. You don't even need to be a mathematician: the SEC has a mutual fund cost calculator on its Web site that allows you to calculate fund fees (www.sec.gov/investor/tools/mfcc/mfcc-int.htm).

Please note that we just said, "assuming the funds give the same rate of return." That's the other half of the equation.

Investors often need to compare and contrast funds not just in terms of expenses, but also on something called **relative performance**. Relative performance is not who's the better bowler—your cousin or your sister-in-law (if in-law relatives count!). Rather, it's more like which fund produces the best returns, assuming a similar investment style, similar assets under management, and similar investment objectives.

Many investors choose **index funds** (also known as **passively managed funds**) because they are cheap and outperform **actively managed funds** more often than not.

An index fund is a fund that's intended to mirror the performance of a certain stock-exchange index as closely as possible by holding each of that index's stocks in amounts equal to the weightings within the index. This process is also called **indexing**. So, for example, you might buy into a fund based on the Nasdaq 100 (the 100 largest companies trading on the Nasdaq) or Standard and Poor 500 (500 of the most widely held U.S.-based common stocks). And there's a bonus with index funds: management expense ratios are lower because management is "passive"—decisions to buy or sell are simple.

A Variety of Opportunities

When talking about mutual funds, Wall Street uses the term **investment style**. As with styles of fashion or decoration, it's a matter of opinion that varies by research firm. For example, Morningstar has 49 categories for stocks and bonds, Lipper Analytical has 29 categories listed in *The Wall Street Journal* every day, and the Investment

Company Institute has a list of its own investment objectives.

As for Dave, he likes to analyze funds using the tic-tac-toe box of investing. Made famous by Morningstar, the style box puts funds into one of nine boxes, according to style and size.

Style, in simple terms, is what you expect from the stocks. Companies that are growing fast go in one column of boxes (**growth**), companies that are growing slowly go in another column (**value**), and those that are somewhere in between go in the middle (**blend**).

Size is a factor of **market capitalization**, or **cap**. As you may recall from Chapter 3, that's just multiplying the total number of shares outstanding by the current price of the stock. Beyond that point, it gets a little more complicated, since not all the folks on Wall Street agree when it comes to translating dollars into the categories—large cap, mid cap, and small cap. Here are three ways to go.

One way is to define the market cap categories in terms of dollars. There are two camps around this flag, differing in the details (and the addition of a fourth category).

Camp One

- **large caps**—$10 billion or more: ,
- **mid caps**—between $1.5 and $10 billion
- **small caps**—below $1.5 billion

Camp Two

- **large caps**—$5 billion or more
- **mid caps**—between $1 billion and $5 billion
- **small caps**—below $1 billion
- **micro-caps**—under $250 million

The third way to define categories, used by Morningstar and others, is by breaking all the publicly traded companies into percentages: the top 5% are large caps, the next 15% are mid caps, and the remaining 80% are small caps.

Stocks in the upper left part of the tic-tac-toe box (large-cap value) are the tamest, stocks in the lower right are the riskiest (small-cap growth), and stocks in the other seven boxes are somewhere in between.

When it comes to bonds, then, the parameters are a little different. What you're looking for here are **credit quality** and **maturity (interest rate sensitivity)**. The farther up the chart (Figure 5-3, bottom), the higher the quality. The farther left the chart, the shorter the maturity. So the safest bet is in the upper left box, with the shortest maturity and the highest quality. The most aggressive would be the lower right box, with long maturities of low quality.

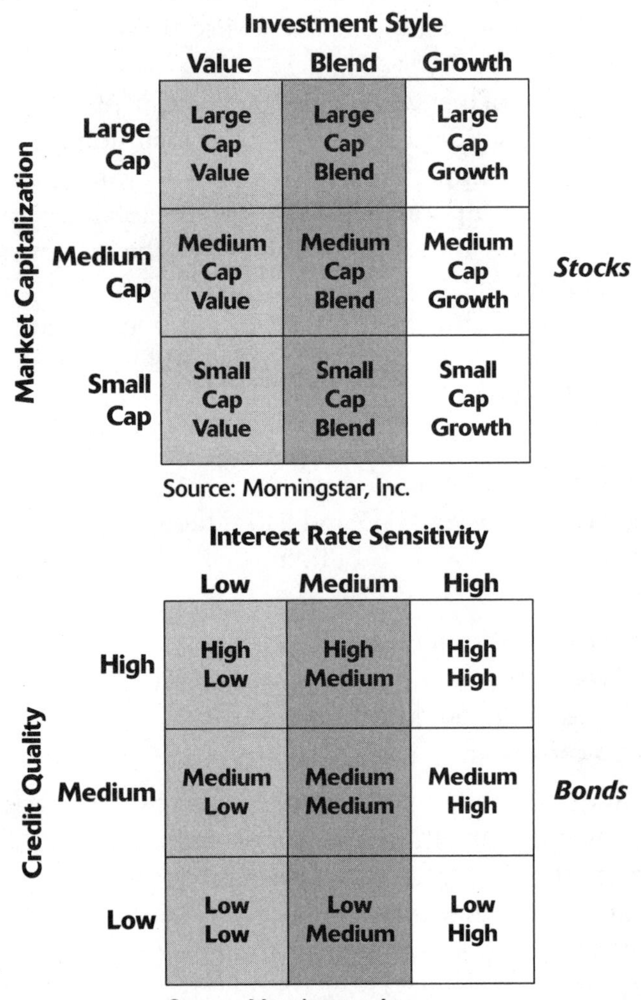

Figure 5-3. Fund styles for stock funds (top) and bond funds (bottom)

Conclusion

That's about it for the basics of "America's Investment of Choice." You're probably concluding that mutual funds have a lot of working parts. Even though a major reason for investing in mutual funds is to delegate the work to a money manager, you have to know what the job description of that money manager is and whether it meets your expectations for your investment.

Diversification, professional management, convenience, flexibility, low costs, and unlimited choices are all really good features. But it's your money and you need to keep an eye on it. In the next chapter, we'll take a closer look at mutual funds.

WALL ST

6

Growth, Income, and More

A Mutual Fund for Every Objective

People and mutual funds have a lot in common. There are lots of them. They come in all sorts of shapes and sizes. Some are built for speed, some are built for comfort, some are built for endurance. Some are dogs and some are stars.

In the last chapter, we discussed the major types of open-end mutual funds: stock, hybrid, bond, and money market funds. In this chapter, we will help you make sense of the various kinds of mutual funds, as defined by their **investment objective**.

An investment objective is simply what the manager of the mutual fund seeks to provide his or her investors. Now, the funny part about investment objectives is this: the three primary reasons why people save and invest are retirement, college education and rainy day fund stuff. But the Investment Company Institute classifies mutual funds into a staggering 33 investment objectives—seemingly an objective for every goal and then some.

So, what terms are used to identify and promote investment objectives and what do they mean?

Stock Funds

Stock funds (technically they're called **equity funds**) are divided into three types: capital appreciation funds, total return funds, and world equity funds.

Capital Appreciation Funds

These funds are designed to do exactly as their name implies. The managers of those types of funds invest in companies that will provide shareholders with capital appreciation; dividends are not of interest. The primary types of **cap app funds**, as they're called on Wall Street, include:

- **Aggressive growth funds**, which invest primarily in the common stock of small, growth companies. (Talk about truth in advertising!)
- **Growth funds**, which invest primarily in the common stock of well-established companies.
- **Sector funds**, which invest primarily in companies in related fields, like precious metals, health care, biotechnology, and (in years gone by) the Internet. Sector investing can pay big returns but it also involves big risks, because the stocks tend to rise and fall together.

Total Return Funds

These funds seek a combination of capital appreciation and income. The major types in this category include:

- **Growth-and-income funds**, which invest in stocks that have the potential to grow and a good history of paying dividends.
- **Income-equity funds**, which seek income first, growth second. The managers look for companies with a good history of paying dividends and that might offer some growth potential.

When it comes to growth stock funds, here's something to keep in mind.

First, the term "growth" is used a lot and with different meanings. There's growth as an investment objective. And there's growth as a type of investment style or discipline: **growth investing** is the opposite of **value investing**.

Second, the term "growth" is often used for virtually every fund in existence, sort of like the way the specific name Kleenex® is used for all brands of facial tissue. Yes, no matter where you put your money, you want it to grow. (Imagine how hard it might be to sell no-growth stock funds!) But since just about any fund will grow over time, it's not quite incorrect to toss this term around.

Just a Bunch of Stocks

Don't forget that these mutual funds are just a composite of a bunch of individual stocks. So if you look at the individual stocks in the year-end 2000 Morningstar stock tools analysis, you would find specific stocks were as follows:

- 7,371 total stocks
- 2,075 growth-style stocks
- 712 blend-style stocks
- 4,254 value-style stocks
- 330 N/A (new companies, not yet in a style box)

And how did these stocks perform over the last three years?

- 1,374 grew revenue at over 40%
- 499 growth-style stocks grew revenue over 40% a year
- 684 value-style stocks grew revenue over 40% a year
- 59 large-cap stocks grew revenue at over 40% a year
- 468 stocks grew revenue over 100%

The fast-growing companies are over all sizes and industries, not just technology, communications, and biotechnology. They cover virtually all of the 10 sectors of stocks. Surprisingly, there were more value-style companies growing their revenue over 40% a year than there were growth-style companies.

So if we haven't totally confused you by now, then just remember that growth comes in all sizes and shapes. Mutual fund managers can invest in virtually any spot and still find rapid growth, if they look hard enough.

Let's Take Some Risks

But there's a down side to growth funds: they tend to be more volatile than value funds.

Figure 6-1 compares returns and volatility for six types of mutual funds over a 10-year period. (Volatility is given in terms of standard deviation, which we'll explain in Chapter 11.) The Morningstar mutual fund universe as of year-end 2000 gives us this:

Number of Funds	10-Year Standard Dev.	10-Year Returns
12,081 funds	12.13%	11.00%
2,320 value funds	14.88%	13.68%
2,420 blend funds	15.63%	13.83%
3,020 growth funds	21.95%	14.72%
4,992 large company funds	16.39%	14.48%
1,664 mid-size company funds	19.33%	14.48%
1,104 small company funds	19.85%	11.41%

Figure 6-1. Fund volatility and returns

The growth funds showed the greatest volatility, with returns only slightly higher than for less volatile funds. Of course the last 10-year analysis is not the be-all, end-all. Every decade has its own special set of economic circumstances and risk/return factors.

Yet these numbers do show that generally speaking, value funds are less volatile than growth funds and had lower returns over the last decade. Small- and mid-sized funds had a wider range of ups and downs than large company funds, yet they really didn't do any better in terms of total returns. The general rule is more risk, more return.

If you look at the latest data from Ibbotson Associates (an authority on asset allocation, providing products and services for investment professionals) going all the way back to 1926, you'll see that smaller company stocks did better, but with higher volatility (Figure 6-2).

So the bottom line here is if you want growth in your portfolio there are a lot of places to go to find it, but stocks are the game. Just be sure when you put your portfolio together it has a bit of everything. Put more in the big companies because they seem to do well

Asset Class	Mean Return	Standard Deviation
large company stocks	11.0%	20.2%
small company stocks	12.4%	33.4%

Figure 6-2. Returns and volatility, large company vs. small company stocks

with less jumpiness. Then be willing to ride out the economic cycles as they inevitably occur.

So, for our final history lesson on risk, then, keep in mind that the stock market goes down as well as up, as shown in Figure 6-3:

Dow Jones Industrial Average Declines	Average Frequency of Declines
5% or more	About 3 or 4 times a year
10% or more	About once a year
15% or more	About once every 2 years
20% or more	About once every 3 years

Figure 6-3. Market events and their timing

World Equity Funds

This is the third and last big category of stock funds. These funds invest in the stocks of foreign companies. When it comes to open-ended mutual funds, there are currently just under 1,800 international funds by objective in the Morningstar database. The major types include:

- **Emerging market funds,** which invest in companies based in developing regions of the world. When markets are good, Wall Street calls these funds "emerging." When markets are bad, Wall Street calls these funds "*sub*merging."
- **Global equity funds,** which invest in companies around the world, including the U.S.
- **International equity funds,** which invest at least two-thirds of their portfolios in companies located outside the U.S.

- **Regional equity funds,** which invest in companies in specific countries or regions, as the name suggests. They're a lot like sector funds in terms of potential returns and risk.

There are many reasons why world equity funds have become popular of late.

First, these funds, especially the emerging market funds, can really outperform all other types of funds. Very rarely does the U.S. have the best stock performance in the world.

Second, despite the fact that 10% of the population controls 90% of the wealth, much of the future growth will occur outside the U.S. Yes, there are an incredible number of people in the world who could use an upgrade in their standard of living. So, from a demand standpoint, there are billions of consumers out there who can drive the world once they figure out how to get a credit card.

Perception of investing in other countries is that it is a risky proposition. The reality is that there are a number of studies that show that putting more of your money into international investments can actually reduce the volatility of your whole porfolio. A good benchmark is 10-20% in international investments.

Year	S&P 500 Performance	Country Funds				
1990	-3%	UK +6%	Austria +5%	Hong Kong +4%	Norway -1%	Denmark -2%
1991	+30%	Hong Kong +43%	Australia +39%	U.S. +30%	Singapore +23%	France +16%
1992	+8%	Hong Kong +37%	Switzerland +17%	U.S. +6%	Singapore +6%	France +3%
1993	+10%	Malaysia +114%	Hong Kong +110%	Finland 101%	Singapore +62%	Ireland +60%
1994	+1%	Finland +52%	Norway +24%	Japan +22%	Sweden +19%	Ireland +15%
1995	+38%	Switzerland +44%	U.S. +37%	Sweden +33%	Spain +30%	Netherlands +28%
1996	+23%	Spain +37%	Sweden +35%	Finland +32%	Hong Kong +29%	Ireland +29%
1997	+34%	Portugal +47%	Switzerland +45%	Italy +36%	Denmark +35%	U.S. +34%
1998	+30%	Finland +121%	Belgium +68%	Italy +52%	Spain +50%	France +42%
1999	+21%	Finland +153%	Malaysia +110%	Singapore +99%	Sweden +80%	Japan +62%

Figure 6-4. Country funds and their returns from 1990 to 1999

Finally, diversification in other countries can actually reduce the volatility of your portfolio. There are number of studies on asset allocation that show that if you increase the amount of money put into international investments you reduce your risk or volatility.

Other Foreign Investments

Of note, besides mutual funds, there are a number of other ways to buy foreign (and we don't mean a Volvo). Those include:

- **ETFs**, exchange-traded funds that are an index of various regions or specific countries. ETFs track indexes like a mutual fund and can be traded like stocks.
- **WEBs**, World Equity Benchmark shares that track the performance of foreign companies, usually in a specific country, and trade like stocks, usually on the AMEX (American Exchange). (If you're thinking that WEBs sound a lot like ETFs, well, you're right!)
- **ADRs,** American Depositary or Depository Receipts, receipts for shares of foreign companies that trade on U.S. exchanges. They help match U.S. accounting standards, so performance is easier to calculate, and they trade in dollars.

Of course, when you're investing abroad, you might expect some problems along the way. So here are a few to think about:

- **Political risk.** The U.S. is the safest democracy in the world. All other countries pose this risk. With emerging and developing markets, you never quite know who's going to be running the show next month. Politics can wreak havoc on investors.
- **Costs.** According to Morningstar, the average management fee on international funds is 1.87%, the highest of any category. If you're buying individual stocks on worldwide exchanges, that also boosts the cost way up because of the transactions and special accounting necessary.
- **Currency.** You can make money in a foreign market, but then lose your profit when you convert it from the local currency into dollars.
- **Accounting.** Here in the U.S. we have the Financial Accounting Standards Board (FASB) to use as a benchmark for our record

keeping. Foreign countries have different standards, if any, although the International Accounting Standards Board is exerting influence on standards in many countries.

- **Regulation.** The U.S. has a flood of acronyms for all the regulatory bodies in the securities business. Things like the SEC, the NASD, and the CFTC (Commodity Futures Trading Commission), not to mention the various state agencies and association watchdogs. Safe to say this is not the case in many parts of the world.

Unless you're a world traveler, then, we suggest you stick to the basics of funds or other securities that trade here in the U.S. Most of the advisors out there don't recommend putting more than 10%-20% into international securities unless you really know what you're doing.

Bond Funds

The next category of mutual funds is bond funds. Bond funds are used by investors who want income and who want to balance the risk associated with their stock funds. Bond funds are broken down into two major categories: taxable and tax-exempt.

Taxable Bond Funds

Corporate bond funds seek income in the here and now, that is, current income, by investing in debt securities by U.S. companies that have good credit ratings. There are four main types of corporate bond funds:

1. **General bond funds** generally invest two-thirds of their portfolio in all sorts of U.S. debt securities, with no restrictions on maturity.
2. **Intermediate-term funds** invest in debt securities with an average maturity of between five and 10 years. These bond funds are less volatile than general bond funds.
3. **Short-term funds** invest in bonds that have an average maturity of less than five years. These bonds tend to act silly (just kidding!). These bonds are less risky than intermediate-term bond funds.

4. **High-yield funds** invest two-thirds of their portfolio in bonds that have a poor credit rating—what Wall Street calls **junk bonds**. Usually these bonds have a Baa or lower rating from Moody's and a BBB or lower rating from Standard & Poor's.

World bond funds invest in the debt securities issued by foreign companies and governments. As with corporate bond funds, there are all sorts of world bond funds, including general global bond funds, short-term global bond funds, and other world bond funds. (Not "other world"—as far as we can tell—but other bond funds from throughout this world.)

Government bond funds invest in all types of U.S. government bonds that have all sorts of maturities. Like corporate bond funds, there are some that invest in bonds with all kinds of maturities, some that invest mostly in bonds with intermediate-term maturities of five to 10 years, and those that invest in bonds with short-term maturities of less than five years. There's also a special kind of U.S government bond fund called a **mortgage-based fund**, which invests mostly in Federal National Mortgage Association (FNMA or Fannie Mae) or Government National Mortgage Association (GNMA) bonds. Those are the bonds that represent the mortgages of millions of Americans.

Strategic income funds invest in all kinds of U.S. bonds. We happen to think that they're a lot like income-mixed funds without the stocks.

Tax-Free Bond Funds

State municipal bond funds invest mostly in municipal bonds issued by a state, like the one you live in. The managers of these kinds of funds invest so as to produce high after-tax income for residents of this or that state. As with most bond funds, there are those that invest in bonds with all sorts of maturities and those that invest in bonds that have maturities of less than five years. Either way, the after-tax benefit can be huge, especially since income can be exempt from state and federal income tax. There are about 1,300 funds that only buy single-state bonds, with the bulk in New York and California.

National municipal bond funds invest mostly in bonds from a potpourri of municipalities. These funds typically generate income that is free from federal tax. Again, there are two types: those that can invest as they please and those that invest mostly in short-term bonds, with maturities of less than five years.

According to Morningstar, there are about 1,850 funds that invest in these kinds of bonds. Historically the tax-free returns have averaged between 4% and 5% or, for someone in 31% tax bracket, the taxable equivalent of 6.5%-7.2%.

If you're into crunching numbers, the formula to figure it out is simple: take the tax-free return and divide it by the reciprocal (1-% tax bracket). Example: .05 (5%) tax-free return divided by .72 (1-.28% bracket) = 6.94% taxable equivalent yield. You can also multiply the taxable return by the reciprocal (1-% tax bracket). Example: .07 (7%) taxable return times .72 (1-.28% bracket) = 5.04% tax-free equivalent return.

Of note, bonds, in general, are likely to produce half the return of stocks. Let's compare the current dividends and the total returns of different classes of mutual funds over the last 10 years (Figure 6-5).

The point of this chart is to show that there are two sides to every income investor, the dividends and interest that we call **current yield** and the **total return** that takes into consideration whether the fund went up or down in value.

As we mentioned in Chapter 4, the prices on bonds change daily, so if you cash out at any time before maturity, you never know what you're going to get back. If you get a nice fat yield on high-yield bonds these days of over 11½%, the bad news is that over the last 10 years your total return would have actually been about 1½% less, due to principal loss. If you're seeking the highest dividend but you still want to be a stock buyer, then think about a **convertible fund**. (These are funds invested in bonds that can be converted into a predetermined amount of the company's equity at certain times during their lives. They tend to offer a lower rate of return, because of the option of converting the bonds into stocks.) If you just want maximum dividends and don't care much about principal, then **high-yield** or **junk bond funds** might make some sense.

Another strategy that we feel works great for retirees or those who want income and keeping pace with inflation is a **laddered**

	Current Yield %	10-Year Total % Return
Stocks		
Growth funds by objective	0.32%	16.63%
Growth and income funds by objective	0.72%	15.08%
Equity income funds by objective	1.49%	14.47%
Stocks and Bonds		
Balanced funds by objective	2.64%	12.14%
Convertible bond funds	3.04%	14.9%
Bonds		
All bond funds	5.77%	7.10%
Government bonds	5.57%	6.89%
Corporate bonds	6.08%	7.32%
Corporate high-yield bonds	11.55%	9.94%
Worldwide bonds	6.69%	5.43%
Municipal bonds	4.5%	6.52%

Figure 6-5. Current and total returns from different classes of funds

portfolio. Here's how it works. Let's assume you have a $100,000 portfolio and you need income. You want to shoot for a 5% current yield, which would be an 8% return minus 3% inflation. So you take that 5% ($5,000) a year you need and lock it up for five years ($25,000). You would do that by putting 5% ($5,000) into a money market account that you could draw checks on for the whole year. Then take the other 75% ($75,000) and buy stock mutual funds. If they average a 10% ($7,500) return, then you should easily be able to replace with your stock returns the $5,000 you spend every year enjoying the good life. If you have a tough year in stocks, then just leave the stocks alone and take 10% next year. Or if it's a really bad two years, then take out 15% in three years. The good

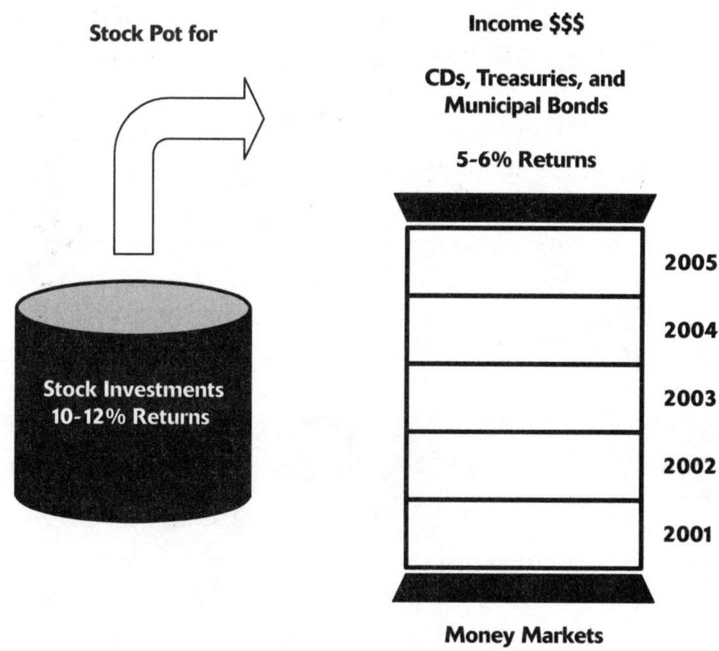

Figure 6-6. Stock pot and ladder investment method

news is that you have five years in absolutely guaranteed investments to hold you over, so you don't have to sell your stocks in bad times. We call this the "stock pot and ladder" method.

Money Market Funds

Money market mutual funds, which should not be confused with something banks offer called a **money market deposit account**, invest in short-term, high-grade (good credit quality) money market securities. Money market securities are short-term IOUs from corporations, the U.S. government, and the like. Investors in these funds are seeking capital preservation and income, although usually nothing more than the going rate.

As with bond mutual funds, there are two major types of money market funds: taxable and tax-exempt. Some focus mostly on short-term securities issued by the U.S government and municipalities, while others invest mostly in non-government securities.

Money market accounts were set up as a matter of convenience in brokerage firms for clients to keep money in something safe while they're waiting to put their money back into stocks or bonds. Today virtually all investment houses have some form of asset convenience account that allow you to tie checking account and credit or debit cards right into your stock accounts. They're all priced at a NAV of $1 a share; although there have been some rare instances where they "broke the buck," it's extremely rare. These assets are not federally insured, but the SEC watches them closely.

The chart shows a sampling of returns on money market funds and their equivalents.

Type	5 Years	10 Years	15 Years
Tax-exempt money market funds	3.04%	2.93%	3.33%
Taxable money market funds	5.02%	4.58%	5.17%
3-month T-Bills	5.35%	4.94%	5.69%
6-month bank CDs	5.50%	5.14%	6.00%

Figure 6-7. Returns on money market funds and their equivalents

Bank money market rates and savings accounts, which are insured, usually produce lower returns than money market mutual funds. One little tip on figuring the direction of these accounts is to find the money market yields in the paper and keep an eye on the average maturity (number of days) listed. If it's getting longer, like 60 days to 75 days, then money market fund managers think rates are going down and so they're locking in longer bonds. If the average maturity is falling, then managers think rates are moving up and want to shorten their yields to get the newer, higher rates.

Hybrid Funds

Hybrid funds are neither equity nor income funds; they're a little of both. As an investor who wants to leave the driving to the mutual fund managers, yet wants to have stocks in there somewhere, sometimes you need a little more esoteric variety to meet your

Year	Passbook Savings	Money Market Account Rates	Lipper Money Market Funds Index	Growth CD Rates
2000	1.65%	2.07%	5.94%	6.64%
1999	1.73%	2.07%	4.74%	5.43%
1998	2.06%	2.47%	5.10%	5.34%
1997	2.10%	2.61%	5.14%	5.71%
1996	2.23%	2.66%	5.01%	5.21%
1995	2.35%	2.82%	5.53%	5.21%
1994	2.16%	2.41%	3.74%	5.40%
1993	2.38%	2.49%	2.72%	2.88%
1992	3.13%	3.22%	3.45%	3.27%
1991	4.90%	5.11%	5.83%	4.95%
1990	5.11%	5.98%	7.93%	7.85%
1989	5.17%	6.27%	8.95%	8.27%
1988	5.16%	5.71%	7.21%	8.15%
1987	5.17%	5.46%	6.26%	6.58%
Avg.	3.24%	3.67%	5.54%	5.78%

Figure 6-8. Bank vs. money market rates

needs. Basically, you want growth (or equity, as they're synonymous) versus income funds. Mutual fund investors look to hybrid funds to bridge this gap into one fund. They invest in a mix of stocks and bonds and something called **derivative instruments**. Derivative instruments are things like **options** and **futures**. (We'll explain derivatives in Chapter 7.)

The major types of hybrid funds are:

- **Asset allocation funds.** These invest in a mix of stocks, bonds, and cash or money market instruments. These funds are typically middle-of-the-road performers, neither rising nor falling as much as pure capital appreciation funds.
- **Balanced funds.** These are a bit like asset allocation funds; they invest in stocks and bonds. But they have a very specific investment objective: capital preservation, income, and long-term growth. To be sure, there are differences between these

funds and income-equity and growth-and-income, but it all gets pretty subtle if you ask us.

- **Flexible portfolio funds.** These invest in common stocks, bonds, and money market securities in the hopes of providing a high total return. These funds are run by investment manager cowboys who have the freedom to roam the range and are bought by investors who like to swing for the fences.
- **Income-mixed funds**. These funds invest in a whole bunch of income-producing securities, including stocks, bonds, and loan shark loans (just kidding), in the hopes of producing income and no capital appreciation.

Index Funds

If you like it cheap and simple, then here's something for you. With a ton of active managers underperforming the indices over the most recent years, this discipline has some merit. It's also nice to get cheap management fees (about half the cost of an average active fund manager), because there are no portfolio managers to pay big bucks to. Index funds use computers to pick their stocks to mirror the selected index.

The most common indices are located on the list below. If you had to pick one all-encompassing stock fund, then the Wilshire 5000 would probably be your best bet, because it's the broadest-based index. The most common would be the S&P 500, followed by the Dow Jones Industrial Average and the Nasdaq.

- **AMEX Composite:** A capitalization-weighted index of all stocks trading on the American Stock Exchange.
- **Dow Jones Industrial Average:** An index of 30 of the largest and most influential companies in the U.S., the oldest and best-known index, often referred to as "the market."
- **Nasdaq 100:** An index of the 100 largest non-financial stocks on the Nasdaq exchange.
- **Nasdaq Composite:** A mid-cap index of all the OTC stocks that trade on the Nasdaq Market System.
- **NYSE Composite:** A capitalization-weighted index of all stocks trading on the New York Stock Exchange.

- **Russell 3000:** An index of the 3000 largest U.S. companies.
- **Russell 2000:** A capitalization-weighted index of the 2,000 smallest companies in the Russell 3000 Index, representing about 10% of the total market capitalization of the Russell 3000 Index.
- **Russell 1000:** An index of the 1,000 largest companies in the Russell 3000 Index, representing about 92% of the total market capitalization of the Russell 3000 Index.
- **Standard and Poor 500:** A market-weighted index of 400 industrial stocks, 20 transportation stocks, 40 utility stocks, and 40 financial stocks.
- **Standard and Poor Mid-Cap 400:** A market-weighted index of 400 mid-cap companies.
- **Standard and Poor 100:** An index of 100 of the companies in the S&P 500 index.
- **Value Line Composite:** A price-weighted index of about 1,700 large-cap, mid-cap, and small-cap U.S. stocks that is not capitalization-weighted.
- **Wilshire 5000:** A capitalization-weighted index of all companies with headquarters in the U.S. for which prices are readily available-now over 7000 companies.

Here's a list of the most common index benchmarks and what they represent. All these are included in the Morningstar database for reference.

- **Barra Indexes** are a subset of the Standard and Poor 500 index, with a combination of size and style categories. They were put together in 1992 by Barra research in collaboration with Standard and Poor. They include indices like large-cap growth, large-cap value, small-cap growth, etc.
- **CPI or Consumer Price Index**, published monthly, measures consumer inflation, a way to know whether your portfolio is keeping up with the standard of living. (For that reason, it's also called the **cost-of-living index**.)
- **CSFB High Yield Index** is compiled by Credit Suisse First Boston to measure high-yield debt securities, sometimes termed junk bonds. The issues are rated BB or below by

Moody's and S&P rating services and have more than $75 million par amount outstanding.

- **DJIA or Dow Jones Industrial Average** is what we see most nights on the news. It's the 30 stocks that represent our industrial economy. They just add up the price of the 30 stocks and divide by an adjusted value to take in changes in splits, dividends, and new additions to the index.
- **JSE Gold** is an index that measures the price of gold by the Johannesburg Securities Exchange of gold-related companies.
- **Lehman Brothers bond indexes** are designed to compare short-, intermediate-, and long-term bond returns. They also group bonds as corporate, government, municipal, and world.
- **Lipper** is a mutual fund evaluation organization that has over 30 representative indexes to measure mutual funds against their respective objectives.
- **Morley Stable Value** is a hypothetical balance of short-term, three-year, and five-year insurance contracts or Guaranteed Investment Contracts (GICs). It's used as a comparison for insurance company-issued returns for investors who want little or no risk.
- **MS EAFE** is the Morgan Stanley Europe, Australasia, and Far East index that includes 21 country returns. It's used as the standard comparison for international investing.
- **Nasdaq**, the National Association of Securities Dealers Automated Quotation System, is a heavily technology-laden index to represent the "New Economy" growth stocks.
- **S&P 500** is the Standard and Poor index of the 500 largest companies that represent our U.S. economy.
- **Wilshire 5000** is an index that attempts to measures all U.S. stocks traded. The broadest index for the U.S. equity market, it measures the performance of "all U.S.-headquartered equity securities with readily available price data." (When this index was created, there were "only" about 5,000 stocks; but now the index covers more than 6,500.)

As we mentioned earlier, you can use index funds as a benchmark for measuring the performance of an actively traded portfolio or buy them directly through open-end funds, closed-end funds, unit trusts, or exchange-traded funds. (A **unit trust**, or **unit investment trust**, is a fixed, unmanaged portfolio of income-producing securities that an investment company purchases and then sells in shares to investors. Just to make it more confusing, this is also called a **fixed investment trust** or a **participating trust**.)

You can even play the sector funds game with these options, by picking a telecommunications fund, a healthcare fund, a financial fund, an international country fund, or just about any specific investment category you could imagine. In fact, these sector funds are good for filling in the holes of a portfolio. For example, let's say your portfolio is light in biotech stocks, but you don't want to buy individual stocks because of the wild volatility. You might just want to plop $10,000 into a biotech exchange-traded fund, unit trust, or open-ended sector to round things out.

A final and big-time advantage of these index funds is that they tend to have very small capital gains at the end of the year. So if you're investing in a taxable account, these funds can make a lot of sense, in particular at the end of the year when all those gains are declared.

Investments Under an Insurance Umbrella

Besides mutual funds, there are two special vehicles that use mutual funds, both of which enable investors to defer taxes: annuities and life insurance. Returns earned under the umbrella of life insurance can defer any income taxes as long as you don't take the money and don't die. If you plan on any or all of the above, then it's time to learn the rules.

Annuities

Annuities are just contracts that allow your money to grow without getting a 1099 tax form every year. The investments *du jour* are either guaranteed rates or mutual funds.

The **guaranteed rate** is very much like a bank CD, with rates being offered from one to 10 years. They are secured (backed by a pledge of collateral) by the general pool of the insurance company but not by the FDIC. There have been a number of cases where an insurance company has run into trouble and assets have been frozen for a number of years. Yet other insurance companies have taken over the troubled companies and, for the most part, investors have gotten their money back, sometimes with a lesser return than promised.

The **mutual fund options** have all the volatility risk of the conventional funds, so you better make sure you've got some pretty good fund companies before you dump your money into them. These mutual funds in a tax disguise are called **variable annuities**.

Here's the way the tax laws work. If you put in $10,000 and it grows to $20,000, then you don't have to pay any income taxes along the way. If you take $5,000 out of that $20,000, then you have to pay taxes on the $5,000 as ordinary income. So if you were in the 28% tax bracket, then Uncle Sam would be looking for $1,400 next April. If you cashed the whole thing in, you would pay taxes on only the $10,000 in gains, not your principal, because that was after-tax money. So our Uncle would want $2,800 by tax day. The method of accounting for all policies issued before August 13, 1982 is called **FIFO** (first in, first out). After that date you use **LIFO** (last in, first out) and the government wants its cash when the funds come out.

Life Insurance

Straight life insurance also has some tax protection. The accumulated build-up in value after the insurance company takes out the cost of pure insurance is tax-deferred. You can get a guaranteed rate from **whole life** or **universal life** policies. If you want to roll the dice a bit with mutual funds, then try **variable life**, which invests the cash values above your cost of insurance into mutual funds.

For tax purposes, you can take out or borrow up to the amount of all the premiums you've put in over the years. On anything that comes out above that, you pay taxes at your regular income bracket.

The Fine Print

It's nice to defer taxes and get some insurance coverage at the same time, yet that doesn't come without some cautionary words. Be sure you understand these items before you plunge into the tax shelters of annuities and life insurance:

- Realize insurance costs. Know that in annuities and life insurance there are very strict disclosures required as to the pure cost of insurance. Ask the agent exactly what those costs are and figure out if you really need insurance. An annuity has mortality and administrative fees that are around 1½% a year.
- Remember that you must be at least 59½ years old before you can take the money out of an annuity. If you do it earlier, you pay a 10% tax penalty.
- Understand that when you die annuities and life insurance do not escape death or estate taxes.
- Know what penalties the insurance company can assess for early withdrawals. They can be substantial.

Building Your Own Portfolio

To finish off our two chapters on mutual funds, we'll end with some words on choosing mutual funds. But not so fast! We're first going to discuss your investment portfolio more generally, because

Capital Preservation		Conservative Approach		Balanced Growth		Moderate Growth		High Growth	
Invest.	Mix	Invest.	Mix	Invest.	Mix	Invest.	Mix	Invest.	Mix
Growth	0%	Growth	0%	Growth	25%	Growth	45%	Growth	70%
Growth and Income	0%	Growth and Income	30%	Growth and Income	25%	Growth and Income	25%	Growth and Income	20%
Income	50%	Income	40%	Income	25%	Income	20%	Income	5%
Cash Equiv.	50%	Cash Equiv.	30%	Cash Equiv.	25%	Cash Equiv.	10%	Cash Equiv.	5%
Returns (assuming hypothetical $2,400 annual investments, 1969-1998)									
Account value: $329,381 Average annual ret. 8.6%		Account value: $476,368 Average annual ret. 10.5%		Account value: $577,116 Average annual ret. 11.4%		Account value: $732,573 Average annual ret. 12.6%		Account value: $860,628 Average annual ret. 13.4%	
Risk/Return Tradeoff (average annual returns, 1969-1998)									
Best 5-year return (1981-1985): 15.5% Worst 5-year return (1976-1980): 4.2% Returns were up: 28 yrs. Returns were down: 2 yrs.		Best 5-year return (1982-1986): 16.7% Worst 5-year return (1970-1974): 1.4% Returns were up: 26 yrs. Returns were down: 4 yrs.		Best 5-year return (1982-1986): 16.3% Worst 5-year return (1970-1974): -2.1% Returns were up: 26 yrs. Returns were down: 4 yrs.		Best 5-year return (1994-1998): 17.9% Worst 5-year return (1970-1974): -5.9% Returns were up: 23 yrs. Returns were down: 7 yrs.		Best 5-year return (1994-1998): 20.9% Worst 5-year return (1970-1974): -10% Returns were up: 21 yrs. Returns were down: 9 yrs.	

Figure 6-9. Choose the right investment

your choice of mutual funds will depend to some extent on what else is in your portfolio.

Your investment portfolio and even your advisor should reflect what you want in your life. If you're a hotshot on the cutting edge, then technology stocks might be your focus. If you enjoy the simple and basic things in life, then maybe value stocks of old-fashioned, quality companies work. If you would just as soon slit your wrists as handle a 10% decline in your portfolio, then stick with bonds and guaranteed CDs.

When we look at a portfolio, we start with two questions:

- How did you mold it?
- What's the current status of your asset mix, your asset allocation?

Allocation is not just how much you have in stocks, bonds, and money markets; it's also what industries your portfolio represents. The high-flying industries tend to be technology, healthcare, and services. The tamer industry sectors are utilities, energy, and consumer staples. The rest—like the cyclicals, financials, and retailers—can go both ways, depending on the economic climate.

The way you pulled together your asset mix is pretty important too. Did you accumulate a lot of one stock or one industry because you worked for the company? Or did you just make a big bet on your brother-in-law's advice? Maybe it was a combination of the last five advisors you had or the last three years of *Money* magazine you've subscribed to. Whatever the makeup, you need to know what discipline and philosophy you're building your financial life on.

If you pick up an asset allocation chart from any mutual fund company, you'll find something that looks like the following.

You can take a bunch of cool quizzes to try and figure out your mix, you can ask a friend, you can consult an advisor, or you can just play it by ear. Whatever the method, you need to track what you've got.

The reason we advise this is that you should try and cut back on the previous year's winners and buy the losers. What? Yeah, that's right. Would our advice make more sense to you if we phrased it differently? OK, buy low and sell high.

The way to do this is to put your asset mix and industries on a piece of paper at least once a year and compare them with the relative indices. For example, if the S&P 500 is 33% technology and your portfolio is 60%, back off a bit—unless you like living dangerously. On the other hand, if last year you were 40% growth stocks and 60% value but this year it's 60% value and 40% growth, then dump some of the value stuff. Why? One reason is that if one style gets much heavier weighting it's likely because it had great performance. The other reason could be because you bought a whole bunch more of last year's winners and sold your losers. That's a deadly problem, because over time styles change: responding to last year's winners could kill you.

If you take a look at Figure 6-10 that we call "investing in the rearview mirror," you can see the results of buying according to last year's returns or in this case returns from the last five years. We've taken the three major stock classes and tested them over 18 five-year time frames going back to 1978, where we get good data on small company stocks. We used the S&P 500 for the large-cap stocks, Russell 2000 for small caps, and MS EAFE (Morgan Stanley Europe, Australasia, Far East) Index for the international benchmark. You'll find that in eight of 18 periods covered, the best became the worst. The worst became the best five times. And five times both reversed. Only two times has the best performer continued to be the best over the following five-year period.

Some may call this contrarian investing; we just call it common sense to stop investors from chasing after hot stocks. On the other hand, if you're a trader, then your discipline will be to jump on hot stocks and dump them when they stop moving. But that jump 'n' dump strategy is not for every investor.

It all comes down to **tactical** allocation versus **strategic** allocation. Tactical is what you do tomorrow in your portfolio; strategic is how it looks over five- and 10-year periods.

Picking and Choosing Your Funds

OK, now that we've reviewed the basics of building your portfolio, we can close our two chapters on mutual funds by discussing ways to choose funds.

Time Period	S&P 500	EAFE	Russell 2000	Best Performer
1/1/79-12/31/83	17.30%	*5.86%*	**26.69%**	Russell 2000
1/1/84-12/31/88	15.24%	**33.12%**	*7.92%*	EAFE
1/1/80-12/31/84	14.77%	*6.52%*	**16.16%**	Russell 2000
1/1/85-12/31/89	20.28%	**34.17%**	*12.92%*	EAFE
1/1/81-12/31/85	14.63%	*12.00%*	**14.87%**	Russell 2000
1/1/86-12/31/90	13.13%	**16.44%**	*2.44%*	EAFE
1/1/82-12/31/86	19.80%	**25.31%**	*15.68%*	EAFE
1/1/87-12/31/91	**15.28%**	*7.17%*	9.29%	S&P 500
1/1/83-12/31/87	16.39%	**31.89%**	*8.62%*	EAFE
1/1/88-12/31/92	**15.81%**	*-0.23%*	15.14%	S&P 500
1/1/84-12/31/88	15.24%	**33.12%**	*7.92%*	EAFE
1/1/89-12/31/93	**14.49%**	*0.36%*	13.99%	S&P 500
1/1/85-12/31/89	20.28%	**34.17%**	*12.92%*	EAFE
1/1/90-12/31/94	8.67%	*-0.19%*	**10.20%**	Russell 2000
1/1/86-12/31/90	13.13%	**16.44%**	*2.44%*	EAFE
1/1/91-12/31/95	16.54%	*7.56%*	**20.99%**	Russell 2000
1/1/87-12/31/91	**15.28%**	*7.17%*	9.29%	S&P 500
1/1/92-12/31/96	15.18%	*6.40%*	**15.64%**	Russell 2000
1/1/88-12/31/92	**15.81%**	*-0.23%*	15.14%	S&P 500
1/1/93-12/31/97	**20.22%**	*9.68%*	16.40%	S&P 500
1/1/89-12/31/93	**14.49%**	*0.36%*	13.99%	S&P 500
1/1/94-12/31/98	**24.02%**	*7.54%*	11.87%	S&P 500
1/1/90-12/31/94	8.67%	*0.19%*	**10.20%**	Russell 2000
1/1/95-12/31/99	**28.49%**	*12.83%*	16.69%	S&P 500
1/1/91-12/31/95	16.54%	*7.56%*	**20.99%**	Russell 2000
1/1/96-12/31/00	**18.29%**	*7.13%*	10.31%	S&P 500

This chart represents a comparison of the rolling 5-year annualized returns for each of the listed equity indexes. The compelling statistic is the inconsistency with which the leading index performs in the following five-year period. The leading index is listed in boldface, with the worst performer in italics.

Instances of best performer becoming worst: 8
Instances of worst performer becoming best: 5
Instances of both happening: 5
Best performer stayed best over next 5 years: 2

Figure 6-10. Investing in the rearview mirror

There's certainly no shortage of opinions these days on how to choose the right mutual fund. Virtually every month, every financial publication lays out the best choices, only to be outdone the next month on the new and better funds.

So unless you plan on doing a lot of trading and hiring a team of accountants to do your taxes, you need a strategy of some sort. So here's the list that lays out our very own top 10 criteria for picking a mutual fund.

#1 Balance. This is rule #1 because it's crucial! Balance your portfolio over different asset classes (stocks, bonds, money markets) and different styles (like those in the Morningstar style boxes in Chapter 5). Don't load up on a single sector or fund, because when (not if) things change, you probably won't know when to change with them.

#2 Industry mix. Knowing the industry mix is key to understanding how much the manager of a fund is gambling. For example, if the performance numbers of a growth fund are great because the manager put 90% of its assets into semiconductor stocks, then you no longer have a diversified fund; you've got a bet. Try to use the S&P 500 sector weightings (10 groups) to see if your portfolio is in line with it.

#3 Management. Your fund is only as good as the people running it, so know about them. Make sure the managers have a tenure of at least three to five years under their belts and then check periodically to make sure those people are still there.

#4 Style. Be sure that the fund manager is keeping to the style of the fund. If the strategy was to buy small emerging companies and now the fund is loaded with big-cap stocks, then skedaddle and find a fund that's managed as stated.

#5 Performance. To play with the famous advice of James Carville: "It's the numbers, stupid." With all the thousands of good managers out there, why pick a loser? The problem is comparing them against the right benchmark and making sure that the manager is not placing too big a stake in a particular stock or industry. So choose managers that are consistently in the top half of their category and in the top quintile over three, five, and 10 years.

#6 Cost. Over long periods of time, even a little cost savings can add up to a lot of money. So try to get a fund that's performing well and is in the lower half of all funds in its category in terms of cost.

#7 Turnover. That's a measure of trading activity, how much a fund manager buys and sells. Every time this is done, it incurs a tax consequence for taxable investors. Obviously, then, low turnover is better. High turnover is also a sign of quick bets in the markets. The average T/O of all stock funds is over 100%; in other words, if they owned 10 stocks, they would sell five and buy five in a year.

#8 Tax liability. If you're investing in a taxable account, be sure you look at the after-tax returns. Also look at the potential capital gains exposure. This is listed in the Morningstar reports and you can call the fund to find out. This is the amount of gains that the fund will have to incur when it sells stocks currently in the portfolio. That figure represents a potential tax liability for fund shareholders.

#9 Risk. You decide what you can handle, but look at the beta, Morningstar risk, standard deviation, P/E ratio, alpha, or Sharpe ratio. Generally the higher the number, the riskier the investment. The exception is the Sharpe ratio, where a higher number is better. These will all help you see the bang that you're getting for your risk buck. (We discuss these and other measures of risk in Chapter 11.)

#10 Size. The size of a fund does matter. If it's a small company fund and it gets too much money, then it makes it harder to invest. If it's a small mutual fund complex, it can also charge higher fees, because of the economy of scale to compete with the larger guys on the block. Most of all, follow the asset flow. If money is pouring into the fund, then it may mean that style of investing has peaked. If dollars are rushing out the door, it can mean negative tax consequences when the manager has to sell stocks to cover redemptions.

The toughest part of investing is, of course, deciding when to sell, because analysts rarely tell you when to do that. When it comes to funds, then you can bet your life that the mutual fund manager, board, or service rep is never going to say, "OK, it would be best now to pull your money out of our fund." (In fact, if that happened, you might suspect managerial insanity—and then it might be wise to dump the fund.) So the best thing is to be sure you're working by our top 10 list of criteria.

Yet here are some warning signs:

- a new portfolio manager
- underperformance for three quarters in a row
- a lot of money coming in or going out of the fund
- a lot more trading (turnover)
- large bets in particular sectors or stocks
- style drift from stated objectives

Finally, when should you hang in there with a fund? Do not sell when your fund is down, especially if the markets are down. This stuff always happens, so wait it out the same way you would a hurricane. (No, we're not advising nailing plywood over your windows and stocking your basement with food and water. Just accept the downs as natural events in the economic world and wait for better times.)

When comparing investment vehicles, you want to compare apples to apples and check your fund's performance against the proper index. It's just like with other vehicles: you wouldn't compare the performance of a sports car, a dump truck, a bus, and a motor scooter. Each of your investments has a different job to perform and a different purpose, so compare each of them against appropriate standards.

7

It's a Mad, Mad, Mad, Mad World:

The Wild and Wacky Markets Where Stocks, Bonds, and Cash Trade

You go to the grocery store to buy food. You go to the shoe store to buy shoes. You go to the toy store to buy toys. Well, the same is true with stocks. You go to the stock store to buy (and sell) stocks.

Well, actually, you don't go in person. You send a messenger. (We'll talk more about that later in this chapter.) And truth be told, it's not quite a store with "sale" signs posted in the windows, either. Instead, the store is called an **exchange**, and there are lots of them all around the world, in actual physical locations and in cyberspace. The exchanges exist simply to bring buyers and sellers of stocks together and to allow some people to make some money along the way. If you want, you might think of the exchanges like big dating services for people who want to sell stocks or buy stocks. (SWM, big dividend, low risk, seeks similar SWF?)

In the United States there are three major exchanges, lots of little exchanges, and some very specialized exchanges. The big ones are the New York Stock Exchange (NYSE), which is conveniently located in New York City, the National Association of Securities

Dealers Automated Quotation System (Nasdaq or NASDAQ), which is located in cyberspace (more on that later), and the American Stock Exchange (AMEX), which is located in New York City. The Nasdaq and the AMEX merged in 1998 to form what is called Nasdaq-AMEX Market Group, but both maintain their separate identities.

To paint with a broad brushstroke, the NYSE caters mostly to large long-established companies, the Nasdaq caters mostly to small companies just starting out in life, and the AMEX caters to what are sometimes called special situations.

The other stock exchanges are often referred to as **regional exchanges** and include Boston, Montreal, and Philadelphia. Those exchanges are mostly country clubs for the rich and wannabe-famous.

The last of the exchanges worth knowing about are the Chicago Board Options Exchange and the New York Board of Trade.

The Exchanges

The Big Board

The New York Stock Exchange (NYSE), also called the Big Board, is the old guy on the block. It's steeped in tradition, with its roots stemming back to 1792, where it all started with 24 brokers meeting under a buttonwood tree on Wall Street. Today, the NYSE is located in lower Manhattan at 18 Broad Street, in a building best known, at least on the outside, for the 11 figures in its pediment that represent aspects of commerce and industry. It's also a building best known, on the inside, for its trading floor, a 36,000-square-foot room that represents the hopes and dreams of millions of investors. (That's 60 million individual investors, according to the NYSE.) Yes, the trading floor is the place where shares of more than 3,000 companies worth a staggering $17.3 trillion are bought and sold Monday through Friday 9:30 a.m. to 4 p.m. How many shares? Well, on average, it's about 1 billion shares a day, which would work out to nearly four shares per American per day.

You often see the NYSE's trading floor on the nightly news when stock prices fall drastically in one day. It's the floor that's covered with scraps of paper and flooded with 3,000 people, wearing different-colored jackets symbolizing different job duties—yelling and gesturing at each other and running hither and yon.

Well, those people are your messengers. They carry your bid to buy a stock or your offer to sell a stock to other investors, who may want to sell you some stock or to buy your stock. Those people have various names, like **commission broker**, **floor broker**, **two-dollar broker**, **registered trader**, **specialist**. Each has a special role to play in the buying and selling of stock, but for the most part they work like a bucket brigade.

Here's an example of the system in action. You want to buy a stock—let's say 100 shares of IBM, which is trading at $100. You place an order with your broker and his or her brokerage firm. The brokerage firm first makes sure that you have the dough to pay for the stock and then puts in the order into a computer. The computer sends the order to the floor of the exchange, either to your firm's broker or straight to the specialist at the trading post where IBM is traded.

The specialist, by the way, is the person who's supposed to match buyers and sellers of certain stocks. If there's an offer to sell a stock, but no bid to buy it, the specialist is supposed to buy the stock with his or her own money. If there's a bid to buy a stock, but no offer to sell it, it's the specialist who's supposed to sell stock out of his inventory. The specialist is the buyer and seller of last resort: it's his or her job to maintain what's called on the floor of the NYSE "an orderly market." (The specialist is usually a Type A personality who you don't want to meet at the end of a bad day in the market.) Once the specialist has found someone to buy your stock or to sell you the stock you want, the order gets placed and—presto!—you have a transaction. You now own 100 shares of IBM at $100.

To be sure, trading stocks may hardly seem orderly to those looking in on the floor of the NYSE from the outside. But the NYSE does have a trading system; there's method to the madness. It uses the time-honored system called the **auction**, the same system as the well-heeled use to buy works of art or kids use when trading baseball cards. On the NYSE, the buyers of stock bid to buy a stock and the sellers of stock offer to sell a stock. Depending on which side of the transaction you're on, the stock is sold to the highest bidder or bought for the lowest offer. The difference between the bid and ask prices, by the way, is called the **spread** or the **bid/ask spread**.

Now, up until 2001, the stock prices were quoted using an antiquated system—fractions: $50½ for $50.50, $50¼ for $50.25, $50 1/8 for $50.125, and $50 1/16 for $50.0625. And once upon a time, a person buying a stock might bid $50.25 while a seller might ask for $50 3/8. Today, however, stock prices are quoted in decimals, in increments of one cent. (Sure, a penny won't buy much, but if you pile up or lose enough of them, it can make a difference!) The world switched to this new system for two reasons: one, technology has improved to the point where trading is less expensive than it used to be, and two, all but Wall Street traders are math-challenged and can't convert 1/8 into real money in their heads.

All-American

The American Stock Exchange is a lot like the New York Stock Exchange. It has a floor where people trade common stocks using the auction system. But, unlike the NYSE, the AMEX trades specialized securities, including index shares and equity derivative securities. **Index shares** are a new type of security (created in 1993) with the advantages of a mutual fund, but none of the down side. **Equity derivative securities** are what are called **options**, which we'll talk more about later.

The Electronic Board

Created in 1971, the Nasdaq is in some ways like the NYSE, too. There are thousands upon thousands of companies, nearly 5,000 at last count, whose stock—worth an estimated $5 trillion—is traded on the Nasdaq. And one billion shares are traded every day. But that's about where the similarities end and the differences begin.

Unlike the NYSE, the Nasdaq has no trading floor—or at least no physical trading floor. The Nasdaq is described as the world's first electronic stock market. The stocks that make up the Nasdaq are traded at many locations around the world; you don't actually see things happening in one place, like the NYSE floor. To help those who need a visual aid, the Nasdaq—which calls itself "the marketplace of the 21st century"—built an elaborate complex in Times Square, called MarketSite, to showcase its trading. It's a 12,000-square-foot sign eight stories high and illuminated 18 hours a day. But all it shows are stock prices.

Speaking of stock prices, the Nasdaq differs from the NYSE in on more significant way. Buyers and sellers of stock negotiate trades and prices rather than use the auction system that's used on the NYSE. If you've ever shopped for a car online, then you know a bit of what it's like to buy or sell Nasdaq-listed stocks. (**Listed**, by the way, is one of those Wall Street words. Listed means a stock is official, sanctioned to trade on such and such stock exchange. Stocks that go belly up get **delisted**, which is a bit like getting neutered in the animal world.)

When you shop for a car online, you send out your specs and the car dealers come back with prices. You then get to determine which car dealer has the best price and you have the chance to negotiate a better deal from any and all of the dealers.

The Nasdaq is a place where the computer is king and traders just "work the box" (the computer). The orders are done by quotes through a network of broker-dealers buying and selling shares based on the Nasdaq computer quotes. There are very restrictive mechanisms in force to make sure that investors, in particular small investors, get a fair quote. That's because firms got into hot water with a major class-action lawsuit for unfair pricing. So in 1997 a new, stricter system reduced the spread (difference between a buyer and a seller) by 40%.

Unlike the NYSE, where there's one specialist at a booth trading the stock, the Nasdaq has a number of brokerage firms that are **"market makers"** in a stock. That just means they maintain an inventory of stock to help match buyers and sellers. The problem here, though, can be that if the markets get tough the inventories dry up because the firms don't want to hold a bunch of stocks that are going down. That can cause more volatility in rocky times. The self-administered regulatory eye that keeps tabs on the traders is called Marketwatch. It monitors news, events, and trades to ensure quality of information and trade regularity.

Like any trading system, negotiation has its pros and cons and auction has its pros and cons. And on the whole, both systems work well for the benefit of investors.

Originally, the Nasdaq was designed to bring together the **Over the Counter** (OTC) stocks. Those were stocks that were not listed on the two major exchanges (NYSE and AMEX). The U.S. Securities and Exchange Commission gave the National Association of Securities Dealers the task of creating a home for those orphaned stocks that "don't get no respect." That's why the image of the exchange is for smaller, younger, more aggressive, and technologically oriented stocks. To this day, three decades later, many big companies that were once itty-bitty companies—such as Microsoft, Intel, Oracle, and Dell Computer—trade on the Nasdaq.

Another interesting difference between the two NYSE and the Nasdaq has to do with something called **symbols**. Each and every publicly traded company has a symbol. Traders use the symbol when seeking the price of a stock. The companies that trade on the NYSE get to use one-, two-, or three-letter symbols, while the companies that trade on the Nasdaq have been forced to with four- or more letter symbols. In the scheme of things, none of this matters except to the corporate big shots who think fewer letters are better. These are the same folks who probably drive Ford Probes with vanity plates. (By the way, the symbol for Ford is "F" and the symbol for Microsoft is "MSFT.")

Investors often watch something called a **ticker tape**, a live account of which stocks are being bought and sold, how many shares, and at what price. The ticker tape uses lots of abbreviations to communicate information; chief among them are the company symbols.

Regional and Specialized Exchanges

Throughout the U.S. there are regional and specialized exchanges that trade securities as well. In some cases, they are kind of an overlap of the Nasdaq and NYSE stocks, because they trade the same securities except they might specialize in a geographic area or sector. For example the Pacific Stock Exchange might focus on technology stocks, while the Chicago Exchange may focus on agricultural companies. The regional exchanges are Pacific, Chicago, Boston, and Philadelphia.

The most specialized of these exchanges is called the Chicago Board Options Exchange, located—you guessed it!—in Chicago. Founded in 1973, the CBOE is a place where **stock options** are traded. When you buy a stock on the NYSE or Nasdaq, you buy a stock. When you buy or sell a stock option, you merely buy or sell the right to buy or sell a stock for a specified price on or before a specific date. What's important about options is this: sometimes, Wall Streeters and sophisticated investors use options to make or lose even more money than they would have if they'd just bought and sold a stock. In other words, average and novice investors need not worry about options just yet. And there are even some pros who ought not get involved in options or their kissing cousin—**futures**. (Some readers may recall the story of the two Nobel Prize-winning economists who ran a company called Long-Term Capital and who lost a ton of money buying and selling futures and who had to get bailed out in September 1998 by Uncle Sam and his Federal Reserve Bank of New York. Enough said.)

Robbing Peter to Pay Paul: Arbitrage

Did you ever walk into a store and buy something, then go to another store and see it priced for a few dollars less? That's called an imperfect pricing system and it happens on Wall Street as well. On Wall Street, however, people can make a lot of money taking advantage of those differentials in the price of a security. They call it **arbitrage**. Simply put, it's noticing price differences and acting upon them.

Let's say, for instance, there's a stock that's trading on two exchanges at different prices. Arbitrage would be the act of buying shares at the lower price on one exchange and simultaneously selling them for the higher price on the other exchange. The difference would end up in your pocket. And it's not pocket change.

Here's an example. You notice that Microsoft is trading in the NYSE for \$60 a share, but on the Pacific Exchange it's at \$60¼ for some reason. Well, if you have a lot of money and a computer that can enter trades immediately, you buy 100,000 shares of Microsoft for $6,000,000 and simultaneously sell them for $6,025,000. We'll do the math. That's a cool $25,000 profit, or .4% return, if all works well. On settlement day you pay the NYSE $6,000,000 and get your 100,000 shares and then immediately send them to the Pacific Exchange where you would get back $6,025,000. You net $25,000 minus commissions (probably 3 cents a share, or $6,000 for the buy and sell transactions). Not bad for a day's work. Of course, it takes money to make money; you need a lot of capital to do these trades. And it's risky: if you don't get the price you wanted, then you can lose a bundle in a hurry as well.

Another, more strategic form of arbitrage is when takeovers occur and there are price differentials between the prices of the stocks based on the combination of the two companies. For example, let's assume that AOL buys Time Warner in a stock exchange where anybody with Time Warner stock will get two shares of AOL for every share of Time Warner. We'll assume that currently Time Warner is selling for $90 and AOL is trading for $50. The market is discounting the price of Time Warner by about $10, because if the deal were done, then two shares of AOL currently at $50 a share would be worth $100, not the $90 it's priced at. In this case arbitrageurs might gamble on buying a whole bunch of Time Warner and then, after the 2-for-1 stock swap, selling their AOL shares for a handy profit. There's a risk that the deal might not go through or both AOL and Time Warner stocks go down in price because of a negative outlook on the companies. That's why arbitrage is a very tricky game: it can take a lot of capital and if things don't go as you expect you end up taking a bath.

Turning Losers into Winners: Shorting the Market

It's been said that you can always make money on Wall Street because you're allowed to play both sides of the market, the downs as well as the ups. Wall Street refers to these two approaches with such terms as **bulls** and **long** or **bears** and **short**. And it can get a little complicated.

You're **bullish** if you expect the price of a stock to go up. You're an owner. You're in what's called a **long position**. You're long. You make money if the stock you own goes **up**. OK so far? Now, the opposite is a little less easy to understand. You're **bearish** if you expect the price of a stock to go down. You're a seller. You're in a **short position**. You're short. You make money if the stock you sell goes **down**. You're un-American. Just kidding! Actually, shorting can be as profitable an activity as buying, especially if you have the dough to play the game. Yes, you have to have money and good credit to use this strategy, because the losses you could suffer are virtually unlimited.

Let's play the game here. You think microchip sales are going to go down because there's an oversupply of chips and demand for the product is slacking. So you get it into your head to sell Intel (the world's leading chipmaker) short. (That means borrowing a security from a broker and selling it with the understanding that you must buy it back later and return it to the broker.)

You go to your broker and get approval to do this. (You need approval because the broker literally has to borrow the stock from someone else at the firm to do this, so there must be enough shares available to be able to short the stock.) So your broker says "OK" and you short 1,000 shares of Intel at $50 a share, which means that they are sold in your account for $50,000 minus commissions—even though you don't own the stock. That balance stays in what's called a **margin position**.

Now time goes by and you must **close** that position at the firm. (That just means eliminating an investment from your portfolio, by selling a long position—selling stock—or, as in this example, by covering a short position—buying back stock that you sold short.) So, you now have to buy back the 1,000 shares of Intel stock that you sold short. Meanwhile, one of three things happens: Intel goes up, Intel goes down, or Intel stays the same.

If Intel is still at $50, you break even when you buy back the 1,000 shares—but you lose your commission and any margin fees that are appropriate (whatever your broker charges for lending you the stock). If Intel goes to $100, then you're in deep donuts, because you're paying $100 a share for stock that you sold at $50: you're down $50,000 plus commissions and any margin costs. If you were right and Intel drops to $25 a share, congratulations! You buy back the shares for $25,000, return the borrowed shares to your broker, and net out $25,000 minus commissions and margin fees.

We mentioned earlier that the losses you could suffer shorting are virtually unlimited. If the stock you short takes off and goes to the moon, you have to buy the shares back at that astronomical price. If there are enough people selling a certain stock short, a rise in that stock price can cause a scramble among short sellers to cover their positions, that is, to buy back their borrowed stock. That flurry of buying can cause the stock price to rise even higher.

Deriving Profit from Derivatives

This is where it gets fun and muddled up all at the same time. Just when you think it's safe to come out and buy a stock or a bond, out pops the derivative ghost that can lead you down a dark and mysterious road to riches or ruins. Here's my first warning: don't try this stuff at home unless you do a lot of homework and figure out the nuances of derivatives. There are three reasons people use these funky investments: to speculate on a quick profit, to hedge themselves against losses, or to cover a number of bases with one transaction.

The term **derivative** refers to any type of security that's derived from a stock or a bond. The two most common derivatives are **options** and **futures contracts**. The characteristics and value of a derivative depend on the characteristics and value of the underlying stock or bond, as you would naturally expect. But dealing in derivatives is trickier, because it may involve leverage—using a little bit of money to make or potentially lose a lot—or a shortened time frame—a stock has value indefinitely, but a stock derivative is good for just a specified time. And, of course, a little Wall Street Speak makes them harder to understand.

Options

An **option** is the right to buy or sell a certain security, usually a stock. As you might guess from the word "option," there's no obligation; you can choose to exercise your option or not. This right is called either a **call** or a **put**, depending on whether the option is to buy or to sell.

A **call** is the right to buy a certain amount of stock at a certain price (called the **strike price**) until a certain time in the future (called the **expiration date**). You do this because you would expect the price to go up within the expiration period. One contract controls 100 shares.

Here's an example. Let's assume you want to buy IBM because you think it's going to go up big. The stock is now (in January) at $100 a share and you think it's going up over $20 in the next six months or so. So you buy what's called a Sept 100 contract, which gives you the right to buy 100 shares of IBM by the third week of September this year for $100 a share. (The three extra months gives you a little wiggle room in case the rise doesn't happen as quickly as you expect.) That contract is trading at $8 a contract. That means you pay $800 (the option is for 100 shares) to control about $10,000 worth of stock (100 shares at $100).

The option has value until its expiration date. You can buy and sell an option, much like a stock or a bond, at any time, and make a profit or suffer a loss. In many cases, the people who buy and sell options don't want to buy IBM stock. In some cases they just want to buy and sell the contracts to make a profit.

The truth of the matter is that most average investors who buy options lose money. Why? Well, let's fast-forward to September. Psychics that we are, the stock is either up, down, or where it was when you bought it. If the stock goes to $130, you'll probably sell the contract for about $30 ($3,000 for 100 shares) and net $22 a share or $2,200 profit, excluding commissions. Do the math! Oh, never mind—we'll do the math. That works out to a 175% gain on your $800 investment over nine months.

By contrast, if you just bought $10,000 worth of IBM, instead of buying the option, and it went to $130 a share, you would make $3000. Very good—yet $3,000 on $10,000 of your capital is only 30% return. It's nice, but nowhere close to a 175% return. That return, if you annualize it, is a 233% gain—which is about 23 times greater than the average annual return of stocks over the past nine decades or so. It's the stuff of dreams. It's like hitting the lottery. It's like … impossible. There are two reasons for this.

One is that options usually trade at a premium to their true value; that is, the value of the contract plus the value of the underlying stock is worth more than the actual value of the two securities. The contract has what's called **time value** and **intrinsic value**. Usually, the longer the contract, the greater the time value and the less likely that investors will make money on the purchase and sale of the contract.

The other reason that few average investors make money using options is that stocks don't always go up. If the price of the underlying stock stays the same or falls, the option will expire worthless and you've lost 100% of your investment. That, by the way, is the way leverage in the market works. You get to use a little bit of money to make a lot or lose a lot—like all of your money and then some.

On Wall Street, for every action there's an equal and opposite reaction. The people who are bullish buy call options: they expect a stock to rise and bring them profit. The people who are bearish, who think stock prices are going to heck in a hand-woven basket from Martha Stewart, expect to make a profit when a stock declines, so they buy put options.

A **put** is just like a call, but in reverse. Instead of hoping the underlying stock goes up, you pray like the devil that bad things will happen to good and bad stocks—that the price will go down. Like call options, put options are speculative investments that usually expire worthless too.

Some investors do, however, use options wisely. The best-known technique is something called the **covered call**. In essence, it works this way. You own a stock that you want to sell for a profit. So you sell a call option at a strike price above the current value of your stock. Then, if the stock hits the strike price, you sell your stock for a profit. And if the stock doesn't hit the strike price, you keep your stock. But either way, you pick up a little cash from selling the call. The covered call—although less risky—is still a fairly sophisticated technique for most average investors.

Futures

A futures contract is an agreement to deliver something at a specified price, on a specified future date. Futures are mainly divvied up into two groups: commodities and financials. **Commodities** include the stuff we eat (e.g., corn, wheat, soybeans, and sow bellies), the stuff with which we build (e.g., lumber and metals), or the stuff that provides power to the world (e.g., oil). **Financials** are contracts on interest rates and stock indices like Treasury bonds and the S&P 500 index.

Many futures contracts are traded on the New York Board of Trade. The two main players are hedgers and speculators.

Hedgers are those who own an underlying commodity, like farmers who are producing wheat or corn or coffee, who would buy contracts to protect their inventory from crazy price swings due to bad weather, or mutual fund companies or investors with big blocks of stocks and bonds, who don't want to get caught with their pants down if the markets take a dive. Currency swings can cause havoc as well, so a lot of big international companies need to protect their earnings. So, because their reporting is in U.S. currency, they hedge currencies on their balance sheet. (It's kind of painful for a company to make a lot of money in a foreign country but then, because the dollar is weak, be forced to book a loss.) By investing in futures contracts, hedgers can offset potential losses.

Speculators are people who try to figure out a system of investing to take advantage of some of the big price movements in the futures markets. Many are professionals called **Commodity Trading Advisors** (CTAs) or **Commodity Pool Operators** (CPOs), who tweak their trading in hopes of developing that magical black box that can make money for them.

Futures are truly high-octane investments that, like options, are best left to sophisticated and institutional investors. Think of it this way. Futures are traded in a place called a "pit." Not a play space. Not a love seat. But a pit. It's a place so loud and wild that the traders have to use hand signals to communicate. Thankfully, there's an entity called the **Commodities Futures Trading Commission** (CFTC), a federal agency created by Congress in 1975 to regulate activities in the commodities and futures markets.

In Closing

So there you have it—the wild and wacky markets upon which stocks, bonds, and other stuff trade. Now let's take a look at the Wall Street firms involved in this thing called Wall Street.

8

The Godfathers: Who's Who and What's What on Wall Street

First and foremost, the thing that you have to remember about the people who control Wall Street, Main Street, and every street in between is that they are nothing more than merchants. Not merchants of death, but merchants of money, merchants of deals, merchants of the intangible, like a safe and secure retirement, like peace of mind. Yes, they are merchants who are ready, willing, and able to sell you whatever you want, whenever you want, wherever you want. They'll sell you products like stocks or ephemeral services like advice. And they sell it with one primary and a couple of secondary purposes in mind. As we've said earlier, these firms exist to make money, for themselves, for their shareholders, and—in some cases—for you. That's the easy part.

The hard part is this. There are lots and lots of merchants out there. Indeed, there are nearly 1,000 brokerage firms, some 10,000 banks, hundreds or thousands of life/health insurance companies, and more than 400 mutual fund firms doing business in the U.S. today.

There are firms that just do deals. There are firms that specialize in selling their research, called the **sell side** of the street.

There are thousands of institutional investors, such as those that manage money for state employee retirement funds and that are often referred to as the **buy side** of the street.

There are firms that specialize in using something called **computer-programmed trading**, like Long-Term Capital (the smart guys that lost a bundle that we mentioned in the previous chapter). There are firms that Wall Street refers to as **boutiques**. No, they don't sell wedding gowns and window treatments; rather, they might specialize in some esoteric aspect of investing.

Oddly enough, some mutual fund firms and investment managers are often accused of doing something called **window dressing**—which is not at all like cross-dressing. Money managers who sell stocks with bad performance and buy stocks with good performance at the end of quarter so that they can show their clients how good they are at stock-picking (not to be confused with the other kind of picking) are often accused of "window dressing" their portfolio.

Those very same money managers, by the way, are supposed to follow something called the **prudent man rule** when buying and selling stocks. Essentially, this means the money manager has to do what a prudent person might do in the same position (as if a prudent person would be seen on Wall Street!).

There are firms referred to **bucket shops** and **boiler rooms**. Like boutiques, these firms specialize in another esoteric aspect of investing—called fleecing the investor. (To be overly fair, we should mention that a bucket shop is a hard-sell telemarketing operation that pushes securities or financial services, commonly using misleading advertisements to entice the public. As for boiler room, well, if you've seen the recent movie *Boiler Room* you know better than we could tell you here.)

There are firms referred to as **wirehouses** (firms whose branch offices are linked by a communications system that enables them to share financial information, research, and prices) and places in those wirehouses aptly referred to as **cages**. (The cage is the place inside a brokerage office where the employees handle the money. It is in no way a reflection on the people who work in the cage.)

There are also nearly one million stockbrokers, 1 million life insurance salespeople, gobs of bankers, and untold numbers of other people associated with what is not so affectionately called the **financial services industry**.

Now on the surface, it seems like a lot of firms and people with which to become familiar. Fortunately, for us (and you) that's not the case. The financial services industry is extremely concentrated (sort of like orange juice) and only a handful of firms really matter. For instance, the top 25 mutual funds control about 80% of the $7 trillion in assets. There are, we think, only seven, maybe nine brokerage firms that are worth noting. Ditto for banks and insurance companies.

But before we dive into those waters, first some background. In years past, post-Depression and pre-Roaring '90s, the financial services industry was fairly easy to understand. Brokerage firms sold stocks and bonds, banks sold certificates of deposit, life insurance companies sold—naturally—life insurance, and mutual fund firms sold—you guessed it—mutual funds. Life was simpler then.

But that was then and this is now. Today, the financial services industry is in the midst of a revolution. The lines—regulatory and otherwise—that once separated firms in the financial services industry have blurred, if not disappeared. Today, banks sell mutual funds, brokerage firms sell life insurance, mutual funds sell certificates of deposit, and life insurance companies sell, well, estate planning (read "life insurance").

Now that you know how things have changed, here's a brief look at who who's on Wall Street today.

The Brokerage Firms

Despite the confusion that the revolution has created, we need only concern ourselves with the household names, the firms that really control Wall Street. By the way, a good place to dig up (and we don't mean Jimmy Hoffa) some additional information about the so-called godfathers is www.hoovers.com. That site provides corporate snapshots for free and offers more detailed information for a fee. The firms on Wall Street are divided into several categories: full-service, retail, discount, trading, and investment banking. Let's take a closer look at the firms in those categories.

Full-Service Firms

The big full-service/retail firms are best known for distributing or pushing products, their own as well as those of other manufacturers. Increasingly, they have their own corporate finance departments pumping out IPOs and the like. They have their own house-brand mutual funds. They have scores upon scores of research analysts who have been named to *Institutional Investor* magazine's All-Star Team. And more and more of these brokers are today offering advice for a fee, rather than access to products, trade execution, and research information. (See Figure 8-1.)

Firm	Broker/Dealer Registered Reps	Rank
Merrill Lynch & Co.	21,200	1
Morgan Stanley Dean Witter	14,708	2
Salomon Smith Barney	12,956	3
The Charles Schwab Corp.	11,202	4
UBS PaineWebber	8,871	5
First Union Securities	8,061	6
Edward Jones	7,560	7
A.G. Edwards	6,996	8
Prudential Securities	6,682	9
Fidelity Brokerage	6,147	10

Source: *Securities Industry Yearbook*

Figure 8-1. Top 10 Firms Ranked by Number of Retail Registered Representatives

Merrill Lynch & Co., with more than 500 offices in the U.S. and more than 13,000 stockbrokers, is far and away the nation's biggest full-service brokerage firm or, as people used to say, national wire-house.

Merrill Lynch offers any and all financial services and products imaginable, especially for the nation's affluent and would-be affluent. What's more, despite its size, the company is capable of launching groundbreaking products. Merrill Lynch, which created in the revolutionary **cash management account** (CMA) in the 1970s, launched a new program in early 2001 called Unlimited Advantage.

With Unlimited Advantage, a client pays a simple flat fee in return for a multitude of services, including consulting, financial planning, investing, and banking. Like the CMA of a generation ago, this product is somewhat revolutionary; it answers the current financial needs and wants of many Americans and is certain to be copied by many in the industry.

The other big national full-service firms are Morgan Stanley (formerly Morgan Stanley, Dean Witter) and Salomon Smith Barney, part of the Citibank family.

Like Merrill Lynch, Morgan and Salomon offer a soup-to-nuts menu of services and products. Most offer tax software, IPOs, bank products, bill-paying services, fee-based investment programs, account aggregation and consolidation, Web and wireless stuff, and a great stable of stock analysts.

Buy Retail or Regional?

Retail firms cater to retail investors. Typically, these firms don't have a strong investment banking department or trading department. But they have an army of people who can move (or "distribute" in more polite terms) product, be it the house brand or that of some other company. The big retail brokers are UBS PaineWebber and Prudential Securities. The small or special-case brokers are A.G. Edwards, Edward Jones, and American Express Financial Advisors. For instance, Edward Jones, which is not a household name, has more than 6,700 stockbrokers and more than 7,000 offices around the world.

A Tisket, a Discount

Discount brokerage firms cater primarily to the do-it-yourself investor. These firms offer lots of investment options, plenty of research, low commission rates, but not lots of personal help, or what Wall Street calls **advice**.

"Advice", by the way, is one of those hot terms on Wall Street these days. Indeed, it seems as if each and every firm is going crazy trying to sell advice to those investors who have neither the time nor the desire to manage their own finances. Advice—it's what America wants and it's what Wall Street is selling these days.

Of course, that wasn't always the case. Prior to 1975, when stock trading commissions were deregulated, and the dawn of the Internet brokerage firm, Wall Street made money buying selling its research or through the commissions it earned when buying and selling stocks for its customers. Way back when, a brokerage firm might be able to charge a customer several hundred dollars to buy or sell a couple hundred shares of this or that stock. Well, today, Wall Street can no longer make money from commissions or research sales. Today, Internet brokerage charge people just a few bucks to buy and sell stock. So, as you might imagine, it's become harder and harder for a big Wall Street brokerage firm to justify charging someone a boatload of money for the privilege of buying and selling stock with a brand-name firm. Ditto for research. Today, information—thanks to the Internet—is everywhere. And no one—save someone who's been stuck on an island trying out for the reality TV show *Survivor*—pays for that stuff anymore.

So, Wall Street has started selling something that people want and presumably can't get from the discount brokerage firms and the Internet brokerage firms—a relationship with a trusted advisor.

Now the big names in the discount brokerage world include Charles Schwab Corp., Fidelity Investments, TD Waterhouse, and Quick & Reilly. Like the full-service and retail brokerage firms, most of the big discount firms have physical locations around the country, as well as Internet-based brokerage services. There are, however, several Internet-only brokerage firms, including E*Trade, National Discount Brokers, Ameritrade, and CSFBDirect.

Worth Noting

Besides the aforementioned firms, which are largely national in scope and capable of moving lots of products, there are several other distributors and manufacturers worth noting. Those include American Express Financial Advisors (4,000+), AIG/SunAmerica (close to 10,000 stockbrokers and advisors), Schwab Institutional (about 6,000 unaffiliated **registered investment advisors**, RIAs), and LPL Financial Services (more than 3,000 advisors). Like the national and regional wirehouses, these firms control much of what gets sold to consumers of financial goods and services.

Trade Ya!

There are some firms on Wall Street that cater either to big institutional clients or to themselves. These firms typically don't have storefronts on Main Street and, aside from the times that someone in the firm loses a ton o' money—say a few billion dollars—on a trade gone bad, you would barely know that they exist. These firms typically buy and sell large amounts of securities and seek to make money on the slightest imbalances in market prices. These are the firms that were profiled in *Liar's Poker* by Michael Lewis or *Bonfire of the Vanities*. The big trading firms include Bear Stearns and Lehman Brothers.

Bank on This

Firms like Goldman Sachs and Credit Suisse First Boston play large, although (to the untrained average American investor's eye) behind-the-scenes roles on the world's financial stage. These firms specialize in raising money on behalf of corporate America, be it through stocks, bonds, or some exotic financial instrument that takes advantage of current fashions on Wall and Main streets or current tax law loopholes. These firms create the securities that we ultimately purchase from a Merrill Lynch or E*Trade.

And Now We Pause for This Commercial

Time was, prior to some recent legislation that broke down the walls between banks and brokers, when banks couldn't underwrite corporate securities and brokers couldn't lend money to corporations. Time was when commercial banks carved out a niche as the institutions from which corporate America borrowed money. Today, the walls have all but vanished. The big commercial banks remain, but their role is changing to that of full-service broker. The big banks include J.P. Morgan (now Chase Morgan) and Bankers Trust.

The Mutual Fund Firms

The mutual fund industry is in many ways like the brokerage

industry. There are lots of firms, but it's really controlled by a few players. There are, for instance, nearly 500 fund firms (as near as we can tell!), but the top 10 control half of the industry's $7 trillion in assets. What's more, the lines of distinction among the fund firms are blurring daily. As of this writing, for instance, one of the nation's largest banks, FleetBoston Financial, is in the midst of buying one of the nation's largest mutual fund firms, Liberty Financial Companies.

Now, once upon a time, mutual fund firms fell into one of two camps: load fund firms or no-load fund firms. In other words, mutual fund companies were defined by their method of distribution. If the company sold its funds through an advisor who received a commission, it was called a **load fund firm**. If the company sold its funds directly to the public without a commission, it was called a **no-load fund firm**. And if a company that sold its funds through advisors tried to sell its funds direct to the public or vice versa, it was called **channel conflict**. Channel conflict is sort of what happens when the gentleman of the house wants to watch *Boot Camp* and the lady of the house wants to watch *XFL* and there's only one TV in the house. People get upset.

Today, there's just one big happy camp. Today, Fidelity Investments sells its funds directly to the public, through advisors with a sales charge, and to institutions that provide 401(k) retirement plans to readers like you. You'll notice, for instance, in Figure 8-2 that Fidelity has the word "combined" next to its name. That's because the assets under management include those from all different channels of distribution—direct, advisor, and institutional.

If you glance at the table, you'll likely notice something else. There are many funds firms whose parent company is a bank, an insurance company, or a brokerage firm.

The insurance industry, like the brokerage and mutual fund industry, is in the midst of huge change. Many insurance companies are merging or being acquired. Many insurance companies are going public or, to use the term of art on Wall Street—**demutualizing**. That's the process of moving from a company owned by the policyholders to one that lines the pockets of the senior management teams.

Rank	Firm	Assets ($Mil)	Market Share (Nov 00)
1	Fidelity (combined)	595,423	13.93%
2	Vanguard Group	483,459	11.31%
3	American Fund Distributors	317,052	7.42%
4	Putnam Investments	217,614	5.09%
5	Janus	166,242	3.89%
6	Franklin Distributors	153,883	3.60%
7	AIM Distributors	102,328	2.39%
8	T. Rowe Price Inv. Services	99,318	2.32%
9	MFS Investment Mgt.	89,513	2.09%
10	American Century Inv.	84,756	1.98%
11	American Express Funds	84,318	1.97%
12	OppenheimerFunds	77,659	1.82%
13	Morgan Stanley Dean Witter	68,984	1.61%
14	PIMCO Advisors	64,877	1.52%
15	Merrill Lynch Inv. Mgt.	61,408	1.44%
16	Van Kampen Funds	55,014	1.29%
17	Alliance Fund Distributors	53,790	1.26%
18	Smith Barney Advisers	52,257	1.22%
19	Dreyfus (combined)	51,602	1.21%
20	Scudder Investor Services	40,579	0.95%
21	Evergreen Funds	36,105	0.84%
22	Prudential Investments	35,852	0.84%
23	INVESCO Funds Group	34,095	0.80%
24	Federated Securities Corp.	32,716	0.77%
25	One Group	31,982	0.75%

Figure 8-2. Top 25 Fund Groups (Long-Term, Open-End Funds Only
Source: Financial Research Corp., Boston, MA

For purposes of decoding Wall Street, it's important to think about insurance companies involved in life insurance, annuity products, and mutual funds. The firms that offer only health and property insurance are of little interest to us Wall Street types.

Multi-Task

The big firms that are engaged in underwriting, marketing, and distributing a broad line of insurance products—including life, accident, health, and property and casualty insurance—would include such domestic and international companies as AEGON N.V.,

Allianz AG, American International Group, AXA, Cigna, Fortis, The Hartford, ING, Nationwide, and Zurich Financial Services.

Throw Us a Lifeline

The big firms that are engaged in underwriting, marketing, and distributing life insurance and related products to individuals and families include Metropolitan Life, Prudential Insurance (parent of Prudential Securities and Prudential Mutual Funds), Metropolitan Life Insurance, The Principal, Lincoln National, Connecticut General Life, Nationwide, Equitable, Anchor National, and John Hancock.

Now, there's something interesting to note about these firms and others like them, if you view them as Wall Street does. He who controls distribution is king. Thus, there are firms in the insurance business as in the brokerage business that are **vertically integrated**. They control the means of production and the method of distribution. They make their own products and they have their own sales force to distribute the products. That sales force is often called a **captive force**. These people aren't behind bars, per se. Rather they have toe (and tow) the company line, which means they're likely to sell whatever the home office tells them to sell. Some firms manufacture products, but sell through people who are called **independent agents**.

The Banks

There are large, diverse financial institutions that serve businesses, government, and consumers called **money center banks**. These banks provide retail banking, investment banking, trust management, credit cards, and mortgage banking over wide geographic regions, both domestically and internationally. The big names include Citigroup (owner of a gazillion types of financial service companies), J.P Morgan Chase, Bank of America, Wells Fargo, Bank One, First Union, and FleetBoston (see Figure 8-3).

The People of Wall Street

The subtitle of this chapter begins with "Who's Who," so we can't close before telling you about all the individuals who work to

Rank	Firm	City, State	Total Assets ($000s) (Dec. 00)
1	Citigroup Inc.	New York, NY	902,210,000
2	J.P. Morgan Chase & Co.	New York, NY	715,348,000
3	Bank of America Corp.	Charlotte, NC	642,191,000
4	Wells Fargo & Co.	San Francisco, CA	272,426,000
5	Bank One Corp	Chicago, IL	269,300,000
6	First Union Corp	Charlotte, NC	254,170,000
7	Taunus Corp.	New York, NY	197,815,000
8	Fleet Boston Financial Corp.	Boston, MA	179,519,000
9	Suntrust Banks, Inc.	Atlanta, GA	103,496,380
10	National City Corp.	Cleveland, OH	88,534,609
11	U.S. Bancorp	Minneapolis, MN	87,336,000
12	Keycorp	Cleveland, OH	87,164,924
13	Firstar Corp.	Milwaukee, WI	77,584,892
14	Bank of New York Co.	New York, NY	77,113,797
15	Wachovia Corp.	Winston-Salem, NC	74,031,652
16	PNC Financial Services Gp	Pittsburgh, PA	69,915,985
17	State Street Corp.	Boston, MA	69,298,347
18	BB&T Corp	Winston-Salem, NC	59,340.228
19	Mellon Financial Corp.	Pittsburgh, PA	50,563, 617
20	Fifth Third Bancorp	Cincinnati, OH	45,856,906
21	Southtrust Corp.	Birmingham, AL	45,164,531
22	Regions Financial Corp.	Birmingham, AL	43,909,839
23	Comerica Inc.	Detroit, MI	42,032,150
24	Summit Bancorp	Princeton, NJ	39,668,367
25	Amsouth Bancorp	Birmingham, AL	38,968,133

Source: *American Banker*

Figure 8-3. The Big Banks (Source: *American Banker*)

make all of the financial companies work. We'd like to be able to tell you about them one by one, with names and photos, to show you that Wall Street consists of people, like you and us—but that would fill many books this size and we could never stop writing and revising. So, it makes more sense to group the players into categories and describe the roles they play in the financial game.

Personal Finance

These are the people on the firing line, talking to you directly to help you get your finances in shape. Dave is one of these creatures. After 20 years of doing this stuff, he knows that the most important thing on the firing line is to disseminate the information from all the gurus—and then to translate their WSS so the small investors understand it. (That's why he wrote this book!) Each of these experts has his or her own areas of expertise and biases, but they should be trying to help you achieve your financial dreams by communicating ideas and concepts ... and then making money for you.

CIMC. The Certified Investment Management Consultant designation is awarded by the Institute of Management Consultants. A CIMC focuses on money manager evaluation and interaction with individuals and institutions. Details can be found at www.icimc.org or by calling 202-452-8670.

CFA. Chartered Financial Analyst. This designation is awarded by the Association for Investment Management and Research to experienced financial analysts after they've passed three levels of exams covering economics, financial accounting, portfolio management, security analysis, and standards of conduct.

CFP. A Certified Financial Planner is the designation awarded to people who have passed a big exam designed to evaluate their expertise in all aspects of financial planning. The designation is overseen by the CFP Board of Standards in Denver. People who have the CFP designation must take continuing education courses and adhere to a code of ethics to keep the right to use the letters after their name. For more information about people with the CFP mark, visit www.cfpboard.org. You can also contact the Financial Planners Association (FPA) at 800-282-PLAN or visit www.fpanet.org.

CPA. A Certified Public Accountant consults with you regarding your tax situation and changes in the tax law by our friends in Congress and the IRS.

CPA/PFS. This designation belongs to the CPA who has taken an exam to become a Personal Financial Specialist.

ChFC. A Chartered Financial Consultant has passed a series of exams from the American College. You can reach this organization at www.amercoll.edu or 888-263-7265.

CLU. A Chartered Life Underwriter, a designation earned by many people who specialize in insurance planning. It's administered by the American College, as well.

JD. A JD is a doctorate in jurisprudence (Juris Doctor). A JD may practice law after passing the bar exam. The designation doesn't indicate any expertise in specific investing and financial planning.

RIA. A Registered Investment Advisor has registered with the SEC and his or her state to offer investment advice. There's an extensive application used to provide the person's background to prospective clients. Called the ADV, it describes the RIA's background and investment style and philosophy.

Stockbroker or **Registered Representative.** The RR is registered with the SEC, the National Association of Securities Dealers (NASD), and state authorities. They usually are an employee of or affiliated with a broker-dealer, a firm that securities. They must pass an examination called a series 7 exam that allows them to trade securities. Other terms used are financial advisor, financial consultant, or account executive.

Odds and Ends

It's Worth More than the Paper It's Printed on

There's one last bit of information worth mentioning about the godfathers of Wall Street. When Wall Street brings a company public, it issues stock certificates. When companies go belly up, those stock certificates become collectibles. The practice of buying and selling collectible stock and bond certificates is called *scripophily*. Oddly enough, some certificates of belly-up companies can be worth a small fortune. You can find out more about this kind of stuff at www.scripophily.com or the Museum of American Financial History, www.financialhistory.org.

WALL ST

9

The Sound of Music: Corporate Finance

Now that you know a little bit about the different orchestras on Wall Street, it's important to understand a little bit about the sections and musicians within those various orchestras. As we said in the previous chapter, the people in the investment banking or corporate finance departments within the various securities firms are responsible for helping companies and governments raise millions upon millions and in some cases billions of dollars to fund their businesses or operations. We like to think of them as the wind section. They need good lungs to talk the talk required to get deals done, which is how they get paid. The more deals, the more pay. Indeed, investment bankers can earn $2 million to $60 million—at least in good times.

Now, in simple terms, this is the deal: investment bankers buy securities (stocks, bonds, or money market securities) and then resell them to the investing public at a higher price. These are the folks who made the term **IPO–initial public offering**—a household term in 1999.

There's a lot of money involved in IPOs. As we write this book, Wall Street is agog over what will be the second-largest IPO ever.

Philip Morris is spinning off—another Wall Street word that means sell off—its Kraft Foods division, makers of Chips Ahoy!, Jell-O and Altoids. The sale of that division, which is the world's largest private food company, was expected to put billions of dollars (maybe 8, maybe 10—who's counting?) in the pockets of a lot of people. (Quick! What's the largest IPO of all time? That would be AT&T Wireless, April 2000, raising $10.26 billion. Now you know.)

Investment bankers are also the folk who provide advice to corporations about mergers, acquisitions, or other financial matters. Besides IPOs, deals of this sort get the most attention on Wall Street. Indeed, as we write this book, there was much ado over several big **mergers and acquisitions**—or **M&As**, as they are known on Wall Street. (For example, in June 2001, a big French firm, Vivendi Universal, bought long-time U.S. publisher Houghton Mifflin for $1.7 billion. More on that later.)

On the surface, investment bankers have glamorous jobs. They earn tons of dough, get driven back and forth to work in long limousines, and wear custom-made suits. But in reality, the work is anything but glamorous—unless by "glamorous" you mean dangerous.

Investment bankers live and die by the times. In bull markets, the number of people who call themselves investment bankers grows like weeds in Bob's backyard. In bear markets, investment bankers are cruising the Internet looking for jobs. In bull markets, investment bankers sell lots of stocks. In bear markets, investment bankers sell lots of bonds.

Looney Tunes

Investment bankers are also living under a great deal more scrutiny than in years past. For you see, the long arm of the law, the Securities and Exchange Commission, reviews the activities of the people who work in investment banking, as well as their brethren down the hall, the securities research department. Why? Because there's supposed to be what's called a **Chinese Wall**, as in long and wide, that separates the activities of the two functions in a securities firm. The folks in investment banking are not supposed to influence the folks in research, who issue opinions, as "this stock is worth buying or worth holding," once the stock has gone public.

Unfortunately, many suspect that's not always the case. Let's give you a 'for example' how and why there's much ado about this.

It's the investment banker's job to search for and work with companies and entities that need to raise money to fund operations. Remember: the more deals, the more money he or she makes. Once an investment banker brings a company public, it's the job of the securities research analyst to follow that company (like a private investigator in trench coat and fedora) and issue investment recommendations—buy, sell, and hold are the most common opinions.

So let's say a new company, called NewCo, goes public at $20 a share and the founder of the company is now worth, at least on paper, $100 million. Now the investment banker wants to keep his client happy; he wants the stock price to go up in the **aftermarket**. (Also known as the **secondary market**, that's when the original investors sell their shares to other investors.) The investment banker also wants to make sure he's in a position to do the next deal when NewCo goes back to market to raise more money.

So, the investment banker saunters down the hall and gently reminds the securities analyst (maybe by way of a sticky note or a sledgehammer) to issue a "buy" rating. A **buy rating**, by the way, usually helps push the price of the company's stock up, since investors (both average and professional) are presumably following the advice of the research analyst. Buy ratings, like the endings of most Hollywood movies, make people happy.

Unfortunately, the analyst—in the percussion section of our Wall Street orchestra—is caught betwixt and between. On the one hand, he wants his firm to do more deals, since the deals generate money. On the other hand, he wants people to follow his advice, since his advice generates money for the firm too—millions of dollars in commission dollars. But for that to happen, the advice has to be pure, free from conflict. If the advice is tainted, no one will follow his advice and he might as well cruise the Internet looking for a job. So the analyst crunches the numbers, talks to management, and ultimately issues a rating. Sometimes it's a buy. Mostly it's a hold—which in the parlance of Wall Street means "Don't buy if you don't own or don't sell if you do own." Rarely is it a sell.

We say, "Rarely is it a sell," because advising investors to sell is bad for business. Bearish views don't generate more investment banking deals for the firm, they don't generate much in the way of commission dollars for the firm, and they can be bad for a securities analyst's career. (In fact, of the 245,390 stock recommendations tracked by Bloomberg in early 2001, only 2% were sells, while 70% were buys and 28% were holds.)

Let's go to the video. Here's Michael Mayo, who lost his job as an analyst after he turned bearish on the entire banking industry in 1999 and issued a sweeping sell recommendation. Imagine the investment banking trying to do deals with a bank when there's an analyst in the company sending the net worth of a some banking bigwig down into the seven digits! Here's Jonathan Cohen, a similar story. He expressed concern over the high stock prices and valuations of many Internet/tech stocks like Amazon.com. For his efforts, his employer gave him—you guessed it—not a bonus but a pink slip.

As of this writing, the SEC has not issued new rules regarding the people in investment banking and securities research and how they should interact or not interact. But many people in the industry were waiting anxiously.

A Day in the Life

Now that you've got an overview, let's get down to the business of the business of investment banking. As we said, the investment banker searches for companies and other entities that need to raise money to finance this or that.

Typically, the process works like this. Investment bankers search high and low for companies and entities. In some cases, they get a phone call from a company executive seeking funds. In other cases, they call around to **venture capitalists**. Venture capitalists are usually the first firms to provide a company with money. They then are typically looking for a way to cash out of their investment.

In any event, the investment banker is typically looking for companies that have a few things in common—a business with a sustainable competitive advantage, solid management, and good financials. Usually, investment bankers move as a herd from fad to fad. In 1998, investment bankers latched onto anything that had a dot-com after its name: that stuff was hot. But investment bankers are a "love 'em and leave 'em" bunch; as soon as dot-coms fell from favor, they moved on to a new fad.

Regardless of how the investment banker finds a company, he or she must follow some standard and legal procedures to bring a company public. The investment banker must conduct what's called **due diligence**. That's the process of investigating a potential investment, checking out material facts to make sure a company is what it seems to be. If the investment banker fails to do an adequate job of due diligence, his firm could get sued later on for what's called a **material misstatement**. That's not when the company says it used rayon instead of nylon; rather, a material misstatement is when a company says it earned a gabillion dollars instead of lost a gabillion dollars. Things like that can lead to a slight interruption in an IB's career.

Paper, Paper, Paper

Once the IB does her or his due diligence, the parties sign a **letter of intent** (LOI). Like wedding banns, the letter of intent sets forth the terms of the relationship. How much money will be raised? In what price range ($10 to $20, for example) will the shares be offered? What percentage of ownership will the owners maintain? And so forth and so on.

Once the IB gets a signature on the LOI, the fun work begins. The IB must then draft a **registration statement**, which is nothing like registering for the draft. The registration statement is a lot of paperwork that must be filed with the SEC. The statement consists of two parts. The first part is the **prospectus**, which contains the important stuff about the company's business. The second part is the **appendix**. By the way, there are two types of registration statements: **Form S-1**, usually associated with IPOs, and **Form SB**, which is usually associated with firms trying to raise less than $10 million or those with a less than robust immediate financial past.

The prospectus, it is worth noting, is the be-all and end-all document on Wall Street. It's the document that's used to sell stuff to investors. The prospectus contains a detailed description of the business, ownership and management compensation, and years and years of financial data, including balance sheets, statements of income, shareholders' equity, and changes in financial condition. It contains information about **golden parachutes**, the severance packages for the company's senior executives.

The prospectus is usually written by what's affectionately called the "sales prevention team"—corporate attorneys who want to make sure the investment banking firm doesn't get sued if something goes wrong with the company or, in the event of a lawsuit, the prospectus contains a disclaimer that absolves the investment banker of any liability. ("What do you mean you didn't read the fine print?") Indeed, the prospectus is filled with sections devoted to the risks factors associated with this or that IPO, so much so that there might as well be a warning from the Surgeon General: "Warning: This IPO might be dangerous to your financial wealth" or "Don't buy this if you know what's good for you." (That's why those attorneys are called the "sales prevention team"—always affectionately, of course!)

Places to Find IPO Stuff

- www.sec.gov
- www.freeedgar.com
- IPO Central at www.hoovers.com
- www.cbs.marketwatch.com

Once the registration is drafted, the investment bankers and the company file it with the Securities Exchange Commission and other regulators, including state securities regulators, as well as the National Association of Securities Dealers (NASD). And then they wait ... and wait ... and wait....

Road Trip

While waiting, the investment bankers and company officials (or at least those who can perform stupid human tricks in public) usually go on the road to hand out the pre-approved prospectus called a **red herring**. That's the document that contains everything but the price, the issue size, and the SEC's final comments and blessing. In what's sometimes called a **dog and pony show**, the IB and company officials go from one financial company to the next, telling their story and getting a sense of how much money they might be able to raise. In other words, they're getting indications of interest. These road shows, by the way, are generally closed to the public, although average investors can sometimes sneak into when the show is held in a hotel conference room, for example. Also, some firms are now webcasting such presentations to average Internet Joes and Joans.

Of note, during the pre-approval time, the company is usually in what's called a **quiet period**. That's a period of as long as three months when the SEC bans promotional publicity. The company can't talk about anything other than what is contained in the prospectus. The company can and usually does publish in *The Wall Street Journal* something called a **tombstone advertisement**. A tombstone gives the basic details about IPO and the underwriting groups involved in the deal. It's a graphically unappealing way of bragging, of saying you've made it to "The Show."

The last part of a day in the life of the investment banker has to do with the afterlife. Before a company goes public, someone has to choose the market where the stock will be listed or traded—the New York Stock Exchange, the American Stock Exchange, or the Nasdaq. The decision is often made by virtue of the company's size. To get listed on the NYSE, the company must meet certain minimum requirements, including pretax earnings of $2.5 million, $18 million in assets, and one million shares outstanding.

Finally, the investment banker and the company set the stage for the IPO. They create a syndicate, that is, they assemble a bunch of brokerage firms that can help sell the stock. Then they start booking orders for the stock. The investment banker is called the **lead underwriter** and receives the biggest slice of the amount to be raised.

It's Showtime!

The night and hours before an IPO can be a bit anxious for the players involved. Usually, the lead underwriter and the members of the selling group are talking to the buyers—the big money managers and mutual fund managers—about how much they would be willing to pay for the stock. Determining the actual price, the **offer price**, is as much art as it is science.

The underwriters need to consider something called **deal flow**. That is, is the pipeline of IPO stock big or is it tiny? If there's a limited supply, they might be able to command a higher price. They need to know the price of similar type of company stock. They need to test the street to find a fair and reasonable price. If it's too low, the underwriters stand to lose out on a lot of money. (Remember: they generate fees on the total amount raised. If a stock goes public and doubles in the first day of trading, it means the bankers made only half as much as they might have.) If the price is too high, the stock won't sell and the investment bankers will have to buy the stock themselves. This one hurts real bad. Instead of not making money, they actually have to shell out dough to make up the amount of shares not sold. Or at least that's the case if the underwriters made a "firm commitment" to sell the stock. If they made a "best efforts" commitment, they're off the hook.

Once the price is set, the stock gets sold and begins trading. Usually, average investors don't have the chance to buy significant amounts of IPO stock. That's a privilege reserved for big money managers and mutual fund managers who can afford to "take down" huge amounts of stock. Think of it this way. If you had the chance to sell 100 shares to 100 people or 10,000 shares to one buyer, what would you do?

Well, that's exactly what the selling group does. The members sell the greatest number of shares to the smallest number of investors and move on to the next deal before someone catches on to the game. Now, once the mutual fund managers buy the stock, they sometimes flip it. That is, they sell the stock to another investor for a tidy profit.

So for example, let's say the opening price for NewCo is $10 a share. A mutual fund manager buys up 100,000 shares. It's a hot issue, so lots of average investors start placing orders to buy NewCo stock. The fund manager and her fellow money managers watch the price investors are willing to pay for the stock rise to $15, $20, $25, $50. Finally, the money manager decides to put her 100,000 shares up for sale at $50. Next thing you know, the fund company, for its $1 million investment in the IPO, has made a cool $4 million profit. Not bad for a day's work.

There are some other things worth noting about IPOs. The senior people who work for the company going public, what Wall Street calls the **insiders**, are restricted from selling their shares for at least 180 days. That period is called the **lock-up period**. In other cases, insiders own what is called **Rule 144 stock**, which likewise can't be sold for a while.

What else do you need to know? Well, a company can go public only once. After it has its IPO, it's likely that a company will try to raise additional capital by issuing more stock. The sale of that stock is called a **secondary offering**.

The Paper Chase

Now, the federal laws that cover IPOs are the Securities Act of 1933 and the Securities Exchange Act of 1934. The first Act says that no stock can be sold to the public unless it is first registered with the SEC and that the registration, the prospectus, must adhere to the truth, justice, and the American way. The second Act requires that a company disclose its dirty and clean laundry at least once per quarter.

The 10-K

The SEC requires that public companies disclose total sales, total revenues, total pretax earnings, and other boring stuff in an annual report called the **Form 10-K**. The 10-K—not to be confused with a 6.2-mile race—is a company's **annual report**.

The annual report—which is the report with the pretty pictures of old white men standing in dark mahogany-walled corporate board rooms—and the 10-K—which is the same report without the pretty pictures—start with management telling you how great the company did or citing the problems during the year that caused them to not live up to their (your) expectations. The report also usually includes a bunch of pretty pictures of the things the company makes and the beautiful people who made or bought their stuff. Next, it gets into the numbers.

The two most important are the **cash flow summary** (also known as the **profit and loss statement**) and the **balance sheet**, which is what the company is worth on paper. The rest is a whole bunch of fine print that your optometrist would love you to read so you would be forced to upgrade your prescription.

Let's take a simple look here at those two biggies of financial statement below and on the next page.

Cash Flow Summary/Profit and Lost Statement	
Revenue or sales from normal course of business	$1,000,000
Operating Income, money from activities that are not a normal part of the business	$100,000
Cost of goods sold, also known as expenses	-$500,000
Amortization, writing off the value of intangible assets–like goodwill, patents, or copyrights–over a number of years	-$30,000
Depreciation, writing off the value of tangible assets–like buildings–over a number of years	-$20,000
Extraordinary items, like the sale of a business	$50,000
Income taxes	-$150,000
Net Income	**$450,000**
Number shares outstanding	450,000
Net income per share ($450,000 divided by 450,000 shares)	$1.00

The 10-Q

The SEC also requires public companies to disclose some of the same information as on the 10-K on a quarterly basis in another form ("Yes, Virginia there is a form for everything."), Form 10-Q, as in quarterly. What's the big difference between Form 10-K and 10-Q, besides the timing? 10-Q is less comprehensive than 10-K and usually not audited by an accounting firm. (Also, when you say, "10-K," nobody answers, "You're welcome.")

Balance Sheet	
Assets (what the company owns)	
Current Assets	
Cash and cash equivalents	$50,000
Inventories (stuff on the shelves)	$50,000
Receivables (what people owe the company)	$50,000
Long-Term Assets	
Building and equipment	$5,000,000
Investments in other companies	$1,000,000
Intangibles like goodwill, patents, and copyrights	$5,000,000
Total Assets	**$11,150,000**
Liabilities (what the company owes)	
Current Liabilities	
Taxes and accounts payable	$25,000
Current long-term debt due now	$25,000
Long-term liabilities	
Long-term borrowing	$4,000,000
Total liabilities	$4,050,000
Shareholders' Equity (what shareholders own) = Assets minus Liabilities	$7,100,000
Total Liabilities and Shareholders' Equity	**$11,150,000**

The Proxy Statement

The SEC requires that a public company provide information to its shareholders before the company votes on certain issues, like the board of directors, a merger, or the selection of a new auditor (especially if the last one screwed up). The **proxy statement** usually comes in the mail with the annual report and contains all the good gossip, like how much stock the insiders own, how much they get paid, and who the directors are and their backgrounds.

Well, "gossip" may be an exaggeration, since the statements are written in a style that only a lawyer could love ... or even decipher. But if you can make it through your first proxy statement, you can be sure that the others will be relatively easy, since they'll be virtually the same in style, form, and language. And, as Martha Stewart would have put it back in the years when she was a successful stockbroker on Wall Street, "That's a good thing."

Knock, Knock! Who's There? Edgar. Edgar Who?

Egads! It's *Edgar*—as in Electronic Data Gathering, Analysis, and Retrieval. Edgar is the system in which the SEC keeps the aforementioned legally required documents, the Form 10-K, the Form 10-Q, and a couple others. Investor types can now scour the documents filed in Edgar—which some do every day, if not even minute by minute. Imagine doing that for a living! Well, if you could make a million dollars a day at it, we guess it couldn't be that bad.

Anyway, there are several sites where you can get Edgar information for free in a hard-to-read format and several places to get Edgar information for a fee in an easy-to-read format. The free ones include www.sec.gov and www.freeedgar.com. The for-fee ones include www.edgar-online.com.

Going Beyond the Forms and Figures

Well, now you know what investment bankers do, how IPOs work, and what information the SEC requires from companies and makes available to investors. You may not want to actually read a prospectus or do more than skim a 10-K or a 10-Q, unless you're suffering from insomnia. But in the next chapter you'll find out all about people who do that stuff for a living and the role they play in the orchestra of Wall Street.

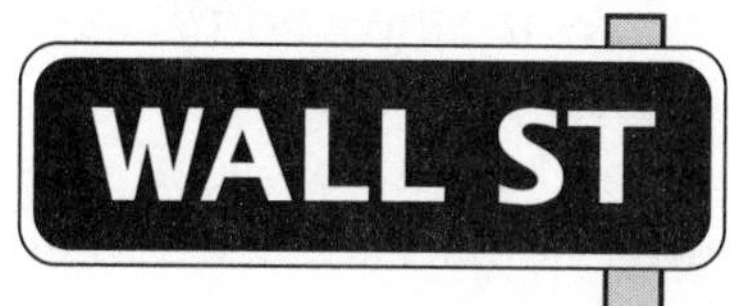

10

The Song Sheet:
How to Read an Analyst's Opus and Other Musical Scores

"Sing a goofy song and you can't go wrong. We-de-do, we-de-do, we-de-do." Well, if you've ever read an analyst's report, then you know how we feel. If you've never read an analyst's report, then you're about to know how we feel.

Yes, the analyst's report can be a bit goofy, especially since it's rare that any analyst is ever taken to task for being "wrong." (You have to wonder how these supposedly bright MBAs who review and rate stocks ever got through school.)

Just What the Heck Is a Report Anyway?

Wall Street analysts, many of whom earn as much as sports stars without having to work up as much of a sweat, issue reports about the companies they follow. On Wall Street, many students who go to Harvard Business School or the Wharton School cut their teeth by analyzing publicly traded companies. More often than not, they follow a specific industry, like utilities or technology.

Peter Lynch, our hero, began his career with Fidelity this way. He went to Wharton and then went to work at Fidelity, the world's largest mutual fund firm, following the chemical industry or some such boring industry. After he paid his dues, he got to run what was to become the world's largest, most famous, and, at times, best-performing mutual fund. Of course, it didn't hurt that Peter used to caddy for one of Fidelity's muckety-mucks when he was growing up. But that's a story for another day.

Anyway, these analysts—many of whom work in relative obscurity, compared with sports stars—usually get another designation along the way—a CFA. As you may remember from the end of Chapter 8, that stands for Chartered Financial Analyst. It's sort of like a mini-MBA and presumably helps the analyst do a better job of analyzing a company's financial health and predicting its future.

Which brings us back to the report. After an analyst reviews a company's financial health, its balance sheet and income statement, and other such financial and business statements, he or she makes a verdict as to whether this or that company's stock should be bought, held, or sold. (More on that later in this chapter.)

The balance sheet reflects a company's assets and liabilities or what is called **net worth** and the income statement reflects its revenue and profitability. Checking those two items to get a sense of a company's financial health is like a doctor checking your blood pressure and heart rate during a general physical.

The reports typically present a conclusion ("buy" or "hold," for example) that is supported by some persuasive language and some complicated analysis of the company's financials. Much like a lawyer making opening or closing arguments, these analysts try to make a case for their recommendation.

These analysts typically write in CFAese or MBAese and they must get paid by the word: some industry reports run 100 pages or so and some company reports run 10 pages or so. If you look at a report in its entirety, you're likely to be overwhelmed by its size and its jargon. The trick to reading a report is to break it down its elements.

Great places to read or buy analysts' reports

Multex.com: multex.com
First Call: www1.firstcall.com
Market Guide (from Multex.com): marketguide.com

So, what are the elements on which you should focus? Well, most reports contain an **executive summary**. The summary typically contains three elements—the analyst's qualitative analysis, a quantitative analysis, and some good old-fashioned gut or gutless instincts. In other words, the report reflects the following:

1. *Number crunching*. That's basic for a report, but the numbers aren't enough. If it were, then mathematicians would rule the world—or at least Wall Street.

2. *Kicking the tires*. Analysts presumably talk with a company's management every so often, either in person or by phone. Some analysts believe that you can tell if management is lying about whether their companies will "hit their numbers" (meet their expected earnings). There's much ado about hitting the numbers on Wall Street. (We'll talk about more about that in just a second or two.)

   At one time a company's management and an analyst could talk in private about the company's prospects, but a new regulation issued in fall 2000 by the Securities and Exchange Commission called **Regulation Full Disclosure** (affectionately known as Reg FD) changed all that. Now a company must disclose all "material" information about its financials and its future to every Tom, Dick, and hairy analyst at the same time. (**Material**, in the parlance of Wall Street, usually means important.)

3. *Instinct*. Sometimes an analyst has a sixth sense that helps him or her divine the future in spite of bad numbers and bad management. Peter Lynch had it, and the world and his shareholders witnessed it most memorably when years ago he bought shares of Chrysler, then on the verge of bankruptcy, and made a ton of dough, a **"ten-bagger"** in his parlance. (That's a stock that gains at least 10 times its original value.)

By the way, the analysts and money managers on Wall Street often move as a herd, together. If someone issues a buy rating, then others are certain to follow. That's why you often hear people accusing Wall Street of having a herd mentality. And that's why people whose instincts move them in another direction tend to stand out in the crowd.

Earn Your Keep

Recall, for a moment, the theme that runs through Wall Street. If you said "money," you're right. If you said something else, just pretend you said "money." (Unless you're reading this book out loud, nobody will know your answer.) To adapt the famous catchword of Rod Tidwell, the Cuba Gooding, Jr. character in *Jerry Maguire,* "Show us the money!"

That's right: the analyst's review of the company's profits or earnings per share relative to its stock price is, we believe, the most important element of his or her report. At the end of the day and the beginning of the night, it's the earnings that drive the stock price up. Sometimes, as we know from the good ol' Internet days, a great story or fad will do the same. But it doesn't last forever—as many people found out the hard way. By the way, if you want a good book on the subject of "bubbles," inflated stock prices that don't reflect true value, try the *Extraordinary Popular Delusions and the Madness of Crowds* by Charles Mackay.

To be sure, it's not easy to figure out a company's earnings. Sure, a company reports its earnings as required by the Securities and Exchange Commission, once per quarter. But sometimes the earnings reflect one-time charges, like the cost of laying off thousands of employees and giving them severance packages. And if that's not hard enough, the analyst has to predict the future: he or she has to calculate the company's future earnings and then determine, in light of that prediction, whether the company's stock price is overvalued, fairly valued, or undervalued.

Analysts—like the shoppers who flock to Filene's Basement stores—often talk in terms of **valuation**. A stock is **undervalued**, and thus worth buying or keeping, if the analyst believes the price should be higher. A stock is **overvalued**, and it should be sold or not bought, if the analyst believes the stock price is too high. And a stock is **fairly valued** if the stock price is just right, in the opinion of the analyst, and we presume worth holding or selling, but not buying. It's a little like the story of *Goldilocks and the Three Bears:* "This stock is valued too low, this stock is valued too high, and this stock is just right."

A company typically reports its earnings in big numbers, like $10.5 gatrillion. But analysts will typically boil that number down into something called **earnings per share** (EPS). The EPS is the earnings divided by the number of shares outstanding. So the $10.5 gatrillion becomes $0.10 after you divide it by 105 gatrillion shares outstanding.

EPS is an important number on Wall Street. But that number requires context and perspective. That's why an analyst will also focus on two other numbers. One is **stock price**, which we just mentioned. The other is something called the **price/earnings ratio** (P/E), which is the single most used ratio in stock analysis.

As we just said, the analyst attempts to figure out whether the stock is worth buying or not. And he or she does this by dividing the price of the company's stock (P) by its earnings per share (EPS). The result is the P/E. The P/E is the Swiss Army knife of stock analysis. It's used in many ways, but its first and primary use is to assess value. Price in the absence of earnings doesn't reflect value and earnings per share in the absence of price doesn't reflect value. But P divided by EPS does.

Now, the P/E ratio must be viewed in context as well. But as a rule, the higher the P/E the faster a company is expected to grow and the more volatile its stock will be as an investment. The lower the P/E, the slower a company is expected to grow and the less volatile its stock will be as an investment. But everything is relative; you should also consider the following:

1. a company's historic P/E, its P/E over the course of its history;
2. the P/E for the industry in which the company operates; and
3. the P/E for the general market.

Let's take an example. A stock is trading at $20 a share and earns $1 per share a year. That means the P/E is 20 times earnings. That doesn't tell you much unless you have some benchmark to compare, which is usually the P/E of the S&P 500. If the S&P 500 is 20 as well, then investors are expecting this company to grow in line with the market averages. If the S&P is at a 10 P/E, then investors would expect this stock to grow twice as fast as the market. If the S&P is 40, then this would be considered a slow grower, at half the market multiple. (A **multiple** is any ratio, usually greater than one, and sometimes specifically a P/E.)

Another way investors have historically looked at the P/E is that the growth rate of the company's earnings should equal the P/E. So if the P/E is 20, the company should be growing its earnings (as they say on Wall Street) at 20%. If you have a 100 P/E, expect a 100% growth rate.

That brings us to another number used in an analyst's report—the **PEG ratio**. That's P/E divided by earnings growth rate. If a company is growing its earnings by 10% and the P/E is 20, you get a PEG of 2. If it's growing at 40% and the P/E is 20, you get a PEG of 1/2. In the scheme of things, analysts—Peter Lynch among them—like to buy companies that have PEG ratios under 1, under ½ in fact. It means you're paying 50 cents for $1 worth of growth.

To estimate a company's future earnings per share, analysts use super computer models. These models, which are the same ones as used to launch space shuttles (but not the Mir), have little room for error. That's why, when a company reports an EPS number that's different from all of Wall Street analysts, fits happen. The analysts have to rerun all the numbers to determine whether the stock is a buy or not. When a company reports lower earnings per share than expected, it suggests that it might be growing slower than expected and hence might now be overvalued. Wall Street refers to this as an **earnings disappointment** and the stock gets **hammered**. (That term means, as you'd expect, that investors sell the stock in large amounts and the price falls.) If a company that reports higher earnings per share than expected, it suggests that it might be growing faster than expected and hence might now be undervalued.

By the way, First Call, a company cited earlier in this chapter, attempts to gather all of the analysts' EPS estimates for a stock and create a *consensus EPS*. And it's these numbers that often determine whether a stock's price gets hammered or not.

(We should also—shhhh!—mention the effect of the **whisper number**. This is any unofficial EPS floating around out there, among Wall Street trading desks and in Internet chat rooms. Whisper numbers are often different from analysts' forecasts and consensus estimates.)

Many analysts view earnings and earnings per share as just part of a company's story. Remember: earnings are just a company's revenue minus its expenses and taxes. There are a lot of things in between that require a "look-see," things that give an analyst a better feel for how a company is doing. One of those things is the **EBITDA**—earnings before interest expenses, taxes, depreciation, and amortization. It can tell you how much cash is actually generated before and after those funky accounting entries show up. In times gone by, analysts would look at EBITDA to determine whether it was worth using junk bonds to finance the takeover of some company.

The Bread and Butter

If number crunching is your thing, if you have designs on becoming a Wall Street analyst, then the best place to get information like EBITDA is in the company's annual report or **10-K** report, which is issued yearly to all shareholders. (Form 10-K is the report that most publicly traded companies file with the SEC annually, within 90 days after the end of their fiscal year. It provides a comprehensive overview of a company's business and financial condition.) Analysts use the numbers in these reports in their computer models.

Let's take a simple look here at those two biggies of financial statements that we saw in Chapter 9, the cash flow statement (Figure 10-1) and the balance sheet (Figure 10-2).

Besides P/E and PEG, analysts use a whole slew of ratios that compare each part profit and loss statement and and the balance sheet with something else. What they're trying to get out of this is some sense of the five major factors that help evaluate a company:

1. Price ratios, which help determine how much you're paying for the company based on things like its earnings, book value, and sales. (**Book value** is the net worth of a company divided by the number of shares outstanding. This is the accounting value of a stock, the value of the assets a shareholder would receive, theoreti-

Cash Flow Summary/Profit and Lost Statement	
Revenue or sales from normal course of business	$1,000,000
Operating Income, money from activities that are not a normal part of the business	$100,000
Cost of goods sold, also known as expenses	-$500,000
Amortization, writing off the value of intangible assets–like goodwill, patents, or copyrights–over a number of years	-$30,000
Depreciation, writing off the value of tangible assets–like buildings–over a number of years	-$20,000
Extraordinary items, like the sale of a business	$50,000
Income taxes	-$150,000
Net Income	**$450,000**
Number shares outstanding	450,000
Net income per share ($450,000 divided by 450,000 shares)	$1.00

Figure 10-1. Cash flow statement

cally, if a company were liquidated.)

2. Profitability ratios, which tell you how much money the company is making, based on the sales, shareholder equity, and assets.

3. Liquidity ratios, which can help you determine whether a company can continue to pay its bills.

4. Debt ratios, which tell you how much a company is borrowing (**leverage**) in order to do business as well as how well it will be able to weather an economic slowdown.

5. Cash flow, which ratios take out the funny accounting entries like depreciation and amortization to give you a truer sense of how much cash the company is plowing back into growth.

Balance Sheet	
Assets (what the company owns)	
Current Assets	
Cash and cash equivalents	$50,000
Inventories (stuff on the shelves)	$50,000
Receivables (what people owe the company)	$50,000
Long-Term Assets	
Building and equipment	$5,000,000
Investments in other companies	$1,000,000
Intangibles like goodwill, patents, and copyrights	$5,000,000
Total Assets	**$11,150,000**
Liabilities (what the company owes)	
Current Liabilities	
Taxes and accounts payable	$25,000
Current long-term debt due now	$25,000
Long-term liabilities	
Long-term borrowing	$4,000,000
Total liabilities	$4,050,000
Shareholders' Equity (what shareholders own) = Assets minus Liabilities	$7,100,000
Total Liabilities and Shareholders' Equity	**$11,150,000**

Figure 10-2. An example of a balance sheet

There are other terms that you're likely to notice in an analyst's report:

- **Gross margin** (aka **gross profit margin**): calculated by subtracting cost of goods sold from net sales.
- **operating margin** (aka **operating profit margin or net profit margin**): calculated by dividing operating profit by net sales or net income as a percent of net sales.
- **pretax margin** (aka **pretax profit margin**): calculated by dividing net profit before taxes by net sales.
- **after-tax profit margin:** calculated by dividing net income after taxes by net sales.

- **pretax return on equity:** calculated as dividing net income before taxes by shareholders' equity.
- **after-tax return on equity:** calculated as dividing net income after taxes by shareholders' equity.
- **current ratio:** calculated by dividing current assets by current liabilities.
- **quick ratio:** calculated by subtracting inventories from current assets, then dividing by current liabilities.

Now, analysts always look for trends in numbers, not just absolute figures. Downward trends in profits and revenues could be telltale signs of a serious problem. Ditto for companies that have grown their profits at 15% or better for 15 years and then post earnings growth of 14%. A stock could get hammered for that kind of disappointment.

Who Does What?

A lot of decisions on Wall Street are made by some very smart people in some very high and powerful positions at some very power-

Wall St Extra

Online References

There are some great places on the Web to go to get definitions of the concepts and ratios discussed in this chapter.

www.spredgar.com: SPREDGAR is an Excel add-in that computes and graphs key financial ratios and cash flow from SEC EDGAR filings with SIC access and stock quotes. This site has a database of a number of these ratios on major companies.

www.edgar-online.com: EDGAR (Electronic Data Gathering, Analysis and Retrieval) Online provides financial statement information to investors.

www.sec.gov: The Securities and Exchange Commission Web site features educational information and access to the EDGAR database of disclosure documents filed by public companies.

www.investment.com: This site from Global Investment Financial Group has a glossary of ratios and terms used in evaluating companies.

ful firms. This direction from above is designed to help institutions and individuals make more money. Sometimes the folks in the tower agree among themselves and sometimes not.

It's a virtual maze of all the people in all the departments who have opinions on the economy, the markets, and individual stocks. There's a whole pecking order of who says what to whom. These are likely the folks you'll see on CNBC or CNNfn giving their take on what's happening. Here's a simplified explanation of each.

Strategists—These are the higher-ups in major investment houses, mutual fund companies, and money management firms who try and take all the data in, to observe the economy, industries, the broad markets, and specific companies and to pick out the strategy for their clients and brokers to use. Many times they'll tell you how to allocate your money among stocks, bonds, cash, and international securities.

Economists—These people try to get a read on the economy to help predict the right places to be going forward. They believe that the economy tends to rhyme over time, as history repeats itself with variations, so they try to bring in a little history put things in perspective. (Yet they almost always defer to their strategists and analyst regarding which stocks to pick.

Portfolio Managers or **Money Managers**—These people are right in the heat of the battle. It's their job to listen to all the economists, analysts, strategists, and company management and to figure out where to invest the money entrusted to them from mutual fund assets, privately managed accounts for individuals, or institutional assets. They have to decide daily how much and which stocks to buy in their portfolio. They have to post their performance figures every day, so it can sure be a pressure cooker.

Analysts—As we've said, these individuals are usually responsible for a particular industry and report to strategists and brokers on the best opportunities. Usually they're Certified Financial Analysts (CFAs), a designation that shows a thorough understanding of stock analysis. They earn that designation by completing a three-part program sponsored by the Association for Investment

Management and Research (AIMR) in Charlottesville, VA. The association can be reached at www.aimr.org or 800-247-8132.

All of these people are the thinkers and the specialists and the doers when it comes to managing money. They're all in a very competitive environment where performance really matters and where time horizons are unreasonably short. But don't start feeling too sorry for these folks, because they get paid very well and the best are truly pampered and rewarded for their right calls. Just figure out why they're making those calls—and understand that even the best make mistakes.

Tools of the Trade

Analysts use several tools when researching stocks. The basic tools include:

1. sources of current market information
2. financial calculator
3. favorite research sources

Source of Current Market Information

We've mentioned a couple of information sources already. Analysts typically review all the documents that the Securities and Exchange Commission requires a company to disclose to the public. In the case of a publicly traded company, those include the 10-K (annual report), the 10Q (quarterly report), and the 8-K (a report of unscheduled material events or corporate changes that could be of importance to shareholders or the SEC, such as bankruptcy, the sudden death of the CEO, the resignation of directors, an acquisition, a change in the fiscal year, or a big lawsuit).

Analysts also review the stuff the big business news operations pump out. *The Wall Street Journal* is required reading or—if, like Dave, you have a fast connection to the Internet—Wall Street Journal Interactive (www.wsj.com). Other staples include CBS MarketWatch (www.cbs.marketwatch.com), Bloomberg.com (www.bloomberg.com), *Investor's Business Daily,* and *Barron's.*

Analysts, like good journalists, also used to do a little detective work. They read the trade magazines for industries in which a company might operate. They go to the trade shows. They keep a close eye on competing companies.

Financial Calculator

Analysts also use a good calculator. Back in the good ol' days, before computers, analysts would typically use the Hewlett-Packard 12-C calculator. That calculator could, if you hit the right keys, determine such things as *internal rate of return* (IRR). Now analysts have Excel spreadsheets and similar tools like the rest of us.

By the way, IRR is the interest rate that makes net present value of all cash flow equal zero. It's the annualized rate of return, considering both the amount of money invested and the length of time it's been invested. The IRR measures how fast an investment is making money: it's a calculation of the time value of money.

How does it work? Well, it's simple—in concept, at least. The IRR takes all of your deposits and withdrawals and the exact timing of each and takes your current account value, to arrive at the single annualized rate of return that matches your current account value to all those deposits and withdrawals.

So how do we calculate IRR? *We* use a computer. Calculating the IRR requires trying rates of return until you find the one that matches all of the deposits and withdrawals with the current account value. It's a tedious chore that really made analysts appreciate that ol' Hewlett-Packard 12-C calculator.

So, once Excel or the 12-C cranks out the IRR, then what? If the investment meets what Wall Streeters call its "hurdle rate," then the investment makes sense.

Favorite Research Sources

We cover the best research sources in Chapter 12, so we'll keep our list short here. When you're trying to get the most out of analyst's reports and the other musical scores of Wall Street, we recommend the following:

- ValueLine.com (www.valueline.com)
- CBS MarketWatch (as mentioned above, www.cbs.marketwatch.com)

- Morningstar (www.morningstar.com)
- *Barron's* (as mentioned above)

Of course, you should also be consulting your broker, who can help you understand Wall Street reports. And if your Uncle Elmer passes along hot stock tips or you find a recommendation in an Internet chat room, you should take a little time to find some of those reports, read them carefully, and then discuss them with your broker. Sure, you may lose a little time checking out what Elmer and strangers are telling you to buy—but that's much better than losing a lot of money.

Putting It All Together to Appreciate the Wall Street Scores

So there you have all you need to read and understand the reports of financial analysts— the major musical scores of Wall Street. Plus, you know a little more about the people behind the scenes and what they do. Finally, you're familiar with some research tools.

Now, you're ready to understand the things that Wall Street tells us in those reports. So, let's dive into the world of buying.

11

Buy, Buy Birdies:
The Institutions and People Who Buy Wall Street's Stuff

The people who sell stuff on Wall Street are called the **sell side**. The people who buy stuff on Wall Street are called "the suckers." Just kidding! Proving once again that Wall Street understands the truth in advertising laws, they're called **buy side**.

This is the group of institutions that have billions and billions in assets under management. In many cases, these are the firms that manage money on behalf of average Americans, on behalf of widows and orphans, and, in some cases, for their own accounts. The firms that make up the buy side of Wall Street can be broken down into two big segments and then a few little ones, in terms of importance.

Pension Plans

Pension plan managers are the institutions that manage what's called **tax-exempt money** on behalf of average Americans. (It's called tax-exempt because the investors don't pay taxes on their earnings until they withdraw their investments, usually during retirement.) Yes, in many cases, these firms—there are thousands of them—manage the money that will fund the average American's retirement plan.

By way of background, there are two big types of pension plans in America: the **defined benefit plan** and the **defined contribution plan**, often called a **401(k) plan**.

The defined benefit plan has been around forever, but has fallen from favor in recent years. With a DB plan, the plan participant (in plain English, that's you, the worker bee) works and then magically starts getting a monthly check after he or she retires. The amount of the benefit is defined in advance. The person retiring will get a fixed amount, say $1,000 a month, for the rest of his or her life. With a defined benefit plan, the manager chooses the funds and investment options and then manages the money.

The defined contribution plan, on the other hand, has been around for only a couple decades, but is now all the rage. With a DC plan, the plan participant invests or contributes part of his or her own salary on a pre-tax basis. With a defined contribution plan, the contribution is defined in advance, but the benefit is not. With a defined contribution plan, the plan participant chooses the mutual funds or investment options, which the money manager then manages.

That bit of background aside, the important thing to know about pension plan managers is this: they're human, they're competitive. And, like their Wall Street sell side brethren, they make a ton of dough, especially if the money they manage rises appreciably. When it comes to decoding Wall Street, here's what you need to know about the people and the process.

The important people on the buy side are the **research analysts** (we'll talk more about those guys in a second) and the **portfolio managers**. The other important group is the **sales and marketing teams**. For a moment, think of a pension plan like you would any manufacturer. But instead of making cars, the product they make is an investment fund. And, as with cars, what sells investment funds is performance.

Portfolio Managers

And what makes the difference in performance between one fund and another is often the portfolio manager, the guy who's down on the line poring over financial statements. That's why most portfolio managers have graduated at the top of their class at Harvard B-School or have a passion for investing the way college students have a passion for cold pizza on Saturday mornings. (Bob once went on an exploratory interview with the director of investment research for Fidelity Investments. The director told him that most of the Fidelity research analysts and portfolio managers had been investing and following the market since they were in elementary school. For his part, Bob spent his elementary school years making dirt roads with toy trucks and flipping baseball cards. Needless to say....)

Investment Disciplines

The portfolio manager is responsible for making buying and selling decisions, that is, which stocks or securities to buy and which to sell. Usually, though not always, the pension plan manager follows a particular investment style or discipline. (We discussed investment styles in Chapter 5, with the boxes made famous by Morningstar.)

Thus, investment disciplines—whether for pension managers or for mutual fund and professional investors—are usually slotted into boxes that are broadly defined by two factors:

- the **market capitalization** of the company in which the PM is investing—large, medium, or small
- the **investment style**—growth, blend, or value.

Market capitalization, as you may recall from Chapter 3, is about the market value of the firm. The market cap is simply the price of the company's stock multiplied by the number of outstanding shares. (As you recall from Chapter 3, there's a discrepancy among those who define cap categories in terms of dollars and those folks who define categories in terms of percentages. But a difference of billions of dollars is just a detail here.)

As for **investment style**, well, that's where things get a bit interesting on Wall Street. The problem is with the labels. Few people agree on what is a **value stock** and what is a **growth stock** and, consequently, what is a **blend stock**, something between value and growth. (There are other investment styles, but these are the most important. And we'll discuss these styles later in this chapter.)

As a rule, growth stocks have high **price/earnings (P/E) ratios** and value stocks have low **price/book (P/B) ratios**. The price to book ratio represents the price of the company's stock divided by the company's book value—its net worth if everything had to be sold tomorrow. Companies that could be sold in a fire sale for twice the current price of the stock are a good value in the minds of value investors.

But there are no rules on Wall Street. And whatever rules there are can be broken at any given moment.

For example, Morningstar believes all things are relative. So it simply creates a measure that examines the P/E and P/B and creates a norm for the respective group. Companies in the norm are blends, companies below the norm are value, and companies above the norm are growth.

Research Analysts

Now, the other important people on Wall Street are the research analysts. Those are the people who work on behalf of the portfolio manager: they screen stocks, talk to the sell side analysts, and (bottom line) try to find bargains and winners for the portfolio managers.

In some ways, it's like most sales jobs. The sell side has to get the attention of the analyst and the analyst then has to get the attention of the portfolio manager. In many firms, as in many companies and schools across America, the PM has his or her list of favorites—analysts who find stocks worth buying and selling.

Sales and Marketing

The other important people inside a pension plan manager are the sales and marketing team. As with other industries, you can make the best darn thing in the world, but it doesn't matter if no one knows about it. So, as you might imagine, pension plan managers have boatloads of people out there shaking the bushes searching for companies in America looking for a new pension plan manager.

In fact, the search for a pension plan manager can be pretty exciting on Wall Street, especially when you think of the millions of dollars in revenue that are at stake. (Yes, we've said it at least once before: most people on Wall Street don't do what they do for the love of it, but for the love of money.)

Let's look at a typical money manager search.

XYZ Company has a pension plan with large-cap growth investment discipline. It wants to fire its money manager for **underperformance**. In other words, the manager failed to deliver the hoped-for investment returns.

So XYZ Company sends out a **request for proposal** (RFP) to the world saying that it wants to place $50 million with a potentially better large-cap growth manager. The RFP outlines what XYZ Company is looking for in a money manager. Lots of money managers—be they large-cap growth or not—then send volumes of paperwork, e-mails, and sales reps to XYZ Company.

And the reason is revenue. The revenue a money manager earns on $10 million in assets under management is typically 50 **basis points**—or 50 bips, as they say in the business. (A basis point is 0.01%.) 50 bips of $50 million is $250,000. For a money management firm, that kind of money is all gravy. That is, after they hire a MBA relationship manager, the rest of the money goes to the bottom line. The money management business, at least in bull markets, can be lucrative.

Now let's take a look at a real money manager search. A little bit ago, a company called Frank Russell Investment Management sent out an RFP seeking a large-cap value manager. The amount to be managed was $1.25 billion. MFS Institutional Advisors, one of the country's largest managers, won the right to manage the money. Estimated revenue? Let's call it $6.25 million per year.

In many ways, the people who work for pension managers are a lot like the folks working in the mutual fund industry, which we'll talk about next. The big difference is this. Usually, pension fund managers work in relative obscurity. Rarely does the newspaper report the price per share of the fund they're running or its investment performance. Rarely are they in the public eye. In contrast, mutual fund managers are out there performing in the limelight.

Mutual Funds

Mutual funds in America trace their roots back to a company called Massachusetts Investors Trust, which was formed in 1924 by a small Boston brokerage firm. It differed in one important feature (redemption on demand) from other pooled investment trusts of the time.

A mutual fund, in simple terms, is just a pool of money managed by a professional manager. The pool of money comes from all kinds of people, people like you and us. Bob, for instance, has a few IRAs with this and that firm. Dave has put the money of several hundred customers into mutual funds, for retirement, college, second homes—you name it. Like the Dallas Cowboys of old, mutual funds are America's investment team. Nearly 90 million individuals and some 50 million households—nearly one in every two American households—own a mutual fund. All told, there was nearly $7 trillion in assets in mutual funds as of year-end 2000 and close to 500 fund firms. Figure 11-1 lists the top 10 fund firms and their assets as of November 2000, to give you an idea of the size of the pools of money managed. We'll talk more about the various types of mutual funds in a bit.

For now, it's important to understand that mutual fund firms—like pension plan firms—are very big players on Wall Street. Like pension plan firms, mutual fund firms buy and sell securities. The people behind these firms are human. They are competitive. And they make a ton of dough in good years and they make a boatload

Institution	Assets ($ Millions)
Fidelity Investments	595,423
Vanguard Group	483,459
American Fund Distributors	317,052
Putnam Investments	217,614
Janus	166,242
Franklin Distributors	153,883
AIM Distributors	102,328
T. Rowe Price Investment Services	99,318
MFS Investment Management	89,513
American Century Investments	84,756

Source: Financial Research Corp., Boston, MA

Figure 11-1. Top 10 fund firms

of dough in bad years. How much dough? Well, stock fund managers are expected to earn on median (we couldn't say "on average," because that's different) $436,500 in 2001, according to a study conducted by Russell Reynolds Associates and the Association for Investment Management Research. And that number is up 35% from two years ago, when the median income was $322,500.

Like pension plan managers, the two most important elements of the firm are money management and sales. The money managers have to put performance numbers up on the boards, which in turn gives the salespeople something to sell.

Now it's true that "past performance is no guarantee of future results." (Those words are the standard legal disclaimer you'll find in ads and brochures and other documents. Mutual funds and especially the banks that sell funds must take extra special care to make that point when they sell their funds to the public.) But the bottom line when it comes to funds is performance ... and Morningstar ratings. (We'll talk more about Morningstar in a bit.)

Performance is indeed king. As with pension funds, the more money a manager manages, the more revenue he or she receives. Thus, performance does two things. First, it increases the amount of money a manager manages (that's a good thing). Second, it attracts new money. New money and good performance are what increase revenue for the mutual fund firms.

By the way, the other way fund managers produce more revenue is to charge more for their services. How much do mutual fund managers charge for their services? Well, stock fund managers charge their shareholders on average 1.5% to manage the money. That works out to $15 per every $1,000 you have invested in a mutual fund. It may not sound like much on the surface, but it adds up quickly.

Take, for instance, the nation's largest mutual fund, Fidelity Investments' Magellan Fund. That fund generated about $710 million in asset management fees or roughly 6% of the $11.1 billion in revenue that Fidelity generated in 2001. (Fidelity has more than 300 funds and close to a trillion dollars in assets under management. Magellan had about $80 billion in assets under management last we checked.)

So, who's managing the money for the mutual fund manager? In some cases, the manager is an individual; in other cases, the manager is a team of individuals. In times gone by, mutual fund managers liked to use the individual as manager, especially when the manager had a hot hand. Hot hands attract what the industry calls **net new cash**. Unfortunately, star managers, like star athletes, move on, either to join another firm with a better financial deal or to open their own firms. Now, when a star athlete skips town, it's unlikely that all the fans will move with him or her. But it's different when a star fund manager bolts. His or her fans sometimes follow. Mutual fund firms realized that they were at risk, so they've shifted to a team money management approach. There are no stars to follow. If someone on the team leaves, shareholders hardly notice.

Research Analysts

As with pension fund managers, the mutual fund management team is supported by a bevy of research analysts. These research analysts work hard for their money. They're constantly on the road, or on the phone, or at their computer, or at the bar.

Take Fidelity, for instance. Analysts there followed 4,669 companies and published nearly 7,000 research reports in 2001—or just about one report for every publicly traded company on the Nasdaq and the NYSE. That's a lot of research and writing.

Sales and Marketing

The salespeople and marketers for the mutual fund managers are a lot like those in the pension fund world, with two big exceptions. First, the sales and marketing team for mutual funds can work with publicly available performance numbers. Second, the funds are required by law to redeem shares on a daily basis, thus making funds a very liquid investment. (That's right—mutual funds report their net assets value, or share price, at the close of each and every business day.)

You've most likely seen an advertisement or two in the newspaper or magazines with some mutual fund touting this or that performance. Many times, they look what's shown in Figure 11-2:

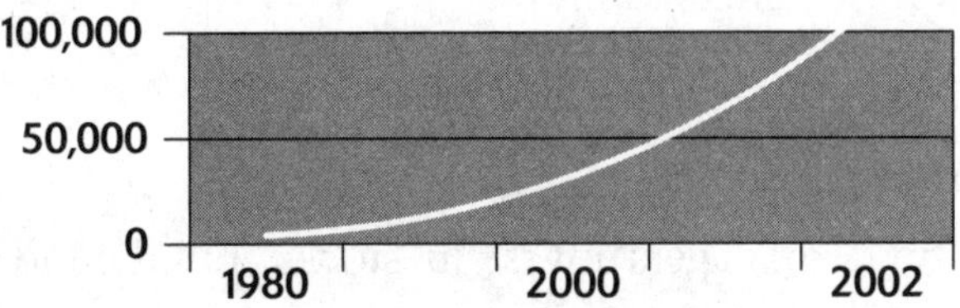

Figure 11-2. Go Gettum Fund chart

Those ads are what people in the industry call **mountain chart** ads. The ad depicts the value of a fund, and presumably a shareholder's new worth, rising to the sky. Fortunately, mutual fund firms have to abide by some usually strict advertising guidelines established by the National Association of Securities Dealers, Inc., the industry's self-regulatory organization. (That's the group of wolves watching the wolves who are watching the chickens.)

Fortunately, too, it's only the one-year wonders that typically resort to using those kinds of ads. Indeed, more and more firms are starting to use brand or image ads to portray what good guys and money managers they are. There's actually a very good reason why fund firms are doing that. It has to do with performance.

Yes, those firms that live by performance die by performance. Money flows in with good performance and out with bad performance, almost like the tides in the Bay of Fundy. If a fund firm starts bragging about performance, it's likely to get new money. But it's unlikely that the money will be **sticky**. As soon as the hot money manager's hand goes cold, as it's certain to do, out go the weasels and up go the redemptions. (While at Dalbar, Inc., an independent financial services research firm based in Boston, Bob worked on research that suggested investors held funds on average for only three years. That's not nearly long enough to capture significant returns.)

Types of Mutual Funds

It's important to note the following about mutual funds. There are thousands of funds, about 8,200 funds really, from which to choose. Fortunately, those funds can be broken down into three or four (depending on your point of view) basic types:

- stock (also called equity)
- bond
- money market
- hybrid.

Stock fund managers invest in stocks, bond fund managers invest in bonds, money market mutual fund managers invest in money market securities, and hybrid fund managers invest in all types of securities—a little of this and a little of that. Most mutual funds come with a prospectus and a stated investment objective that outlines the type of fund and its investment style or objective.

Most stock mutual fund managers invest according to market capitalization and investment style (growth or value), like pension fund managers.

Most bond fund managers can be placed in similar boxes. However, as we discussed in Chapter 5, instead of market cap, bond fund managers evaluate bonds based on **credit quality** (how likely the bond issuer will pay off the debt) and **interest rate sensitivity** (how much the value of the bond will rise and fall as interest rates go up and down). Bonds with high credit ratings and low sensitivity usually pay a lower rate of interest, while bonds with a low credit rating and a high sensitivity pay a higher rate of interest and cry when their feelings are hurt.

Now, funds have a variety of investment objectives, ranging from aggressive to conservative. In fact, the Investment Company Institute, the big mutual fund trade/lobbying group, has created 33 broad categories according to investment objectives. (No, we're not going to list them here or box them up for you.) By choosing funds according to their objectives, an investor can achieve degrees of investment variety.

Funds also offer a different kind of variety within the fund, called **diversification**. Diversification is one of the major reasons that people invest in funds, the other major reason being professional management. Yes, most individuals have neither the money to buy enough stocks to achieve diversification nor the time to manage their portfolio. And that's why funds have become popular.

Why is diversification so important? Well, a diversified portfolio, according to the Investment Company Institute, helps reduce risk. That is, if you own enough stuff spread out enough, a loss in one security will be offset by a gain in another.

Other Things to Know

As you may recall from Chapter 6, way back in the 1990s people in the industry used to fuss and fret about **distribution channels** and **channel conflict**. Firms that sold load funds did so only through their advisors. Firms that sold no-load funds did so only direct to the public. Ah, life was simple way back then! But life has changed. Today, very few fund firms even talk about channel conflict. Today, Fidelity sells its funds through every channel imaginable—direct, through advisors, through institutions, through gift shops, and on the Internet.

Another important thing to know about funds is that they have minimum investment requirements, so you should find out for any particular fund the least money you must invest at the front end. But don't worry: you don't have to be rich to get into mutual funds: nearly two-thirds of funds have a minimum of $1,000 or less.

You should remember from Chapter 5 that funds come in two basic types—**open-end** and **closed-end**. The **open-end fund** is continually selling shares to the investing public, while the **closed-end fund** issues a fixed number of shares. The value of the open-end fund always reflects the underlying prices of the companies it owns. The value of the closed-end fund may be different from the actual underlying value of the securities held.

And how do you keep up with the values of your mutual funds? You read the newspaper. Each fund family is usually in bold-faced type. The name of the fund is below the fund family name, usually abbreviated and looking very foreign, such as "EuGr" or "AABal" or "FL Tx." (Don't worry: you'll quickly learn to recognize your holdings.) The second column is the NAV, the **net asset value**. That's the price of a fund share as of the close of the preceding business day. The next column is usually how much the NAV has changed in value from the preceding day (Figure 11-3).

NAME	NAV	NET CHG	YTD %RET
Babson Group			
Bond L	1.56	-0.01	-13.8
Enterp	14.33	-0.05	+14.9
Gwth	10.00	-0.10	-29.7
Intl	13.06	-0.10	-36.9
Shadw	12.35	-0.10	+9.8
Value	40.20	-0.03	-8.6

Figure 11-3. *Wall Street Journal* mutual fund quotation

Individual Investors

The last of the big players on the buy side are individual investors. Not the kind who ride the subway to work with you, but the big guys, the people like Carl Icahn who have big amounts of money to buy (usually) whatever they want. (In case you don't recognize the name, he's the chair of Lowestfare.com. As we write this book, Ichan is trying to invest $400 million to buy National Airlines.) The sell side of Wall Street spends some time courting these folks, of course, but the big money is still with courting the pension plans and mutual fund managers.

Learning the Fundamentals

Analysts typically fall into one of two broad camps. To do their jobs, they use either **fundamental analysis** or **technical analysis**.

Fundamental Analysis

The analysts who use fundamental analysis (who, for what it's worth, are the more common of the two camps) review the following information:

1. Management and the people who run the company
2. The numbers: earnings and the balance sheet
3. The industry
4. The competition
5. Where the company is in the economic cycle

Management

Fundamental analysts have a tough job. Typically, they have to develop a deep understanding of the companies they follow. Not just the numbers, as we discussed, but the people—the people who run the company, who answer the phones, who work in shipping and receiving. The analyst looks for people who will talk to him about the real deal, what's really happening inside the company with regard to sales, profits, competition, and trends. The analysts also look for simple telltale signs.

A good value-style money manager that Dave knows once paid a visit a company to evaluate whether to buy its stock. He walked into the corporate offices and saw some of the most extravagant ostrich chairs and original works of art he'd ever seen. Then he met with management. After a few minutes, he came to the conclusion that the top managers couldn't get a handle on corporate spending and were not living up to their own values, never mind those of his value investment philosophy (which we'll discuss shortly).

The Numbers

Analysts review a lot of numbers. They want to make sure that management is consistent in its commitment to the numbers and the direction of these numbers. If the analyst sees a deterioration of a series of these ratios or growth trends, it's usually a warning sign that things are not rosy. That's why analysts pay special attention to management's integrity, especially when it comes to projections of company's growth.

The Industries

Analysts don't look at a company in a vacuum. They review the company against its peers. So, often the analysts will crunch the numbers and create ratios for a company and compare and contrast them with the industry benchmarks and pinpoint problems. They can gauge how a firm measures up in comparison with the industry growth rate, how much leverage or borrowing a company is doing, and whether its profit margins are in line.

Here are the big industries that Wall Street analysts follow:

- **Utilities**—the electric and gas companies that we all pay every month to keep the lights on, the appliances running, and the heat and AC going so we stay comfortable.
- **Energy**—the companies that take oil and gas out of the ground to produce the fuel to run our economy and rip us off at the pumps.
- **Financials**—the banks and credit unions, insurance companies, and investment houses that want our money so they can lend it back to us or get us to invest it.
- **Industrial Cyclicals**—companies that produce goods that are sensitive to the business cycle and price changes, a category that includes companies in aerospace, construction, machinery, machine tools, chemicals, metals, paper, and building materials.
- **Consumer Durables**—companies that produce things that last more than three years, like cars, golf clubs, furniture, toys, and shoes—unless you have kids.
- **Consumer Staples**—companies that sell us things that we don't expect to last, such as food, beverages, tobacco products, and household goods.
- **Services**—phone and cable TV companies, restaurants, hotels, newspaper and magazine publishers, theaters, transportation companies, personal and business services, and (for all those consumer staples and durables) waste management.
- **Retail**—the stores at the mall that sell us all those consumer staples and durables.
- **Healthcare**—drugs and hospitals to keep us alive and looking good.
- **Technology**—cool new stuff that will make us more effective (well, in theory!), neurotic, and poorer.

Competition

The competition is very keen in America these days, so if an analyst can stack up companies side by side, he or she can then identify the winners and the losers. That's why the analyst likes to talk to people at a company about their competitors, especially who's toughest and why. The analyst also knows that the company's management is also very happy to point out competitors' weaknesses. The analyst also visits the competition to get a better sense directly.

The Economic Cycle

The economy, like the various industries, tends to run in cycles. Does that matter? Maybe yes, maybe no. It depends on the approach of the money manager.

Some analysts prefer to start a review of a company's prospects by evaluating where we are in the economic cycle—boom, bust, or somewhere in between. This is called the **top-down** approach. It's called that not because the people who coined the phase drove convertibles, but rather because these folks think a company's fortunes must be viewed in the greater economic context. In some cases, money managers will attempt to identify which industries will do well in light of the economic cycle and then the best stocks in those industries.

Figure 11-4 can give you a sense of where to be and what does well when.

The other type of money manager doesn't give a hoot about the economy and instead focuses on good companies, regardless of the industry or the economy. That style of analysis is the **bottom-up** approach. (By the way, that approach is not to be confused with **bottom fishing**. That's the practice of going after stocks whose

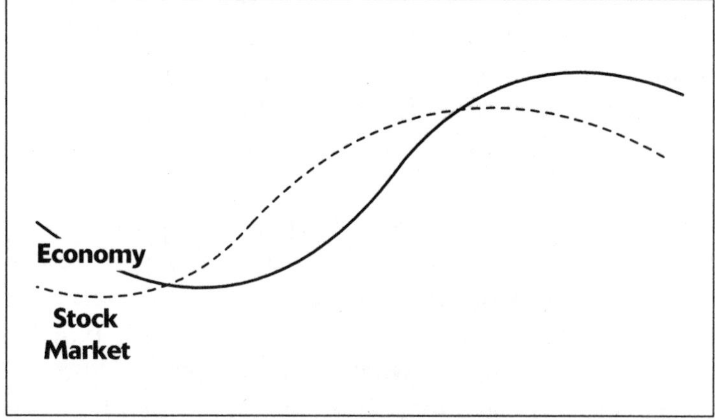

Figure 11-4. The economy and the stock market cycles

prices have dropped dramatically or even bottomed out.)

The bible of fundamental analysis is *Security Analysis* by Benjamin Graham and David Dodd, which came out in 1934. Warren Buffet, the successful investment billionaire, was actually a student of Ben Graham. Another good read is *The Essays of Warren Buffett: Lessons for Corporate America* by Warren E. Buffett and Lawrence A. Cunningham.

Technical Analysis

A **technical analyst** isn't concerned about the state of the economy, the company and what it makes, the people who are running the company, its competitors, or the financial ratios. A technical analyst simply cares about a bunch of squiggly lines and dots that make up what's called a **stock chart**. The stock chart depicts the price of the stock over a period of time. The technical analysts like to consider the **52-week high** and the **52-week low**, the numbers that represent the stock's highest and lowest prices over the last year.

Besides price and price changes, the technical analysts like to keep close tabs on **stock volume**, the number of shares of a company's stock being bought and sold. Technical analysts believe that stock volume is a good indicator of demand. Using the "where's there smoke, there's fire" motto, technical analysts believe higher-than-average volume suggests higher demand and usually higher prices, while lower-than-average volume suggests lower demand and usually lower prices. This, by the way, is sometimes called **momentum investing**.

As the term implies, technical analysts are not generally long-term investors. They tend to jump in and out of stocks, which can create for some investors lots of short-term gains (or higher taxes) and commissions.

A stock chart plots the price movement and indicates volume; there's also some type of moving average to help you see whether the trend is up or down. For more examples than you ever wanted, go to Big Charts (bigcharts.marketwatch.com) and plug in any stock symbol. The results are what make technical analysts salivate.

A stock tends to have **support levels**: that's when it goes down to a certain level, then tends to hold that level. It also has **resistance**

levels: it will move up to a price, then stop as it runs into resistance. The most convincing moves are when stocks break support levels (sell and get out!) or break through resistance levels (buy it and bet the farm!).

Unfortunately, there's no absolutely perfect way to interpret these charts, so there's a lot of guesswork and assumptions on the decisions. Also the time frames can be short-term (daily or weekly), intermediate (three to 12 months), or long-term (more than a year). So it's up to you to find a system and a time frame that work for you. These strategies are becoming more common because of the vicious swings of investors doing **sector rotation**, which is moving from one sector or more sectors to one or more other sectors, to find the momentum in a stock.

There are hundreds if not thousands of books and disciplines on technical analysis. One of the oldest systems and one that the two of us really like is the "point and figure" system invented by Charles Dow (who founded *The Wall Street Journal*) back in the late 1800s. The system just uses a bunch of Xs (when momentum is up) and Os (when momentum is down).

According to a study, 80% of a stock's price movement is based on the market and the industry it's in and only 20% is fundamental research. So it's crazy to follow fundamental research without keeping an eye on the market and the industry. The intricacies of this strategy can best be found in *Point and Figure Charting* by Thomas J. Dorsey. His Web site is www.dorseywright.com.

Investment Styles

Analysts and money managers use different investment styles, the two most common of which are **value** and **growth**. The growth and value disciplines are the Hatfields and the McCoys of Wall Street.

Good Stuff Cheap with Value Investing

With **value investing**, the analyst/money manager is seeking a bargain, like 50 cents of goods for $1. Typically, a value investor is looking to buy companies that have low P/E ratios or hidden assets that others don't see. It might even be a turnaround story, where new management is coming in to whip the company into shape and kick in the profits. It might even be a dirty old industry that's using new technologies. An example might be Williams Companies, which was an old energy company that decided to start installing fiber optic lines over its right of access. Maybe it's an old assembling company that is now putting together high-tech components instead of widgets (whatever a widget is!). Value investing can take time; value investors are best known for their patience.

Many of the disciples of this discipline are bottom-up managers, folks who don't care what the economy or the industries are doing, who are buying the stock just because the price is lower than they expect it to be when all the pieces are working right or when Wall Street decides it's a decent company after all. Many times, the analysts and money managers who are value-style investors must wait years for their picks to work out.

It's Going to the Moon on the Growth Ship

With **growth investing**, managers are looking for the companies that will let you take a pill and it will make you smarter, cure baldness, make you immune to cancer, and help you lose weight all at once with no side effects. Growth managers are not a patient crowd either, because if you don't deliver on your earnings, look out!

That's because the stocks they seek are driven up on positive momentum in a hurry and can be knocked down just as quickly. The best examples: the Internet stocks of late 1999 and early 2000. The prospects were tremendous and assumed that we would never leave our homes to go shopping, that we would just click a mouse or hit a button to buy houses, cars, medicines, and clothes. As you may have heard, that hasn't quite come to be (yet!), as many of those Internet stocks either have closed shop or are struggling to be profitable.

These growth stocks typically have high P/E ratios, because the growth of the company is intended to be high. As a rule, the analysts and money manager say growth companies should be growing earnings at least in line with their P/Es. So a P/E of 100 would be warranted if they can grow earnings 100%. Money managers also look at the high P/E relative to other industries. Faster-growing companies are priced richer and higher because their prospects are perceived to be better. Whether that happens or not will be reflected in the way the markets will punish or reward the stock price, the P of P/E.

The World According to GARP

Value investing and growth investing typically move in opposite directions. When value is in favor, growth is not and when value is out of favor, growth is in. (More on that in the next section.) By the way, the folks on Wall Street love talking about things as being in or out of favor. Like the economy, it's impossible to predict when something will be in favor and for how long. But one thing is certain: nothing lasts forever on Wall Street and you can bet your bottom dollar that as soon as something is in favor, like value investing or growth investing, it's likely to be soon out of favor.

As you might expect with any two extremes, there's a compromise, a hybrid between value investing and growth investing. It's called **GARP—growth at a reasonable price**. Of course, what "reasonable" means is open to many interpretations. Yet GARP allows managers and investors some middle ground without the heartburn of pure growth and the boredom of great value.

Growth or Value?

Neither style—growth or value—is "the right way" or "the wrong way." They're just different. Over time, both disciples have about the same total returns, yet their styles go in and out of favor as Wall Street decides which discipline it wants at the moment.

Historically, when the future is bright and very promising (greed), then growth wins the race. But when we're a little worried and we're pulling in our horns a bit (fear), then value wins out.

The Path Less Traveled with the Contrarian

Earlier in this chapter, we discussed Wall Street analysts and their instincts and we mentioned the tendency of Wall Streeters to move in herds. But not all of them follow the crowd.

Contrarians are investors who behave in opposition to the prevailing wisdom, whether buying when others are pessimistic and selling when they're optimistic or buying stocks that are out of favor. Simply put, the contrarian strategy says that the Wall Street herd is usually wrong. It tends to move in extremes on the up side and the down side like a bipolar basket case. It sometimes even takes the best and the brightest analysts right along in its stampede.

Contrarian investors tend to have more of a value bias of buying good stuff cheap. The major difference is that they salivate when good industries get smashed. They say, "Throw out the goods and I'll be glad to buy them when you momentum guys head out of town." The tough part, though, is making sure that company or industry is not going belly up. It has to still have a viable product.

Lots of people describe themselves as contrarians, but the real contrarians are people who don't use that label.

Warren Buffett is probably the best example. He's made a ton of dough buying depressed stocks (when the prices are low and/or the companies have management problems). His company, Berkshire Hathaway, today represents the investments of many companies. But it was his first big investment, a textile/shirt-making company that had fallen on hard times.

One of the premier contrarian investors is long-time *Forbes* columnist David Dreman, who wrote the book *Contrarian Investment Strategies*. His discipline is very strict in that he prefers to buy stocks with P/E ratios in the lowest 20%. Then, if you just hold onto them, they will go up faster than the market as a whole because they've already been abandoned by investors. With the bad news already out, then this bottom 20% will rise faster when the momentum swings back.

Risky Business

Wall Street has long sought ways to quantify and measure risk. In the case of a stock, risk is volatility, how much it goes up and down in price. And to that end, Wall Street has created several indicators of risk. As you might imagine, the problem with any of the risk indicators is that volatility is no big deal when a stock is going up; it's on the down side that risk raises its ugly head. That said, here are some of Wall Street's more popular risk measurements:

- **alpha**—That's the difference between the actual return of a stock and an expected return, depending on the type of company. A positive number means it did better and a negative number means it did worse than you would have expected.

- **beta**—This is the volatility of the market compared with a benchmark like the S&P 500 index. If the beta of a stock is 1, then it has the same volatility as the market as a whole. If the beta is .5, then the stock is half as volatile. If it's 2, then it's twice as volatile as the market.
- **standard deviation**—If you're up on statistics, you recognize this term. If not, well, let's just say that it's a way of measuring the distance of data (in this case, stock prices) from their mean. The more spread out the data, the higher the deviation. The higher the standard deviation, the more volatile the stock.
- **bear-market rank**—This is an analysis that Morningstar and other services use to see how a stock has done against its peers when the market is down. Morningstar uses numbers from 1 to 10. The best bear-market rank is 1: the stock should perform better in bear markets than 90% of all stocks. The worst rank is 10: the stock is expected to perform worse than 90% of all stocks. Other services may use A-E letters like we had when we were graded in high school.
- **Morningstar risk rating**—This is a broad asset category comparison to see how one fund is doing against its peers. The norm is 1. A fund with a risk rating of 1.25 is 25% riskier than the other funds in its class. A 1.75 would mean 75% more volatility.
- **Morningstar risk-adjusted rating**—Also known as "the star rating system," this rating subtracts a fund's Morningstar risk score from its Morningstar return score. If a fund scores in the top 10% of its broad investment class, it gets five stars (highest). A fund in the next 22.5% gets four stars. Funds in the middle 35% are given three stars. A rating of two stars mean a fund is in the next 22.5%. And, if you're doing the math here, you can guess that one star goes to funds in the bottom 10%. If you're concerned about risk, avoid 1-star funds; 5-star funds give you the best bang for your risk buck.
- **R-squared**—This is the last of the three amigos after alpha and beta that attempt to figure out the expected returns of a stock

relative to a market index like the S&P 500. Instead of using 1 like beta, R-squared is based on a 0-100 scale, with 100 being exact correlation to the index. If the R-squared is 45, then 45% of the total return can be attributed to the market and the other 55% to the stock's unique properties.

- **Sharpe ratio**—This is a risk-return calculation devised by Nobel Laureate William Sharpe to figure out the best return for the risk. We'd like to explain the calculations, but unless you've got a Nobel Prize in your trophy case, you're better off just understanding the essential: the higher the number, the better the return for the risk.

Another tool that Wall Streeters use is a **quadrant analysis**. This is a chart (Figure 11-5) that gives performance numbers on the vertical axis and volatility on the horizontal axis. So, ideally, you would like to be way up in the northwest corner with no risk and big returns.

The lines through the middle of the chart represent the relative index you're using as a point of comparison. You can chart these comparisons using stocks, mutual fund managers, private money

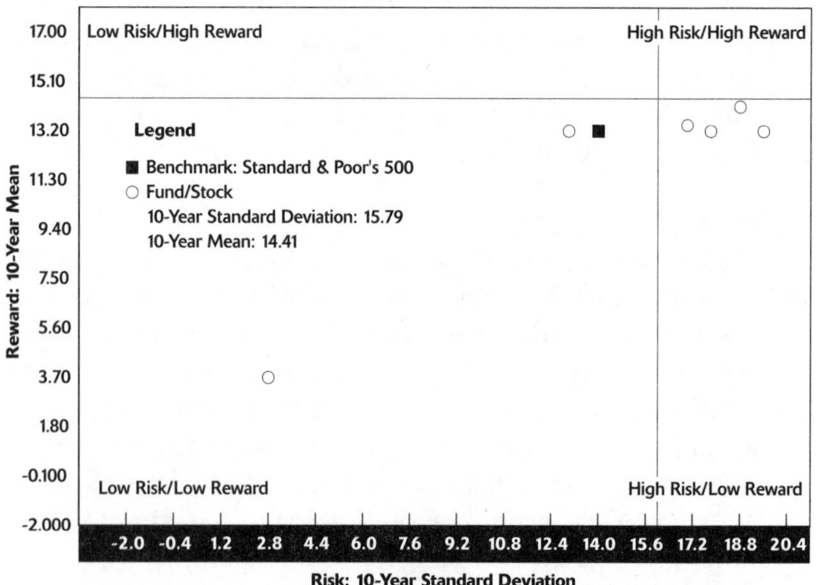

Figure 11-5. Risk/reward chart (continued on next page)

	10-Yr Standard Deviation	10-Yr Mean
■ Benchmark:		
Standard & Poor's 500	15.79	14.41
○ Fund/Stock:		
Fidelity Magellan	17.14	14.62
Franklin Adj U.S. Gov't Secs	1.52	4.84
Idx: Barra Large Cap Growth	18.37	13.63
Idx: Barra Large Cap Value	15.31	14.72
Idx: Russell 2000	19.64	11.81
Janus	19.31	14.30

Figure 11-5 Continued

managers, or virtually anything else for which you can get a performance number. These types of charts are also called **scattergrams, risk return charts**, and **matrix analyses.**

Bye, Buy Birdies!

Well, now you know about the folks on the buy side of Wall Street, the institutions and people making lots of money by managing pension plans and mutual funds for millions of people. And you understand about how they choose their investments according to their objectives and their disciplines. Finally, you're familiar with investing styles and probably bewildered by the many ways in which Wall Streeters measure and assess investment risks. Now it's time to look at some of the Wall Street messengers.

12

Don't Shoot the Messengers

The world has always been divided between the white hats (the good guys) and the black hats (the bad guys). Well, the same holds true on Wall Street. Many of the people who make up Wall Street—the sell side, the buy side, the investment bankers and corporate finance departments, the sales and marketing departments of mutual fund firms—are the black hats. And many of the people who watch and report the goings-on on Wall Street—the journalists, the industry watchdogs, and the third-party research firms—are the white hats.

The white hats are always trying to uncover the truth about what's happening on Wall Street. And the black hats are trying either to hide or shade or spin the truth or to use the white hats to achieve their objectives. At times, the black hats hate the white hats. And at other times, the white hats hate the black hats. But no matter who hates whom or who loves whom, they both need each other.

Yes, it's a love-hate relationship. And you should understand that and recognize and appreciate some of those white hats. After all, they could help you know more about Wall Street . . . and maybe even make a fortune. So, let's take a look at Wall Street's messengers.

What You Need to Know About Aggregators and Consolidators

Wall Street, as we've said, has a habit of speaking in a language that's difficult for "outsiders" to understand. And it has a habit of using a lot of that language, of cranking out reams and reams of paper, everything from A (analyst's earning estimates) to Z (zero coupon bond analysis). On Wall Street, there are several firms that have made a business out of aggregating and consolidating the pieces of paper flying about in the Wall Street blizzard and trying to make sense of the gobbledygook for people—sometimes for a fee, sometimes for free.

First Call

The first company worth noting is First Call. Founded in 1984, the company tracks and reports on the hundreds if not thousands of earnings estimates that Wall Street analysts issue on the companies they follow. First Call compiles all of the earnings estimates and then creates what's called a **consensus earnings estimate** for the hundreds of publicly traded companies out there. First Call takes all the numbers for any company and boils them down into one simple number, **mean earnings per share**. For example, there are 11 analysts who follow Toys 'R' Us, according to First Call. And as a group, those analysts predict that Toys will lose 6 cents a share for the quarter ending July 2001. On the day that the company announces its quarterly earnings, the stock may go up if the company loses less money than the consensus estimate. That's called a **positive earnings surprise**. And the stock will may fall if the company loses more money than that. That's called—you guessed it!—a **negative earnings surprise**.

Wall Street has begun to place a great deal of credence in the mean or consensus estimates. It's easier to keep track of that one number and it's easier to measure a company's actual performance against the mean than against estimates from 11 or more analysts. So, as you might imagine, First Call has become a really big deal on Wall Street, commanding a great deal of power and respect.

Now, we said that a company's stock may rise or may fall in the wake of an earnings announcement because it's impossible to predict Wall Street's reaction to **in-line earnings** (earnings that meet the consensus estimate) or to negative or positive earnings surprises. That's why there's usually a bit of a minuet that takes place between a company's investor relations department and Wall Street analysts prior to an earnings announcement. The people in investor relations are charged with talking to Wall Street analysts about the company's financials and prospects. In times gone by, the IR department would try to steer analysts' estimates up or down prior to the quarter's end, so that the company's stock wouldn't get crushed in the wake of the earnings announcement. Nowadays, thanks in part to **Regulation FD** (more on this in Chapter 13), the IR department can't disclose material information to a select group of analysts; the company must open its kimono to all or not at all.

And that means each analyst tries to keep track of what the others are saying and estimating, often trying to stick close to the consensus. Keep in mind, the best Wall Street analysts are those who can identify which stocks to buy and sell and how much each company might earn on a quarterly basis. Analysts who are unable to issue good buy and sell recommendations and estimate a company's earnings usually don't have a long career on Wall Street. And therein lies the tricky part for Wall Street analysts. Estimates that are close to the mean don't differentiate them from the other Wall Street analysts ... and estimates that are far from the mean can be risky, especially if they're on the wrong side of far.

In some ways, First Call has added support to the contention that the Wall Street folks move in a herd, with little originality or courage. Its system puts everyone in a box. On the other hand, it has created a system that helps people better understand the investment process and can hold people accountable. Remember, way back when, there were just a few people that might know how an analyst felt about a company, what his or her earnings estimates were. And those were the big buy-side investors, the pension plans and mutual funds. Today, that's no longer the case. (First Call's Web sites, by the way, are www1.firstcall.com and www.thomsonfn.com.)

Other Hunters and Gatherers

First Call focuses on earnings estimates. But you should also know about a whole new group of mostly Internet companies that are aggregating and consolidating the other piece of Wall Street's intellectual capital—the analysts' research reports and their buy, sell, and hold recommendations. Like earnings estimates, a research report and the buy, sell, and hold recommendations can drive a company's stock price up, down, and every which way in between.

Time was when it was nearly impossible to know what analysts thought of a stock. Today, however, companies like Briefing.com, CBS MarketWatch.com, and Yahoo are tracking down everything Wall Street does or says and tying it up in one pretty bow.

Just Read the Paper

The daily newspaper provides all that you need to know to decode Wall Street. Quite frankly, *The Wall Street Journal* is still the mother and father of all business news and analysis. Charles Dow and Eddie Jones, who joined forces in 1882 to report stock market news, founded the parent company of *The Journal,* Dow Jones & Co. And today *The Journal* supplies information on every important aspect of Wall Street, from annuities to zero coupon bonds. The paper contains the closing prices of every major security that trades on Wall Street, including options, currency, bonds, mutual funds, and stocks. It's all there.

The novice reader, of course, will be overwhelmed by the sheer amount of information in the paper, most of which is not relevant. So here's a quick guide to finding what's relevant:

- The first section always contains the big business and economic news and analysis of the day. Usually, the first section is filled with news of mergers, tax cuts, interest rate cuts, and the like.
- The second section is filled with trend stories, sprinkled with some news of the day—who's moving up and down the corporate ladder, which firm is launching an advertising campaign, and so on.
- The third section is filled with market news, including the

much beloved "Heard on the Street" column. That column is intended to provide insight into what those who move markets are doing. The rest of the third section is filled with the closing prices of thousands of securities.

Financial professionals and everyday people read *The Wall Street Journal*. And in many ways, it's all that you need to become acquainted with the goings-on on Wall Street. But financial professionals and everyday people interested in the market read and watch other stuff. Here's a look at that.

Who's Doing What and What's Worth Reading, Watching, or Surfing

Wired for Success

Besides *The Journal*, financial professionals play close attention to several other sources of news and information.

One of those sources is the infamous Bloomberg, which is a financial news-gathering and disseminating service for which people have to pay more than a $1,000 month. Founded by Michael Bloomberg, a former bond trader, the news service that bears the founder's last name distributed hard-to-get bid and ask prices on bonds. Over time, the service became a powerhouse in the world of business and financial news and is now as much a staple of every money management operation as *The Journal*.

Bloomberg is what's called a **newswire service**. Like Associated Press and UPI of old, it's supposed to disseminate news real time, 24 hours a day, from around the world. Plunging yen prices in Japan get reported with the same tenacity and accuracy as rising bull markets in the U.S. Average investors and would-be investors can get a taste of what Bloomberg offers at www.bloomberg.com. Other real-time business wire and financial data services to which the world pays attention are Reuters, Bridge Information Systems, ILX Systems, and Dow Jones Newswire (kin to *The Wall Street Journal*).

Financial professionals read and watch these sources of news and information for any little bit of news that can affect the price of butter and, well, stock, and any other securities for which there's a market and buyers and sellers. Some people are able to make split-second decisions based on the news they're reading and make or lose millions in the time it takes to say, "Good morning."

Now the people in the financial news business knows that the people on Wall Street can make or lose fortunes based on what they report. And to be relevant to the people on Wall Street, the people in the financial news business fight to deliver the news first, before their competition. That's what the news business is all about—delivering news before anyone else. And if you can deliver news first, the people on Wall Street will read or watch you instead of the competition.

We say "watch" because another important player in the business news world today is CNBC, the all-business news cable station. That television station, which is owned by NBC, broadcasts all sorts of business news all day long—breaking news, analyst commentaries, and CEO interviews. You name it, you're likely to see it on CNBC. And you're likely to see CNBC on the television in most brokerage offices and in most health clubs and in the early morning and at lunchtime. Other business television stations include CNN Money (formerly CNNfn) and Fox Business News.

Web Sources

The newswire services and television have played a long and important role in business world. But another medium has surfaced of late, a medium that makes it easy to report and disseminate news. Here, the big dot-com players are CBS MarketWatch, Yahoo, MoneyCentral, Quicken, AOL, and Morningstar.

CBSMarketWatch is a bit like Bloomberg, without the expense and for a slightly different audience. Born in the land of stock options, California, CBS MarketWatch began its life catering to high-technology investors and employees. Today, the site—cbs.marketwatch.com—offers all that the most sophisticated investor could ever want from a news source.

For its part, Yahoo—www.yahoo.com—delivers news and information packaged by other news outlets, as well as news disseminated by scores of average investors in its chat rooms and on its bulletin boards. In this way, Yahoo has given new meaning to the "democratization of information." Average investors, some of whom are bulls and some of whom are bears, get to talk up or down stocks at Yahoo.com, with some interesting tidbits popping up along the way. For instance, as we write this book, a major Wall Street firm issued a buy rating on a company called Global Crossing. Unfortunately, many of the investors who own stock in Global Crossing and who have access to a computer posted a number of comments slamming the report and the company. "Management has no credibility with the street. This is a hated company," said one Yahooster.

Of course, chat rooms and bulletin boards are not the place most professionals go to ferret out information. But it sure makes for good entertainment for some and for others it's as good a place to vent as the corner bar. In fact, some people have taken advantage of the inexplicable faith that many tend to have in strangers on the Internet and have touted companies just to drive up stock prices. So, if you wouldn't believe a stranger on the street trying to sell you something (watches, bridges, land in Florida, or whatever), don't believe people talking in chat rooms and posting to bulletin boards.

Our Weekly and Monthly Bread

We've focused much of our time on the real-time disseminators of business news. There are several other business news publications, most of them weekly or monthly, that can affect the price of tea in China, although not nearly as much—as a rule—as wires and the Web. Those include *Barron's, Business Week, Forbes, Fortune, Money, Kiplinger's, Smart Money*, and *Worth*.

Most of the above publications, but especially *Barron's*, offer professional investors and average investors the chance to put things into perspective and context. During the workweek, when the you-know-what is hitting the fan or radiator, it can be hard to take a step back and reflect on the news of the week. The weeklies and monthlies offer that chance.

How to Be a Discerning and Discriminating Consumer of the News and Hype

If we had to choose just one word to describe how to be a discerning and discriminating reader and viewer of the news and hype that surrounds Wall Street, it would be "skepticism." Yes, the key to success when it comes to reading *The Journal* or watching CNBC or surfing CBS MarketWatch is to be first and foremost a skeptic. And the reason we say that is this: risk aversion. Skeptics might not make as much money as other people, but they don't lose as much either.

Now, we don't want you to doubt and disbelieve every report that's published. For instance, we think we can trust the Federal Reserve when it publishes its data, or even a company when it releases its quarterly earnings report. But we do think you should read with a high degree of skepticism what analysts have to say about the Federal Reserve or a company's earnings report. We say that, in part, because Dave and Bob have lived through their share of earnings reports and analysts' commentaries. And to live it is to understand it.

You see, Wall Street can be broken down into two camps when it comes to publicity.

There are firms that desire publicity and seek out opportunities to get their name in the press, to generate some brand name recognition for their firm, to get some order flow. Sometimes, these firms and their spokesman are what we in the financial journalism business call "shameless self-promoters." Indeed, many firms in the financial services industry have built television studios on their trading floors and research departments so that they can feed the beast—when CNBC calls they want to be ready to put a talking head on the air. To be fair, these self-promoters aren't necessary lying when they are quoted in the paper or on the air. But the average Jane and Joe need to know that it's just a point of view. It may or may not be true. It may or may not be colored by circumstances and motivations of which the viewer or reader is unaware. The analyst may or may not have an agenda. So it's important to read an analyst's commentary with a degree of skepticism.

And then there are some firms that are publicity-shy. Financial journalists, despite their best efforts, rarely get the people who work for these firms to say a word about anything, or at least anything that's newsworthy or valuable. And when they do, it's probably for a reason. Like the publicity-hungry firms, they speak with an agenda—to promote some activity that will likely result in near- or intermediate-term revenue.

Now that you understand about the shameless self-promotion and agendas, it's time to examine other sources of information about Wall Street.

WALL ST

13

Lifelines and Other Forms of Survival

Like everywhere in life, there are all types of people who work on Wall Street, ranging from the ultra good to the ultra bad. Fortunately, there are a bunch of white hats patrolling the canyons and prairies of Wall Street, seeking to regulate the ne'er-do-wells and protect innocent lambs—average investors—from being fleeced by the greed machine.

Now, the white hats come in all sizes and shapes. Some work for the federal or state government, some work for quasi-governmental, self-regulating professional and agencies, and some work in the private sector. The feds need to get involved because securities have a habit of trading across state lines. The states get involved, too.

But regardless of who's doing the enforcement, much of the regulations revolve around the issues of full disclosure of information and preventing fraud.

As this book went to press, Wall Street was grappling with a new SEC rule called **Regulation Full Disclosure** (Reg FD). That regulation was intended to create a level playing field for average and institutional investors. Under the regulation, publicly traded companies have to make information about the financial condition of the company, management, and general operational activities available to everyone all at once. No more are they allowed to disclose some information to some investors and not to others. The regulators want to make sure that the investing public has all the *material* (Wall Street speak for "important") information it needs to make informed investment decisions.

As for fraud, well, as this book went to press, the SEC was in the midst of investigating a growing number of companies, more than 200, for cooking their books. (That's a fancy was of saying, "They lied about how much money they made or lost.")

When it comes to stock, bonds, and mutual funds, the law enforcement agencies with the biggest clout are the Securities and Exchange Commission and the National Association of Securities Dealers Regulation, Inc. The others include the New York Stock Exchange and the state securities regulators. Other lifelines include investor associations such as the National Association of Investor Clubs and the American Association of Individual Investors. The following represents a brief snapshot of those and other folks seeking truth, justice, and the American way.

Securities and Exchange Commission

The Securities Exchange Act of 1934 created the Securities and Exchange Commission (SEC). The SEC, which is an independent federal agency governed by Congress, enforces the securities industry laws. It oversees the mutual fund industry, the money management industry, investment advisors, brokerage firms, and the securities exchanges. It regulates the self-regulators, the National Association of Securities Dealers. It tries to rid the securities of rogue brokers and cyber rogues and stop insider trading. It is truly the nation's top stock cop.

The SEC was created to administer The Securities Act of 1933. That Act called for the registration of all new securities, required full disclosure for new securities, and prohibited fraud and deception in security dealings.

(It's hard to imagine now, but fraud and deception were the rule way back when. Take, for example, Charles K. Ponzi. In 1919

Ponzi created the Securities Exchange Company in Boston. He based his business on trading international postal reply coupons and selling promissory notes paying 50% profit in 90 days. Of course, investors went crazy and Ponzi quickly became rich. By the time his investment bubble burst, he had collected $9,500,000 from 10,000 investors. Investigation revealed that there were no coupons or profits—earlier notes were paid at maturity from the proceeds of later sales. Because of the simplicity and grand scale of his scheme, Ponzi became famous: any swindle of this nature, once known as a **bubble**, is now called a **Ponzi scheme**.)

Anyway, the SEC consists of five commissioners appointed by the President of the U.S. The chair of the SEC is also appointed by the President. As we write this book, the SEC was about to get a new chair, Harvey L. Pitt. Arthur Levitt, Jr. who served as chair for a gabillion years, retired in February 2001. For many, his retirement was a sad event: Levitt was what you might call a friend of the investor, always seeking ways to protect and educate investors.

But we digress. Over the years, there have been other pieces of legislation that have helped bolster and broaden the powers of the SEC. The SEC became responsible for the **over-the-counter** or **OTC** market in 1936. It was given power over the mutual fund industry in 1940. The Investment Advisers Act of 1940 required people who sell investment advice to register with the SEC. The Securities Investor Protection Act of 1970 created something called the Securities Investor Protection Corporation (SIPC), which insures investors against losses when a brokerage firm goes belly up. And the Insider Trading Act of 1984 was designed to discourage **insider trading**. (That's when people who have information about a company that no one else has buy and sell stocks based on that knowledge.)

When all is said and done, the SEC is here to make sure investors have the information they need to make intelligent investment decisions. There are lots of rules we could bore you with. Some address what mutual fund firms can and can't say in their sales literature. Some address what are called **tender offers**. (Although it sounds like a marriage proposal, a tender offer is when a company is trying to acquire and offers to buy shares of the target company from its shareholders, often at a price above market.) Anyway, add up all the rules and here's what you get.

The SEC requires that companies about to go public disclose any and all substantial information on their registration and that existing companies issue timely and detailed reports.

The SEC attempts to prevent the manipulation of security prices. It does this in part by regulating the activities of corporate officers and directors. The SEC also makes sure that insiders (people who are in the know, as opposed to outsiders, who are out of the know) register to buy and sell securities.

The SEC, as we mentioned, regulates the mutual fund industry and supervises the regulation of brokers. For instance, the SEC requires that stockbrokers must perform due diligence prior to selling a security to a customer. In essence, the stockbroker is required to make sure the investment fits the client's needs.

The SEC also supervises securities dealers and member firms of the National Association of Securities Dealers, Inc. We talk more about the NASD in a second.

But first, this commercial. The SEC holds itself as the investor's advocate. No person should ever invest without first going to the SEC Web site, www.sec.gov, and checking out all the investor education material there. The site is full of information. There's the SEC Complaint Center, where investors can lodge complaints (sorry—praise is handled in another center!) about a bad broker or firm, an unfair practice in the securities industry, or the latest Internet fraud. And there's the Investor Education and Assistance section of the Web site; it's the place where investors should go to learn about the risks and rewards of investing.

There! Now we can talk about the NASD.

National Association of Securities Dealers

Created in 1938, the National Association of Securities Dealers, Inc. is "the largest (or at least so says its Web site, www.nasd.com) securities-industry self-regulatory organization in the United States." It regulates the Nasdaq Stock Market and over-the-counter securities markets. Through its subsidiaries, which we'll list in a moment, the

Subsidiaries of NASD

- **NASD Regulation, Inc.**, which oversees the securities industry "through the registration, education, testing, and examination of member firms and their employees, and through the creation and enforcement of rules designed for the ultimate benefit and protection of investors"
- **The Nasdaq Stock Market**, home to many small-cap stocks, as we've discussed
- **NASD Dispute Resolution, Inc.**, another place for investors with complaints about being sold unsuitable investments or being victimized by excessive or unauthorized stock trading (by a broker, not self-directed) can go to seek justice through arbitration or mediation
- **The American Stock Exchange**, as described in Chapter 7

NASD (or at least so says its Web site) "develops rules and regulations, conducts regulatory reviews of members' business activities, disciplines violators, and designs, operates, and regulates securities markets and services (raise the flag and wave it proudly!) all for the benefit and protection of the investor," whatever that means.

According to one of those books used to train brokers, the NASD was set up to:

- Promote investment banking and the securities business
- Standardize the industry's practices and principles
- Make sure its members observe securities laws and keep "high standards of commercial honor"
- Adopt and enforce rules of fair practice in the securities business
- Promote self-discipline among members
- Investigate grievances between members and between the public and member
- Promote "just and equitable principles of trade" for the protection of investors.

As near as we can tell, here's what the NASD does. It oversees all the brokers in the U.S. And with some 681,530 people (as of

May 2001) who have what's called a Series 7 license, that's a job unto itself. (By the way, the folks who hold that license are technically called "registered representatives" or "stockbrokers." In the olden days, they were called a "customer's man." When the market was down in 2001, no one called them at all.) Anyway, those folks have to pass an exam to become stockbrokers. It's not an easy test, in part because you have to learn lots of things that you never have to use.

The NASD also oversees all the brokerage firms in the U.S., from Merrill Lynch to the itty-bitty firm in the center of your town. In case you're wondering, there are close to 5,600 brokerage firms in the U.S.

These brokerage firms and brokers must comply with the NASD's Rules of Fair Practice, which were written to prevent fraudulent acts and manipulative practices and to protect investors against unreasonable charges and commissions. (Imagine if doctors and lawyers had such a code!) Anyway, those rules say such things as:

- All advertising, sales literature, market letters, and recruiting materials from a NASD member must be truthful.
- A NASD member must always search for the best price for the securities it is buying or selling for its customers.
- A NASD member can't sell stock to a customer unless the customer has agreed to pay for the securities (hmmm).
- A NASD member that holds securities in street name (that is, in its own account) for its customers must forward all proxy material and annual reports to the customers.

When it comes to persuading investors to buy and sell securities, the NASD also has rules about brokers can and cannot do. These are sort of like the broker's 10 Commandments. First, a NASD member must know its customer (and not in a biblical or superficial sense) before it makes any recommendation. The broker must review any and all things about the customer, including assets and liabilities, income and expenses, and aunts and uncles, to figure out if the investment being recommended is suitable or not. Customers who feel wronged will typically file a complaint with NASD Resolution. alleging that the broker made an unsuitable investment recommendation. If, by the way, you feel wronged by a broker or brokerage firm, you should visit NASD Regulation, www.nasdr.com.

How can an investor be wronged? Here are some of the more common violations.

- **Pitching penny stocks** without getting to know the customer. (A penny stock is a stock that typically sells for less than $1 a share. All are traded over the counter. Penny stocks are high-risk, highly speculative investments.)
- **Churning** (officially called "excessive trading," to increase broker commissions).
- **Trading mutual funds.** (Remember, mutual funds are supposed to be long-term investments.)
- **Setting up fake accounts and concealed transactions.** Brokers have to set up accounts with real names and inform the powers that be which securities they're buying and selling for their own account.
- **Taking advantage of what's called discretionary authority**. A broker who has discretionary authority can buy and sell on behalf of the customer without his or her consent. Customers who give their broker discretion do so at their own risk. We should also note that brokers have to make an **order ticket** (or **ticket**). That's the record of the securities transaction. They must indicate whether the order was solicited or unsolicited. (A **solicited trade** means the broker persuaded the customer to make the trade. An **unsolicited trade** means that the customer told the broker to make the trade.) Sometimes, unscrupulous brokers will check off "unsolicited" even if they solicited the trade, to avoid getting caught breaking the rules.
- **Pitching securities that are inconsistent with the customer's financial profile.**

The NASD also gets a say in commissions, especially with over-the-counter securities. In essence, a member firm has to charge fair and reasonable prices for the stuff it sells.

Group	Numbers
Member Firms	5,579
Branch Offices	82,126
Registered Representatives	672,489
Regulatory Actions	
Customer Complaints Received	6,584
Customer Complaints Resolved (including carryover complaints)	6,932
Firms Expelled (not including failure to pay fines)	13
Firms Suspended	2
Individuals Barred	388
Individuals Suspended	281
Investigations	246
Advertisements and Sales Communications Reviewed	76,475

Figure 13-1. 2000 NASD Regulation statistics

New York Stock Exchange

The other big self-regulator on Wall Street is the New York Stock Exchange. Like the NASD, it reports to the SEC. Like the NASD, it has it own set of rules, which are a lot like the NASD rules. No one is allowed to manipulate stock prices, commit fraudulent acts, and so forth—the usual stuff.

(If you'd like to know more—or to get a good night's sleep—check out the regulations section of the NYSE Web site, at www.nyse.com/regulation/regulation.html.)

Federal Reserve Board

Another force to reckon with on Wall Street is the Federal Reserve Board. We've already talked about the Fed and its focus on making sure the economy is growing steadily. Well, the Fed also plays a role in the securities industry, watching over banks and their activities as well as watching over U.S. government securities markets—which happen to be larger and more important to the economy than the stock markets.

If you're curious about what the Fed does to regulate and supervise, you can find out a lot, lot more at www.federalreserve.gov/regnsup.htm. (Warning: it's not very interesting reading.)

States

Not all regulation is federal. Each state has laws and regulations to make sure Wall Street folks play fair.

You may have heard of something called **blue sky laws**. Well, those are essentially state laws that deal with the regulation of the securities business. Once upon a time, some companies would sell stock in a company that had no more assets backing it than a piece of blue sky. Blue sky laws, which can vary from state to state, establish the standards that a company must meet before it can sell stock in a particular state. The laws also license brokerage firms, brokers, and investment advisor representatives.

Every state has a securities officer. Those officers, who are represented nationally by a group called the North American Securities Administrators Association (NASAA), make sure that investment advisors obey state securities laws. Those regulators oversee investment advisors who have less than $25 million under management. Organized in 1919, NASAA (no, not the space agency) is the oldest international organization devoted to investor protection.

Like the NASD and the SEC, NASAA is happy to take an investor's complaint. It's also happy to prevent complaints from happening. Indeed, the NASAA Web site—www.nasaa.org—is filled with information for people who want to protect themselves from securities fraud. (By the way, it's a wonder why anyone would ever invest after reading all this investor fraud protection stuff, but that's a chapter for another book.)

Organizations

Besides the formal regulators, there are plenty of organizations out there throwing lifelines to anyone in need. Here we'll quickly review a few of them.

The education arm of the Investment Company Institute has a partnership with the National Urban League, "Investing for Success," to teach African-Americans about investing. The Web site is www.ici.org/investing_for_success.

The National Endowment for Financial Education is doing its part to educate people about financial literacy and investing. For instance, it offers a course to high schools called the High School Financial Planning Program (www.nefe.org/pages/educational.html).

Another useful Web site for would-be investors is www.investoreducation.org. That's the Alliance for Investor Education, which is a coalition of financial services industry and investor advocacy groups established in 1996.

One more organization to help you navigate Wall Street is the American Association of Individual Investors (AAII). It's one of the best organizations to join if you fancy becoming an investor after reading this book. AAII recently partnered with the NASD to create online financial education that uses video and audio streaming technology. You can learn more at its Web site—www.aaii.com.

But before you take off to go online and check out these great Web sites, we suggest that you keep reading. The next chapter talks a little bit more about online stuff—as in online trading.

14

The Tools of the (Online) Trade

Teach a man to fish and you feed him for a day. Teach a man to invest online and he'll buy his own yacht and have someone else fish for him.

That's how a recent letter about online investing addressed to Bob began. The letter, from a person who shall remain nameless operating out of Utah, went on to say (comments within parentheses represent the opinions of the authors):

> Dear Friend (Sucker),
>
> The Internet has dramatically changed all of our lives... And, if you haven't noticed, fortunes are being made (by people like us who like to prey on the gullible and naïve) using the Internet.
>
> The power of online trading is incredible. In fact, according to Boston Consultant estimates, online trading currently contributes 70 percent of all e-commerce revenue. (That doesn't mean investors are making money; it just means that lots of people are—or were—doing lots of trading.)

> The best way to consistently make money in the stock market is to do your own investing.... It's easier than you might think, especially if you have someone like me to help you along. (Right. And we have this really neat bridge in Brooklyn to sell you, too!)
>
> There are really only three key elements for consistent success in the stock market (fools, money, and more fools).
>
> - Key Element #1: Knowledge. You need to understand how the stock market works and how to recognize a good stock investment from a bad one. (So far, so good.)
> - Key Element #2: Information. Armed with the right, timely, and crucial information, you can knowledgeably determine when is the right time to not only buy a stock, but you will know when to sell it before you ever buy it. This way you can maximize your profits and minimize your risk. (We can't but think of that famous bit of investment advice, "Buy low and sell high," that people have been trying to follow for a long, long time.)
> - Key Element #3. Confidence. You have to have confidence in yourself that you really know what you are doing. (We know, by the way, plenty of confident people who have marched into bankruptcy—but that's a chapter for another book.)

The letter goes on to invite Bob to a free workshop that will help him "immediately get started on (his) way to personal wealth and financial security." And included among the free gifts he would receive at the workshop:

> - How to Place a Trade Online or Covered Calls: The Ultimate Cash Flow Strategy for Personal Wealth in the Year 2000 or Beyond. (We hope it's "beyond" because the year 2000 has long come and gone.... Also, we suggest avoiding covered calls as a strategy until you figure how to buy a stock.)

- The 5 Step Online Investing Wealth Building Formula. (We suspect this is a little bit like the Texas two-step.)
- Tax Tips for Traders. (The IRS really likes this one.)

Are the authors a little cynical? Yes, with good reason. To cite only one example, Bob has a friend who—prior to the crash—was running his business with his right hand while trading with his left hand. As near as we can tell, he made more than 230 trades in one year—or at least one trade for every day the market was open. And, as near as we can tell, he didn't make any money—unlike the accountant who prepared his tax return.

And so it goes, the online madness is still around in the year 2001, although it seems a bit less mad, especially now that the bull has gone out of the market. Still, you should understand what online trading is all about. But we promise to keep this chapter brief.

Doing Your First Trade

Doing your first trade online is a little bit like the first time you did ..., well, you know, the first time you did anything for the first time. You're just not sure if you did it right. Did you inhale? Was it as much fun for you as it was for the other person? All those questions. So, as the letter from our friend(?) in Utah said, it's all about confidence.

The first thing you need to do is to open an account, if you don't have one. To do that, simply contact any of the firms mentioned in Figure 14-1 and send them your money. Then sit back and watch the dollars roll in. (Just kidding!)

To open a brokerage account with an online trading firm, you first need to do some paperwork, which means that you need to understand something called the **brokerage account form**.

Actually, whether you venture into the world of online trading or choose to open an account with a human broker, you have to become familiar with the brokerage account form. It's the form that details who you are, what kind of investment experience you have (don't lie or you won't be able to sue the brokerage firm later on!), and your investment objectives.

Customer Service	Web Address
Fidelity Investments	www.fidelity.com
TD Waterhouse	www.waterhouse.com
Charles Schwab	www.schwab.com
Products and Tools	
Merrill Lynch Direct	www.mldirect.com
Fidelity Investments	www.fidelity.com
Morgan Stanley Online	www.msdwonline.com
Ease of Use	
Merrill Lynch Direct	www.mldirect.com
Fidelity Investments	www.fidelity.com
National Discount Brokers	www.ndb.com
System Responsiveness	
Charles Schwab	www.schwab.com
Morgan Stanley Online	www.msdwonline.com
Ameritrade	www.ameritrade.com
Cost	
Datek	www.datek.com
Scottrade	www.scottrade.com
A.B. Watley	www.abwatley.com

Figure 14-1. Best online brokers (Source: *Money* magazine, June 2001)

The typical form, according to Bruce Sankin, author of *What Your Stockbroker Doesn't Want You to Know*!, addresses the following:

1. **Dog tag information**, including name, birth date, Social Security number, etc.
2. **Residence: own or rent**. (If you own a house, odds are that you might be a tad more sophisticated—or at least aware of the fact that real estate isn't a marketable and liquid security. **Marketable** means that there's a market in which to buy or sell

something quickly. Stocks are marketable because they can be bought and sold frequently. Real estate sometimes takes a few months to buy and sell. As for **liquid**, well, it's a question of how easily an asset can be converted into cash.

3. **Legal residence.** If you have more than one mailing address, other than a PO box, odds are that you are worth a pretty penny—or an ugly nickel.
4. **Employment/occupation.** If you're the senior vice president of a major consumer goods company with a graduate degree from a world-renowned business school, odds are slim to none that you'll get any money back when you go to sue your online or offline broker.
5. **Annual income/net worth.** If you're earning lots of dough or you've got a well-diversified portfolio, you're not likely to win any money when you sue your broker for malfeasance, churning, and unsuitable investments.
6. **Fixed income.** If you're on a fixed income, you're likely to be a conservative investor. If your stockbroker advises you to buy hog futures or cow pasts, it's likely to be an unsuitable investment.
7. **Director, officer, 10% stockholder.** If you're one of these, you probably know a little about risk and return.
8. **Citizen of the USA.** If you're a citizen, you're in the clear taxwise. If you're not a U.S. citizen, do tell here. Otherwise, you're likely to face some tax penalties on capital gains (if you're lucky enough to have any), dividends, and interest.
9. **Other brokerage accounts.** If you have other accounts, it might suggest that you know what you're doing when it comes to investing. Of course, the only thing that we think proves that you know what you're doing is results. Have you made or lost money in the market? If you've made money, you know what you're doing. If you've lost money, well, maybe you should be playing Monopoly™ with play money.
10. **Investment profile.** This is where you describe your investment objectives. If you want growth, say so. If you want income, say so. If you want safety of principal (that is, you don't want to lose money), say so. Also, don't lie about how many years of experi-

ence you have investing in stocks, bonds, etc. This document can and will be used against you when you sue your broker.

11. **Introduction.** How did you come to open this account? Some people clicked on a banner advertisement. Some people took a cold call. Some people went to a seminar. You should be honest in answering this question, because the brokerage account form can and will be part of the public record.
12. **References,** as in the name of your bank. If you go to sue your broker, these references will be checked. The brokerage firm and arbitration folks (more on that in a second) will investigate your activity in these other accounts to demonstrate knowledge of the risks and rewards of investing.
13. **Power of attorney.** This is the person to whom you give the power to act on your behalf (if you so choose), the person who can buy or sell stuff in your name, if you are unable to do so. Don't assign a power of attorney without first checking with your spouse.
14. **Account description: cash or margin.** A **cash account** is one in which you buy and sell stocks and bonds with cash, like the checkout line at the supermarket. A **margin account** is like a home equity loan account: the brokerage firm will let you borrow money to buy more securities. (More on this later in this chapter.)

Now you know the basics of the brokerage account form, so you can open an account. But wait just a moment!

Look Before You Leap

Before you start, here—courtesy of the Investor's Streaming University, an educational Web site co-sponsored by the National Association of Securities Dealers and the American Association of Individual Investors—are some more tidbits that might prove useful in the world of online investing.

First, we should define **online trading**. It's the buying and selling of securities from your computer, hand-held personal digital assistant, or other electronic device. It's a techie update on the traditional method of calling up a broker and placing an order. ("Two cheeseburgers, easy on the onions, and a large cola—and could I have 100 shares of FriesCo with that, to go?") It's also different from **day trading**; that's the process of buying and selling sometimes in a matter of seconds so as to make (or more often lose) money.

As Mary Schapiro, the president of the NASD Regulation, says in the www.streamingu.org course on online brokerage accounts, "Online investing requires the same hard work and thoughtful preparation that investing always has." But she warns that the Internet has created as much high-quality information about investing as there is unsubstantiated speculation and misinformation.

So what's an investor to do? Well, when it comes to investing online, the best offense is a good defense. Be a skeptic. Heck, be a cynic even. Trust no one over 30—or under 30. (Except us, of course!) (Indeed, as we write this chapter, we read that a 15-year-old boy was dispensing legal advice to people on the Internet who thought him to be a qualified expert. What's the world coming to?)

Anyway, Ms. Schapiro is kind enough to tell us in her online course about online investing that the NASD Regulation is doing all it can to pursue securities fraud, but that it's impossible to monitor every investment-related posting on the Internet. "The best protection for investors is for them to know what they are getting into," she says.

Online investing is also a lot like traditional investing in this regard. There's the same risk of losing money online as with a broker.

However, there's a risk associated with online investing that's not often associated with traditional investing. Online investors place their order directly from their computer with their online brokerage firm. In some cases, stuff happens. Maybe you have a slow connection to the Internet and your order doesn't get placed fast enough and you lose millions in a matter of seconds. Or maybe the computer system crashes at your online brokerage firm and your order never gets placed. To be sure, there are always computer problems of one sort or another with traditional investing, but somehow those problems seem easier to resolve. Or at least that's our perception.

Speaking of perceptions, we should note that many people, at least before the Internet bubble popped, believed they could start trading online and—presto!—own an island. Some readers may remember watching one online brokerage firm advertising the fact that a tow truck driver was able to buy a tropical island as a result of trading online or another online brokerage firm showing a young office copy boy teaching the stodgy old company president how to trade online. Well, the Securities and Exchange Commission took issue with what some viewed as "promissory" ads. The online brokerage firms, by the way, don't advertise such stuff anymore.

Even if they don't actually expect to get rich and buy an island, investors are attracted to online trading because it's less expensive to wheel and deal electronically. Sure, the price of buying and selling stocks online is sometimes less than with a human. In many cases, you can trade stocks for $9.99 online. But we should point out that many full-service brokerage firms today have online discount firms or package deals that enable investors to buy and sell as much as they want online or offline, provided they maintain a certain balance in their account.

News, Analysis, and Commentary

Now you know about online trading. If you decide to give it a shot, we'd recommend tapping into some information resources for Wall Street news, analysis, and commentary.

We think it's a good idea to check out a Web site such as www.briefing.com. Founded in 1995, Briefing.com—touted as "The Perfect Companion to Online Trading™"—offers online investors a chance to learn as much or as little as they want to know about the daily droppings and happenings on Wall Street, including:

- Earnings calendar
- Earnings estimate upgrades and downgrades
- Stock splits
- Economic calendar
- IPO calendar

The site consists of three parts. One is free, another costs a low monthly fee, and access to the whole site is available for a larger monthly fee.

Once you become versed in the subject matter, it's time to open an account and do your first trade. Say Roger Clemens for Manny Ramirez .... (Our apologies to all of those who don't believe that life revolves around professional baseball and the exchange of pieces of cardboard with the likenesses of athletic millionaires.)

The Dangers of the Margin

Earlier in this chapter, we discussed some general risks of online trading. Here's another that could ruin you.

In our outline of the items on a brokerage account form, we described a margin account as being similar to a home equity loan account. Well, just as with a home equity loan, a margin account offers advantages and disadvantages. Here's how a margin account works.

Let's say you buy $10,000 worth of stocks in a margin account. Well, given that you know what you are doing (right?), the brokerage firm will let you borrow 50% of that amount, or $5,000, to buy more securities, so that your total portfolio would be worth $15,000. That's great, eh?

Well, yes, sometimes. This strategy works well during a bull market, but not so well in a bear market. In a bear market, as the value of your portfolio declines, the amount that you can borrow declines, too. And that means the brokerage firm will ask you to pay back the amount of the loan in excess of 50% of the current value of your portfolio.

Let's continue with our example. You owned $10,000 worth of stock and borrowed $5,000. Then, the stock you owned went south, declining in value to $5,000. That means that the maximum amount of your loan would be only $2,500—which means that you would have to repay $2,500 of the loan so as to bring it down to 50% of your portfolio value. That would be, what they call on Wall Street, a **margin call**.

Margin calls are the worst. Typically, it means that you have to sell some of the stock that you own to pay back the part of the loan over 50%. And so it goes, in a vicious cycle. The stock falls again, you get another margin call, you sell some more stock, the stock falls again, you get another margin call.... It's a risky business. By the way, all securities purchased with margin must be held in street name. That means that the securities are registered in the name of the securities firm—so the firm can quickly liquidate the securities as collateral in a hurry if necessary. So there's a certain expectation that at least occasionally some investor will fail to keep up with a vicious cycle.

Anyway, if you're a novice investor, stick to cash accounts. If you're a sophisticated investor, wait until there's a bull market to use a margin account.

15

Your Money, Your Life:
Put Your Investments into Context

We all come into the money game with some baggage. Our "money roots" are all the things that surface when it comes time to make a money decision. They're kind of mixed in there with self-worth, values, mores, and the like. They're part nature, part nurture, and a lot of question marks. Our friends, relatives, teachers, employers, and others have probably added to the database of weird thoughts we have about money.

Whether those things in our baggage are right or wrong is always subject to debate, but you do need to get a fix on them before you can truly understand the money game. It's not what you learn and know that affects your life, it's how you react to those things when you make decisions. The toughest thing is not just learning the basics but unlearning the wrong stuff! So we're going start with the top things that you think you know but that ain't so.

Investment Myths

1. I need to really know a lot about investments before I can be successful. Not! Unless you're an investment advisor, you have a real job and a family. It's that job that will provide the fuel to create your net worth and the family that will draw it down.

Sometimes I think there's an inverse correlation between intelligence and successful investing. That's because when you think about investing or anything else too much, you get paralysis by analysis and end up doing nothing. If we think about everything that can go wrong and investigate every option available, then we'll just be slaves to information overload. What you do need to know is how to save money, be patient, not jump around too much, and have a discipline that reflects your mindset and family values and lifestyle. Then have the discipline to stick to it.

2. You must diversify. Tell that to Bill Gates, Larry Ellison, Steven Case, Ted Turner, and the rest of the billionaires who have invested their whole lives into their companies. Even if you look at those relative paupers, those millionaires in our midst, you'll find that many of them made their money by running their own small businesses and investing their lives in their profession—which just so happened to make them wealthy.

That doesn't mean that diversification isn't a safer and less volatile route to financial success. In fact, most every one of these rich folks will end up diversifying later in life. They do that to take something off the table, so if bad things happen to their companies, they don't have to start all over again. The two contrary points are to not put all your eggs in one basket or to put all your eggs in one basket and then watch it like a hawk!

3. You need professional help. At some time in your life you probably will need some help from an attorney, accountant, or investment expert. In fact, the really rich folks almost all have advisors who keep an eye on the money they've made while they go out and make more. I've said many times that as an advisor I'm the "keeper of the wealth" and the client is the "maker of the wealth." If you enjoy dealing with investments and are good at it (not just that you think you're good at it!), then go for it. Maybe once in a while pay an hourly fee to get a second opinion to make sure you're not on the brink of financial destruction. After all, many people fix their own cars and do their own painting, carpentry, plumbing, and landscaping. Some even do their own taxes! Even if *I* wouldn't do those things with a gun to my head, it doesn't mean that *you* shouldn't.

4. You must put your retirement money in only safe investments. "Safe" is on of those relative words that means a whole lot of things to a whole lot of people. To investors, in most cases, it means bonds, money market funds, or CDs. The problem here is that, even if you retire at age 62, you can still expect to live 15 more years, on the average. That means you still have to keep pace with inflation after you pay Uncle Sam his cut. Some say this means investing only in stocks to do this. However, we're not saying, "Don't own bonds," because you probably need more of them at retirement when the paychecks stop. Just don't abandon stocks because your company has given you a nice gold watch and an opportunity to lower your golf handicap.

5. Growth style stocks are the only way to go. We spent a lot of time earlier in this book talking about all those tricky differences between value and growth stocks. It's impossible to pick when the tech stocks are going to outperform the more defensive old economy stocks. Looking at long-term performance, the sure bet is that they'll all average out. In good times (like 1995-1999), the growth stocks did great. When things slow down, then investors get cautious and go back to the less volatile value stocks because they hold up better (early 2000-2001). Since 1973 the Lipper large-cap *growth* funds have averaged 14.9% a year; compare that with the annual rate of the Lipper large-cap *value* funds at 14.5%. With only .4% separating the two and with it being virtually impossible to time when either will win, it seems wisest to own both types of stocks.

6. A good income is the best determinant of financial success. It's a good determinant, but not the best. We've all heard of the hotshot athletes who made millions and are now busted. So, other than having a lousy agent or financial advisor, the best determinant of financial success is how much money you save every year. I'll take someone with an average income who saves well over someone with a high income who doesn't save any day of the week.

It's key to understand that your income will reflect your standard of living over your lifetime. If your lifestyle doesn't change much at retirement, then those extra savings can improve your lifestyle geometrically. That's assuming, of course, that you have a solid investment portfolio, not just low-return guaranteed stuff. Getting back to that comment about net worth, "It's not what you make, it's what you keep."

7. Your house is your best investment. It's not—because it's not an investment, it's a lifestyle decision. Your home, whether you own or you rent, is a conscious decision about how much money you're willing to spend to put a roof over your head.

Unless you plan on retiring on a warm island in a tent, then you'll continue to need a roof over your head. More than likely when you retire, you may want a couple of roofs, one near warmer weather (unless you love the cold stuff) and one around your lifetime friends and family. If you're lucky enough to live near family and warm weather, then you'll probably want to stay put. If I'm wrong and you downsize to a smaller house, then just consider your gains a bonus due to a "lifestyle reduction dividend." If you think you made a great return on your house, then just think about what would have happened if you'd put your mortgage payment into stocks. Over the last 30 years, if you'd taken $200 a month and invested in the S&P 500 index, it would now be worth $1,087,235 (annualized return of 14.88%). The odds are pretty good that if you bought a house 30 years ago and paid $200 a month on a mortgage, that house is not worth more than $1,087,235.

8. Your goal is to not pay any taxes at all. It's not what you pay Uncle Sam that matters; it's what you keep after he gets done. For example, if you earned a 10% return on your investments (stocks that are taxable) and had to pay the taxman 28% of that, you still netted out a 7.2% return. If you decided to buy a 5% tax-free bond so that Uncle gets nothing, you're short 2.2% for the privilege of not paying taxes.

Don't get me wrong. I'm not in favor of supporting $500 U.S. government-issued toilet seats, but just be sure you don't short-change yourself because of taxophobia. When you put taxes ahead of returns, we call it the tax tail wagging the dog. Those of you below the 28% bracket ($43,850 income jointly) probably don't need much in the way of tax benefits.

9. Online is the only way to invest. If you don't know what you're doing, online investing just allows you to pay a lower commission to lose money faster. Somehow we managed to buy stocks and make money before we invented the microchip and I think that will continue. Most of us still buy our cars, clothes, and food without the aid of a laptop. We'll probably continue to do this, just like we'll still use that old tech thing called the phone to call up our brokers to buy and sell.

Whether they use advisors or not, I personally think that more people will invest online as a matter of ease and convenience, not necessarily for better returns. I've got to admit, though, that getting information with the box and the 'Net is much faster than without. The problem is that if the customer isn't comfortable doing it that way, then remember that the customer (that's you!) is always right!

10. You've got to figure out how to time the markets to succeed. Not even the best of the investment professionals in the business with the super-inflated wallets and egos will admit to being able to do this. So we mere mortals shouldn't even think about it.

There have been 17 bear markets since 1946 and only nine recessions, according to Ned Davis Research. So if you think you can pinpoint these times, then you should be *writing* this book, not *reading* it. Just work on that diversification thing we've been harping on and leave the timing alone.

Plan, Plan, and Plan Some More

Now that you can free yourself from the chains of the financial myths that may have financially shackled you over all these years, it's time to do something about it. Just as Moses came down from the mountain with the 10 commandments, you now have the 10 myth busters to carry around like tablets of financial hope and discipline to guide you on the rest of your financial trip. Although Moses had some serious stuff to do with his tablets, like selling those commandments to people who were killing each other and coveting their neighbors' wives, our mantra is simpler—plan, plan, and plan some more!

Just like real estate is location, location, location, planning is plan cubed. When it comes to the process of planning, there are five basic steps:

- What have you got?
- What do you want?
- What do you need to know?
- How do you implement the plan?
- How do you keep on top of the plan?

Figure Out Where You Are

Step one in the planning process is find the biggest counter or floor area you can and start dumping all your financial stuff on it. Bring out the musty insurance policy from your parents, the brokerage statement that's unintelligible, the savings account that's paying a whopping 2%, the 401(k) with 500 choices, and the benefits statements on all the stuff your company is providing you that you don't feel you want or need. Next, get out a pen and a pad of paper. Then, let the organizational games begin!

We'll deal with how these things stack up later. For now, just figure out what you've got. If you get this far, then congratulations! You're doing better than most.

We've included two simple charts here (Figures 15-1 and 15-2) to use when it comes to lining up your ducks. The two components you need are your **net worth statement** (what have you got?) and your **budget** or **income statement** (where does your money go?).

Two quick points here:

- For the net worth statement, make sure, if you're a couple, that you sort by noting **single** ownership or **joint** ownership.
- For the budget, you can either break things down on a monthly basis or annualize them.

Your budget or income statement should show more coming in

than going out. If not, then make a beeline to the Consumer Credit Counseling Service or The National Foundation for Credit Counseling (www.nfcc.org). It's a non-profit national organization that helps people sort out their debt woes before they get eaten up by credit cards or bill collectors.

Net Worth			
Assets (what you own)	**Self**	**Spouse**	**Total**
Cash or Equivalents			
Cash	______	______	______
Checking Accounts	______	______	______
Savings Accounts	______	______	______
Money Market Fund	______	______	______
Certificates of Deposit	______	______	______
Savings Bonds	______	______	______
Life Insurance (Cash Value)	______	______	______
Total Cash and Equivalents	$______	$______	$______
Retirement Assets			
IRAs	______	______	______
Pension/Profit Sharing	______	______	______
401(k), 403(b), 457 Plans	______	______	______
Keogh Accounts	______	______	______
Annuities (surrender value)	______	______	______
Total Retirement Assets	$______	$______	$______
Investment Assets			
Stocks	______	______	______
Bonds	______	______	______
Mutual Funds	______	______	______
Rental Properties	______	______	______
Other	______	______	______
Total Investment Assets	$______	$______	$______
Lifestyle Assets			
Home	______	______	______
Cars	______	______	______
Furniture	______	______	______
Clothes/Jewelry	______	______	______
Collectibles	______	______	______
Other	______	______	______
Total Lifestyle Assets	$______	$______	$______
Total Assets	$______	$______	$______

Figure 15-1. Figuring out your net worth (continued on next page) (Used with permission of Dee Lee, Harvard Financial Educators, Harvard, MA)

Net Worth			
Liabilities (what you owe)	**Self**	**Spouse**	**Total**
Debts			
Medical/Dental	______	______	______
Taxes Owed	______	______	______
Personal Loans	______	______	______
Mortgage	______	______	______
Pledges	______	______	______
Loans	______	______	______
Credit Card Balances	______	______	______
Other	______	______	______
Total Liabilities	$______	$______	$______
Total Assets	$______	$______	$______
Minus Total Liabilities	$______	$______	$______
Net Worth	$______	$______	$______

Figure 15-1. Figuring out your net worth, continued
(Used with permission of Dee Lee, Harvard Financial Educators, Harvard, MA)

Decide Where You Want to Go

If you're not in hot water with creditors, then step two is to figure out what you want. Sit down, play some music that makes you relax, have a drink, and try and figure out why you're on this planet. List anything that pops into your mind, from the little stuff like the meaning of life to the really important things like a new car. Then start to prioritize this wish list.

When all is said and done, then, have a top 10 list of the most important things you want to accomplish in your life. If you need money to achieve your goals, start putting price tags on them in terms of what it will cost to get the job done. Even if the goals are not financial, figure out the steps necessary to fulfill your dreams. I'm sure you can go to the self-help section of the book store and find some books to pump you up to get going on this "life's to-do list." All I ask is that you put it in writing! Then have a monthly appointment with yourself to see how things are going and see if you need to change direction somewhere.

Budget		
Monthly Expenses	**Budget**	**Actual**
Basic Expenses		
Mortgage/Rent	______	______
Real Estate Taxes	______	______
Utilities	______	______
Other Household Expenses	______	______
Home Insurance	______	______
Food	______	______
Clothing	______	______
Car Expenses	______	______
Car Insurance	______	______
Other	______	______
Total Basic Expenses	$______	$______
Other Expenses		
Books, Magazines	______	______
CDs, Music	______	______
Entertainment	______	______
Gifts	______	______
Pet Expenses	______	______
Lunch at Work	______	______
Internet Service Provider	______	______
Vacations	______	______
Other	______	______
Total Other Expenses	$______	$______

Figure 15-2. A sample budget form
(Used with permission of Dee Lee, Harvard Financial Educators, Harvard, MA)

Know the Rules of the Game

The third step is to know the rules of the game. The key strategy of winning in the investment game is beating inflation after tax. Then reflect a little on those asset allocation strategies we spoke about in earlier chapters.

The most important part of the game is using this thing called "the logic alert." That's a bell that ought to go off in your head when someone or something sounds too good to be true. This will absolutely be your best single indicator to back off from something and think about it a bit. If things are happening and there's a lot of pressure to do something right away, then take a line from the anti-drug campaign—"Just say no." Even if you're wrong, with 40,000 stocks and 12,000 mutual funds, you'll probably get a second chance somewhere else.

Do Something

Step four is brutal: you actually need to make a decision to do something. You have to implement the plan or, as Wall Street likes to say, execute it. (Doesn't that sound like a bad Western hanging?)

You have to decide at this point whether you're going it alone or hiring an advisor. Whatever your path, you can choose something that fits your personality. You can play the toe dipper and do a little at a time. You can move at a brisk pace and get the big stuff done, then move gradually into the peripheral items. Finally, you can say, "Geronimo-o-o-o-o-o!" and plunge off a cliff and never look back. You know your hat size best, so find what fits.

Just do one very important thing—set a specific date to get it all done. Have a deadline and abide by it and not cheat yourself after all the hard work. Or, if you're going it alone and can't do it, then find an advisor to make you live up to your plan.

Keep Track

The final step is to keep track of the results of your investment decisions. That's not easy for most of us.

But here's something that might help you follow your investments. Obligations are coming at us from all directions. You probably find yourself wondering at times, "What about me?" Well, a financial plan is about you and about accomplishing what you want so your life has meaning and you can afford to do the things that really can make a difference in your life and impact your family.

If that thought can't motivate you to keep on top of the stuff, then (again) go the self-help section or hire somebody to do it for you. Just do it!

The time it takes is really not more than a few hours a month—a lot less than shoveling the snow or keeping up with the yard. If you've got one of those expensive boxes on a desk somewhere that you plug in occasionally, then buy a software program for it to keep tabs on things, like Intuit Quicken or Microsoft Money. You just need to track your finances, to see if you're progressing every year (making money). If not, then you need to know why.

That usually means that your allocation is out of whack or you've got some real dogs in the portfolio. If so, then make some changes and move on. The key here, though, is relative performance: you have to compare your returns with some benchmark to see how you're truly doing. If you're up 10% in a year, you may be happy, but if the averages are up 20%, you now have a problem!

The Emotional Enemy

In most investment and planning decisions, it's best to remember the wise words that Walt Kelly gave Pogo: "We have met the enemy and he is us." That's because we're human, we're emotional, and we feel things as much as we analyze them. We're not Spockian humanoids making intellectual decisions all day long. We react and overreact every single day about one thing or another.

The financial markets themselves move like a pendulum from bull to bear to bull again in a single day. That's to be expected because the markets are just a bunch of human beings—traders, analysts, and portfolio managers trying to do their jobs. Of course they're judged and compensated on how well they do every single day. That leads to a pressurized microcosm of very wealthy neurotics looking to be the first one in or out of a market trend.

So, as an amateur looking into that world, it would be virtually impossible for you not to feel the same things as Wall Street. There's only one difference: if you do lousy, you may not lose your job—just your future.

If you remember nothing about the markets or the psychology of markets, understand that they move in cycles. These cycles are actually used by Wall Street in charting stocks to see the pattern of movement. Let's take a walk down the investment road.

First we visit motivation, which is "Why are we taking the investment road?" After this period of wonderment and reflection, we move into action by buying the stock. We feel good about things because we've just made a commitment for self-betterment.

Next, we start following the stock. We may even be right as the stock starts going up in value. We now feel joy and esteem as our hard work has led us to pick the right stock. Then the stock moves even higher and we feel almost jubilant as we begin to bond with this stock because it's treating our net worth so well.

But then comes disappointment as the markets and our favorite stock are now stalling out and even moving down. We feel we should weather the storm with our little buddy and hang in there as it continues to weaken.

Now the stock is where we bought it and anxiety sets in as we've left all that money on the table and now we're actually losing the game. It falls further and we're downright ticked off at our old best friend. Anger sets in. Then we panic and dump our savior stock turned enemy and dog.

We feel a sense of relief now, as we've made a firm decision to end the relationship and move on. As thinking beings, we still think of the good times and bad times we had with that stock. We wonder if we can ever have a successful relationship again and our self-esteem starts to flounder. So we go back to ponder our motivation again. We think about what we should do next. Then the cycle begins again.... We buy another stock!

The reason for this emotional exercise is to see that all of us question our decisions constantly and all of us make mistakes. The key to keeping your emotions in check is to understand that even the best make mistakes, a lot of mistakes. So if you're a perfectionist, get over it! The key is to understand these cycles of the market and recognize that every **correction** in the market (that's Wall Street Speak for a drop in the market following a rise) has led to a higher ground eventually. We need patience: it's imperative to long-term happiness and returns as we try and tame the emotional tiger (see Figure 15-3 for the evidence).

So don't get drawn into the daily minutiae of market sentiment and media madness. Use your long-term emotional stability, not your street-fighter ferocity.

The Things You Need to Know When Divvying up Your Assets

You must remember that time is of the essence. That doesn't mean your time horizon is short; it just means that it's defined. If you have a whole bunch of those goals we talked about earlier, then

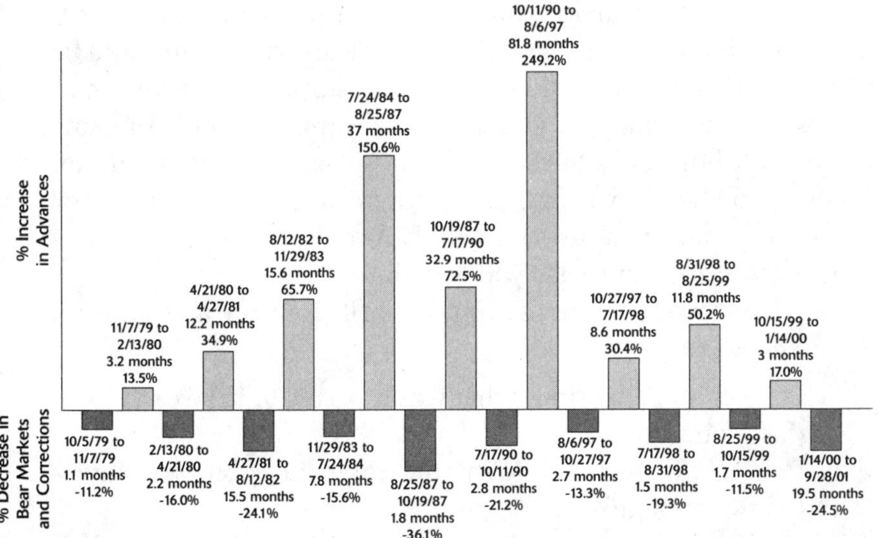

Figure 15-3. Bull Markets (Advances); Bear Markets (Corrections)

you need to also have timelines for achieving them.

You should think of those deadlines as short-term, intermediate, or long-term. We define short-term as three years or less, intermediate as three to 15 years, and long-term as 15 years and beyond. So you need to take all those baskets of investments that may be in many different accounts and under different ownership and meld them together to match your intent.

How you spread out your wealth is based on how many baskets you want to keep an eye on. There are several possibilities.

If the time frame is the most important factor, then what goes where? Short-term money needs to find a home in cash, bonds, or maybe balanced investments (stocks and bonds). Intermediate money should be primarily in stocks, with some bonds, depending on how much volatility you can stomach. For the long haul, stick with stocks, because you *never* would have lost money in the stock market if you invested over 20 years. Those are pretty good odds.

The second way to divvy up your assets is by the actual account name. That gets really tricky because you have to understand the rules of joint ownership, estate planning, financial aid for education, and tax planning.

The third way to divide your investments is by the actual investment as well as the custodian. For example, the custodian could be a brokerage firm that would hold all your stocks, mutual funds, or bonds in one account. It could also be a mutual fund company that would hold only the mutual funds that are in its family of funds. Your shoe box is also an option; just let the cleaning crew know this somewhere in your will, before they toss out your fortune when the big guy calls you upstairs.

So divide and conquer, as you deem fit! Here are a few tips on the breakdown:

- For ease of paper flow, what works best is to have one custodian you trust.
- Putting money in a child's name can reduce his or her potential financial aid.
- Keeping all assets in joint name can be a major estate planning blunder.
- Putting assets in an irrevocable trust can increase your income taxes.
- One investment does not fit all needs.
- Ownership changes in IRAs can cause big tax problems.

Pulling together all of the pieces of your financial puzzle is very difficult to do alone. This is where you may need to get some help from a pro to make sure your asset allocation picture is in line with your goals.

Time in the Market

Investing experts often advise investors that what matters is not *timing the market,* but rather *time in the market.* In other words, let time be on your side, working for you. Don't try to guess at where the market's going.

Time heals all. When it comes to down stock markets, you'll need this time, regardless of how painful, to allow your portfolio to heal.

In the last section, we saw the stats on how many times you would have lost money based on the number of years you would have held onto your stocks. Now let's take a closer look at just how often and how ugly things can get.

How many times would you have lost more than 5% (about a year's worth of interest at the bank) in the Dow Jones Industrial Average this past century? About three times a year. 10% corrections happen about once a year. 15% dives happen about once every two years. The market declines 20% every three years. The best way to handle these financial downturns is to expect them and prepare, not just try to react when they're happening.

Another way to get timing out of your head is to look at how your performance would have changed if you'd missed the best days in the market. For example, if you'd missed the 10-50 best days, your returns would have been 1.2%. By comparison, if you'd just bought and held, your returns would have been 6.2%. On the other hand, if you'd been a genius and missed the 10-50 worst days, you would have made 11.7% returns (Figure 15-4). If you still believe you can get in and out accurately, then good luck!

	Days Excluded				
	10	20	30	40	50
Best	4.7	3.6	2.7	1.9	1.2
Worst	7.9	9.0	10.0	10.9	11.7
Best and Worst	6.4	6.3	6.3	6.3	6.4

Figure 15-4. Gain per Year of S&P 500 Excluding the Best and Worst Days (1/4/1928 - 3/15/2000)

The method that works best to keep you away from temptation of timing is to find a good mutual fund and do **dollar cost averaging** (DCA). Next to compound interest, DCA is the greatest investment tool ever.

How does it work? It's simple. Just set an amount of dollars to put into an investment regularly. Then do it—no matter how the markets are moving.

The more frequently you do it, the better. Here's an example to prove that point. If you invested $100 a month for the last 30 years into the S&P500, it would be worth $543,629. If on the other hand, you'd invested the same amount but only every year, your investment would be worth only $524,086. That's a difference of almost $20,000.

$100 a month	$543,629
$300 quarterly	$538,975
$600 semiannually	$530,170
$1,200 annually	$524,086

But maybe you don't believe that DCA works. The proof is mathematical: your average cost will always be less than the average price per share. Figure 15-5 shows how many shares the set amount of investment ($100) will buy as the price per share rises and falls.

$ Amount	Price per Share	# Shares Bought
100	50	2
100	40	2.5
100	30	3.3
100	35	2.9
100	40	2.5
500	39	13.2

Figure 15-5. Buying Shares at Different Prices

Do the math: the average price per share is $39, but $500 ÷ 13.2 shares gives an average cost per share to you of $37.88. It's not magic, just mathematics!

You've Just Got to Have Faith

All the numbers on the good and bad times show that it doesn't pay to be a pessimist on the U.S. stock market. It's important to remember that point.

For every dip in the cycle, the market has continued to ultimately climb higher. If you were smart enough to get out of the market before a bump, then you would have to be doubly smart to decide when to jump back in.

If you want to time the markets, then good luck with that strategy! If you want to be successful over time, then remember that the objective of investing in stocks is not to get out when they drop 30%, it's to be there when they go up 300%. See Figures 15-6 and 15.7 for an idea about the difficult nature of market timing.

Beginning Date	DJIA	Ending Date	DJIA	% Gain	Days
6/17/1901	57.33	11/9/1903	30.88	-46.1%	875
1/19/1906	75.45	11/15/1907	38.83	-48.5	665
11/19/1909	73.64	9/25/1911	53.43	-27.4	675
9/30/1912	68.97	7/30/1914	52.32	-24.1	668
11/21/1916	110.15	12/19/1917	65.95	-40.1	393
11/3/1919	119.62	8/24/1921	63.90	-46.6	660
3/20/1923	105.38	10/27/1923	85.75	-18.6	221
9/3/1929	381.17	11/13/1929	198.69	-47.9	71
4/17/1930	294.07	7/8/1932	41.22	-86.0	813
9/7/1932	79.93	2/27/1933	50.16	-37.2	173
2/5/1934	110.74	7/26/1934	85.51	-22.8	171
3/10/1937	194.40	3/31/1938	98.95	-49.1	386
11/12/1938	158.41	4/8/1939	121.44	-23.3	147
9/12/1939	155.92	4/28/1942	92.92	-40.4	959
5/29/1946	212.50	5/17/1947	163.21	-23.2	353
6/15/1948	193.16	6/13/1949	161.60	-16.3	363
1/5/1953	293.79	9/14/1953	255.49	-13.0	252
4/6/1956	521.05	10/22/1957	419.79	-19.4	564
1/5/1960	685.47	10/25/1960	566.05	-17.4	294
12/31/1961	734.91	6/26/1962	535.76	-27.1	195
2/9/1966	995.15	10/7/1966	744.32	-25.2	240
12/3/1968	985.21	5/26/1970	631.16	-35.9	539
4/28/1971	950.82	11/23/1971	797.97	-16.1	209
1/11/1973	1051.70	12/6/1974	577.60	-45.1	694
9/21/1976	1014.79	2/28/1978	742.12	-26.9	525
9/8/1978	907.74	4/21/1980	759.13	-16.4	591
4/27/1981	1024.05	8/12/1982	776.92	-24.1	472
11/29/1983	1287.20	7/24/1984	1086.57	-15.6	238
8/25/1987	2722.42	19/19/1987	1738.74	-36.1	55
7/16/1990	2999.75	10/11/1990	2365.10	-21.2	87
7/17/1998	9337.97	8/31/1998	7539.07	-19.3	45
Mean				**-30.9**	**406**
Median				**-25.2**	**363**

Figure 15-6. Bear Markets 6/17/1901 - 12/29/1998, as defined by Ned Davis Research (DJIA = Dow Jones Industrial Average)

Beginning Date	DJIA	Ending Date	DJIA	% Gain	Days
9/24/1900	38.80	6/17/1901	57.33	47.8	266
11/9/1903	30.88	1/19/1906	75.45	144.4	802
11/15/1907	38.83	11/19/1909	73.64	89.7	735
9/25/1911	53.43	9/30/1912	68.97	29.1	371
12/24/1914	53.17	11/21/1916	110.15	107.2	698
12/19/1917	65.95	11/3/1919	119.62	81.4	684
8/24/1921	63.90	3/20/1923	105.38	64.9	573
10/27/1923	85.76	9/3/1929	381.17	344.5	2138
11/13/1929	198.69	4/17/1930	294.07	48.0	155
7/8/1932	41.22	9/7/1932	79.93	93.9	61
2/27/1933	50.16	2/5/1934	110.74	120.8	343
7/25/1934	85.51	3/10/1937	194.40	127.3	958
3/31/1938	98.95	11/12/1938	158.41	60.1	226
4/8/1939	121.44	9/12/1939	155.92	28.4	157
4/28/1942	92.92	5/29/1946	212.50	128.7	1492
5/17/1947	163.21	6/15/1948	193.16	18.4	395
6/13/1949	161.20	1/5/1953	293.79	81.8	1302
9/14/1953	255.49	4/6/1956/	521.05	103.9	935
10/22/1957	419.79	1/5/1960	685.47	63.3	805
10/25/1960	566.05	12/13/1961	734.91	29.8	414
6/26/1962	535.76	2/9/1966	995.15	85.7	1324
10/7/1966	744.32	12/3/1968	985.21	32.4	788
5/26/1970	631.16	4/28/1971	950.62	50.6	337
11/23/1971	797.97	1/11/1973	1051.70	31.8	415
12/6/1974	577.60	9/21/1976	1014.79	75.7	655
2/28/1978	742.12	9/8/1978	907.74	22.3	192
4/21/1980	759.13	4/27/1981	1024.05	34.9	371
8/12/1982	776.92	11/29/1983	1287.20	65.7	474
7/24/1984	1086.57	8/25/1987	2722.42	150.6	1127
10/19/1987	1738.74	7/16/1990	2999.75	72.5	1001
10/11/1990	2365.10	7/17/1998	9337.97	294.8	2836
8/31/1998	7539.07	3/24/2000	11112.72	47.4	571
Mean				**86.8**	**738**
Median				**69.1**	**614**

Figure 15-7. Bull Markets 9/24/1900 - 3/24/2000, as defined by Ned Davis Research

It's All About You

This chapter started by addressing the 10 myths of money, showing that it's not what you don't know that really hurts, but what you know that isn't true. We then gave you our five-step process of getting all your stuff together, figuring your wants, knowing the basics of the game, playing the game, and keeping score on the game as the game evolves. Finally, we discussed the greatest obstacle we each must face—ourselves. We warned against letting your emotions run your intellect down to a frazzle and we advised you to accept that we are all emotional animals down to our core. Keeping that fact in mind will help you keep your sanity whenever the markets yank your chain.

In the next chapter, we'll help you keep track of all the paper generated by Wall Street ... and the paper required by the IRS and other taxing authorities that get a piece of your action.

16

Paper, Paper, Paper: Forms and Records and Taxes

The last (phew!) part of decoding Wall Street involves all the paper and the paperwork the Street and friends of the Street generate. It's especially necessary if, after reading this book, you decide to move from voyeur to investor. So before you waltz off and start investing in dot-com this and dot-com that, read this final chapter. It will provide you with guidance on dealing with all that paper.

First off, it should come as no surprise that Wall Street produces lots of paper. Some of it, like the letters that come into your house inviting you to attend an estate planning seminar, is designed to persuade you to buy or sell securities. Some of it, like the research reports or the treatise on changes in the required minimum distribution for your retirement account, is intended to educate you. And some of it, like your quarterly statement or the proxy statement, is required by law. In the next few pages, we'll try to shed some light on the three types of paper that you might encounter along the way.

Wall Street Paper

Each and every day, with the exception of Sunday, paper produced by Wall Street firms is delivered to people around the country, in each and every state, on each and every street. In fact, you might be one of those people receiving some of that paper. That will certainly be the case if you decide to become an investor or subscribe to a personal finance magazine. (Magazines will often sell the names and addresses of subscribers to list brokers, who in turn will sell the information to stockbrokers looking for potential investors.)

And not all of those words that Wall Street is sending out are on paper. If you're an investor, it's likely that you can sign up to receive electronic copies of your monthly and quarterly statements. Many firms are now encouraging their customers to go electronic, which saves the firms money on paper, printing, and postage.

Types of Paper

Wall Street can easily overwhelm you with its paper. That's why we recommend following Dave's method for classifying all paper produced by Wall Street into three types.

The first type of paper is junk mail. We suspect we don't need to explain junk mail. It's likely that you've opened a piece of junk mail once or twice in your life. The envelope is typically addressed to you or the current resident and the letter starts something like this: "Dear Mr. ____: How would you like to save millions of dollars in estate taxes…?" And if you haven't opened a piece of junk mail in your life, we liken it to pornography—you'll know it when you see it. You should immediately deposit that mail into the circular file. Do not pass "go," do not collect your million dollars, do not be tempted to go to this or that seminar to save millions of dollars in estate taxes.

You're especially prone to getting this kind of mail if you've ever purchased an investment (your name goes to a list broker) or if you live in a nice neighborhood. Time was when rookie stockbrokers would use something called the Cole's directory to prospect for wealthy clients. The Cole's is like the white pages, but instead of listing names in alphabetical order, it lists streets, followed by names. And next to the street name is a little letter, indicating whether it's a rich street or a poor street. Needless to say, whether they're using Cole's or newer tools, the rookie brokers send lots of direct mail to people living on the "A" streets. Also needless to say, most of the people on the "A" streets already have relationships with two or three financial advisors or happen to be financial advisors themselves.

The next type of paper produced by Wall Street is what Dave refers to as the to-be-looked-at type. Typically, this paper is worth reading, but not worth keeping forever. It might be a reprint of an article that your broker thought you might enjoy, like the one that tells you how to bump off your spouse without fear of being caught (just kidding!), or it might be an analyst's research report on the company you are interested in buying. Wall Street is fond of this type of paper. It's the stuff Wall Streeters often refer to as "value added." It's stuff brokers send to persuade you to invest or to switch brokers.

But in the end, it's just stuff. In fact, from a paper management point of view, Dave considers this type of paper to be the most dangerous of all. It accumulates, the way dust bunnies do under your bed. And you and your spouse certainly don't need to get into arguments over whether you have to save it and you certainly don't have to rent a storage garage for the piles of paper that accumulate. Dave (OK, so it's really his wife) uses something called the three-inch system. When the pile gets higher than three inches, out it goes. Bob has a friend who uses a similar system. Once the pile gets too high, he takes the bottom half and throws it out.

Pile 1: Junk stuff to scan and trash

Marketing letters
Retail fliers
Mini newsletters with those no-lose ideas
Quarterly stock and mutual fund reports
Credit card offers

Pile 2: I want to get to that stuff when I have time

Magazines
Research

Catalogues
Books to read
Articles of interest

Pile 3: Essential stuff I need to file so I don't lose it

Bank statements
Investment accounts
Retirement things
Bills
Tax information

The final type of paper Wall Street sends out is the stuff people need to keep for review or tax reporting purposes. For every account that you have, you'll typically receive a quarterly statement that details the activity in your account. That activity might include purchases, sales, dividends, stock splits, and the like. In some cases, the statement will tell you how much money was in your account at the end of the previous quarter and the value of your account at the end of the most recent quarter.

Wall Street has never had an easy time of doing this, though, in part because it hates telling people if they've lost money. (Customers who lose money typically blame the broker. In fact, there's an old saying on Wall Street that goes something like this: if the stock goes up, it was the customer's pick; if the stock goes down, it was the broker's fault.) Bob knows several firms that produce a statement that details the number of shares the customer owns and the price of those shares—but not the total value of the account. To be fair, not all firms are afraid of telling their customers whether they lost or made money over the past quarter. In fact, American Century actually prints the value and the percent gain or loss since the investor got into the fund.

You can use these statements to review whether performance is meeting, exceeding, or falling short of expectations. Brokers will typically do this on a quarterly or annual basis for their best clients. Investors who don't have a broker will typically do this for themselves, using a personal finance software program.

The other important thing about statements is this: they're the only evidence you've got to prove you have money in investments.

There is absolutely nothing else to show evidence of your intangible assets.

For taxes, Wall Street produces several documents. One is called a **1099-DIV**. That's the form brokerage firms send to you and the IRS stating the amount of dividends this or that company paid to you. Then there's something called the **1099-INT**, which describes how much interest someone paid you, and then there's the form that details your capital gains, if you're lucky to have any of those. You might also get one or more of the following:

- **Form 1099-R:** report to recipients of distributions from pensions, annuities, profit-sharing and retirement plans, IRAs, insurance contracts, etc.
- **Form 1099-B:** report on proceeds from broker or barter exchange transactions
- **Form 1099-OID:** report to recipients of interest that is treated as original issue discount

You'll need to keep those documents in a safe place for the fun time when you or your accountant try to figure out how much you might owe Uncle Sam. Then you'll want to keep that stuff around in the basement or attic for a few years, just in case you get audited.

Keeping Good Records

No, we're not talking about the Beatles White Album and other relics from the Age of Vinyl that you've got piled up here and there. We're talking about how you deal with those piles of the third type of paper that Wall Street produces.

First, the **financial statements**. The financial statements contain information about the stuff you own but can't really touch—your stocks and mutual funds. These are pieces of paper that say you own X hundred shares of something and it's worth Y gabillion dollars (wishful thinking). The statements will often contain lots of details, so much that we could probably write a whole 'nother book just on that subject. First, there's ownership information, the details of the specific ownership: single name, trust name, custodian, jointly held, or other. Then, there's information particular to the type of account.

The financial statements that contain information about your intangible assets can be broken down into **taxable accounts** and **tax-exempt accounts**. It's important to understand the difference between these categories of statements because they're handled very differently for income taxes and estate tax planning purposes. So keep them separate, stupid.

The taxable accounts need the most yearly attention. Those are things like your investment accounts, checking accounts, savings accounts, and company stock purchase plans. You even need to report the income earned from tax-free bonds even if you don't have to pay taxes.

If you take a **distribution** from tax-deferred accounts, such as an IRA, tax-deferred annuity, life insurance, 401(k), or any other pension accounts, you will have to report the amount to the IRS.

Why So Much Paper?

There are several reasons why Wall Street is fond of paperwork.

One reason is to make sure there's proof of ownership. This is protection for you, the investor.

Another reason is to document all buying and selling activity. This is protection for the brokerage firms against charges of churning and unsuitable investments. (**Churning** is when a broker trades excessively in a client's account, to maximize commissions, without regard for the financial interests of the client. As you might guess, that's a violation of the rules set by the National Association of Securities Dealers. **Unsuitable investments** are, well, investments that are inappropriate for a specific customer in terms of depth of investment experience, net worth, annual income, investment objectives, and other factors.) That's why a **trade confirm**—the paper that confirms the sale and purchase of a security—typically states whether the trade was **solicited** or **unsolicited**. A solicited trade is when the broker asks you to buy or sell something. An unsolicited trade is when you ask the broker to buy or sell something. It may not sound like a big difference, but believe us, it is.

The third reason Wall Street produces paper is because it's required. The IRS wants to keep track as best it can of all the money it should be receiving. So, as we mentioned, come tax time, Wall Street sends out stuff in duplicate—one for you and one for Uncle Sam.

The IRS wants Wall Street to help investors establish the **cost basis** of what they buy. (That's the purchase price, including commissions and other expenses.) That way, when investors sell this or that security, they can determine whether they made or lost money. If they make money, they'll owe taxes on the capital gain. If they lose money, they get to take a modest deduction. All this stuff is reported on the 1099-B.

Determining cost basis, by the way, is the worst part of Wall Street. It's hard to do unless you're a math whiz. It's especially hard if you sign up for a **dividend reinvestment plan** (DRIP). With a DRIP plan—a term that's as redundant as "ATM machine" or "PIN number"—an investor buys a preset value of stock each month. So, one quarter the stock is $10 a share, the next it's $11, and the next it's $12. When the investor goes to sell the stock, he or she has to determine the cost basis for the stock sold.

File This

Some people are overwhelmed by financial documents. They stuff old tax forms and paid bills and warranties and insurance policies into desk drawers or shoeboxes or grocery bags.

If you're among these paper-challenged people, here's a little list of all the files you should create to help you organize your life. And, if you decide to become an investor, it will definitely help you handle the paper blizzard that will result from dealing with Wall Street.

1. Tax Information
   Old tax returns and backup support
   Cost basis information on investments
2. Banking Statements
3. Investments
   Mutual fund statements, investment accounts, private investments and loans, savings bonds, limited partnerships, collectibles, investment real estate
4. Insurance
   Life

Medical
Homeowner's
Auto
Disability

5. Credit Card Statements
   Visa, MasterCard, Discover, American Express, retailers
6. Tangible Assets
   Home mortgage records
   Automobiles
   Recreational vehicles
   Home projects
7. Warranties
8. Personal
   Wish list
   Where assets held
   People to contact
9. Bills
10. Work Information
    401(k) or retirement statements
    Year-end benefits summary
    Stock purchase and option plans
    Employee contracts

Here are a couple of pointers on the system.

First of all, you may notice that we did not do a "miscellaneous" file. That's because it's deadly; it will be the weakest link in the whole system and will probably end up being the biggest file that you can't find anything in.

In your tax folder, you need to always keep the original cost of anything you buy. Every time you buy a security, you get a confirmation slip. Keep that in the file; then, when you sell the security you'll have it at your fingertips come reporting time, so you have the cost data immediately accessible. Also in your tax folder you should keep the most recent tax return, so it's handy. Returns for previous years (you should keep at least the last seven years' returns) should go into storage: get an old shoebox or a $2 plastic container (the one with your mother-in-law's name written on it with indelible ink) and stick those old returns in the cellar. If you own mutual funds or reinvest dividends, then you should also have a permanent file for tax purposes, because you have to account for every dividend that's reinvested from the day you bought the fund or stock. Your adjusted cost (the cost basis) and adds all the dividends over the years so you don't pay taxes twice.

Your tangible assets file is for keeping all titles—or you can store them in a fireproof lock box. If you don't have a title or an updated statement (within the last six months to a year) to show ownership of any possessions worth more than $500 (or any other figure that makes sense to you), take a picture of each of those possessions or videotape them all. In case of a disaster, this evidence will help you minimize your losses. You should also keep your home mortgage records and bills for any home projects that increase the cost basis. (You'll thank us when you sell your house.)

The personal file is really key. You should maintain on one piece of paper a list of where all your assets are being held (including account numbers and addresses) and the contact person and phone number. This too you should put in a box, just in case a disaster hits and you lose all your records or your number gets called.

Yes, this is the 21st century and a whole lot of stuff is stored electronically. It might make sense for you to buy a personal finance software program that can help you keep track of a lot of these records. The two big sellers are Intuit Quicken and Microsoft Money. They're both good programs and can make the filing on the investment stuff a lot easier. Lots of times the software is even free when you buy a computer. Imagine spending $2,000 so you can get a $29 software program. (But, honey, it was free with the computer!)

The Government Take on Profits

One third of your working day goes to pay federal, state, and local taxes. Or, put another way, if you're the average U.S. taxpayer, you had to work until May 3, 2001 to pay your 2000 taxes (national Tax Freedom Day).

But nobody is really average. A lot of us are making less than the average taxpayer and consequently paying less in taxes, while many of us are making more and paying more. Figure 16-1 showswho pays the taxes, according to a 1998 study:

% of Taxpayers	% Share of Total AGI*	% Share of Taxes	Average Tax Rate
Top 1%	18.5%	34.8%	27.1%
Top 5%	32.9%	53.8%	23.6%
Top 10%	43.8%	65.0%	21.4%
Top 25%	65.6%	82.7%	18.2%
Top 50%	86.3%	86.3%	18.2%
Bottom 50%	13.7%	4.2%	4.4%

*Adjusted Gross Income

Figure 16-1. Who pays the taxes

So, in general, the more money you make, the larger the piece of the pie you pay. That's a pretty good case for keeping up with the tax laws and paying only your fair share. The place to start here is to understand some of the jargon the IRS throws at you when it comes to your investments and deductions.

Understanding the 1040 is a good place to start. There are 69 lines on the standard 1040 return. We obviously can't go over all of them, but here are some that you ought to focus on a bit:

Line 7 is for wages. It would sure be nice to have a ton of these, even if you have to pay Uncle Sam up to 39.6% of your income. You can, by the way, reduce wages by taking advantage of things at work like a 401(k) plan, a flexible-spending account, or a non-qualified plan. The latter provides big tax deferrals for higher-ups in the company.

Lines 8a and 8b are for interest, both taxable and tax-free. If you need income and are in a 28% bracket (taxable income over $43,850 if filing jointly or $26,250 if single), then you should probably have a lot more in tax-free stuff than in taxable.

Line 13 is your schedule D. You better get used to this form if you own stocks or mutual funds in taxable accounts.

You've got to keep good records here, but this should also be a prelude to year-end selling where you can sell your losers and take the tax losses. Each year you can take advantage of net losses up to $3,000.

Line 23, IRA deduction, is where you might be able to throw a little more into your retirement before the taxman takes it forever. There are strict guidelines here in terms of who qualifies for a tax-deductible IRA, but check out the new Roth IRAs to see if you can open an account and never ever have to pay taxes on the income when you take it out.

Line 33, Adjusted Gross Income (AGI), tells how awesome or puny you are when it comes to your earning power. It's used for a lot of other calculations regarding taxes due for other things. Basically, the rest of the lines on the tax return are to reduce to lessen your IRS burden by finding deductions to reduce line 33.

Line 36 is the itemized deduction area, where you take off a standard deduction ($7,200 married filing jointly or $4,300 single) or, if your itemized deductions are higher than this figure, use the higher figure. They include things like medical expenses, taxes, interest deductions and charitable contributions.

Line 39 Taxable Income (TI) is just your AGI minus your itemized or standard deductions and your personal exemptions.

Lines 66a and 68 are truly the bottom line, because 66a is how much the IRS owes you because you've overpaid and 68 is what you owe Uncle, even though he's already received the lion's share from your paycheck deductions through the year.

The IRS and Your Investments

There are a number of ways the government treats (and shares) the profits from your investment portfolio. If your money is in a **qualified** retirement plan, then the only concern you really have is when you take the money out. With the exception of the fairly recent

Roth IRA, it all gets taxed at whatever your tax bracket is. If you make the mistake of taking the money out before age 59½, then you could face a 10% penalty, unless you use some tricky exceptions to sidestep around the tax whack. The **non-qualified** money (retirement stuff that's not tax-deferred) also faces taxes of many shapes and sizes, depending on the type of investment. So it's best that we give you a little water torture here to see how the feds get their share.

Stocks and bonds are governed by the capital gains tax. Your tax is figured out primarily on two factors: the time you held the investment and your personal tax bracket. If you bought and sold a security within a year, your profit is considered a **short-term capital gain** and is taxed at the rate of your incremental tax bracket. The highest bracket is 39.6%, the rate you pay if you earn more than $288,350 (for joint or single filers in 2000). If you held the security for longer than a year, what you earned is taxed as a **long-term capital gain**. If your tax bracket is 15% (under $43,850 for joint filers and under $26,250 for singles in 2000) or lower, then you pay a maximum 10% tax on your profits. If you're in a 28% bracket or higher (taxable income is over $43,850 jointly or over $26,250 single in 2000), then the maximum rate on long-term capital gains is 20%.

(At one point they even had a mid-term capital gain, which drove everyone nuts. Fortunately, with the Taxpayer Relief Act of 1997 they got rid of it.)

Be aware that in 2001 a really long-term capital gains tax kicks in, for profits from assets held over five years. It makes the maximum tax rate 18%—if they don't change the rules by 2005, when it really takes effect.

Here are a couple of points to keep in mind. You must be sure to include all the commissions you've paid on the buys and sells when you calculate the net gain of each of your transactions. If you have a bunch of transactions, then you have to net them out to a final figure. The maximum loss you can take each year is only $3,000. If you really blow up and have a lot of losses in a given year, then you can carry them over to subsequent years indefinitely—well, as long as you're alive and filing a tax return. The form you to use is Schedule D, Capital Gains and Losses. If you want to really learn this stuff, then get IRS Publication 544, Sales and Other Dispositions of Assets. You can download it from the IRS Web site, www.irs.gov, or call 800 829-3676.

Mutual Funds: Same but Different

Mutual funds suffer through the same capital gain and loss rules as straight stocks and bonds. But there's an important difference: even if you don't sell any shares of a fund in a given year, stocks are bought and sold within the portfolio and the gains or losses are passed on to you the shareholder.

The average turnover of equities in the Morningstar universe in 2000 was 112% (theoretically bought and sold 56 stocks of a 100-stock portfolio), which opens up a lot of holes for taxes to be sucked out. So you get taxed on transactions every year and you have no control over it. You can call up your broker or the mutual fund company to try and get some idea what that number is, but unless you want to cash in the fund and have to pay taxes on all the gains you've made since buying into the fund, this information is almost irrelevant.

What matters is your timing. If you're planning on buying a mutual fund near the end of the year, you need to find out when the year-end dividend is going to be paid. If you buy the fund and it declares a dividend right away, you'll have to pay taxes on a whole year's worth of capital gains even though you just bought the fund.

Don't forget, too, that when you sell the fund, you have to keep records not just on what you put into the fund initially (original cost basis) but also on all the dividends that you've received over the years (adjusted cost basis) even if you reinvested them. If you neglect to add all the dividends over the years, relax: you won't incur the wrath of Uncle Sam, because you'll be allowing him to tax you twice on the same money.

There are four methods that you can add up your basis: specific shares identified, first in first out (FIFO), single category average cost, and double category average cost. We're not going to go off on a diatribe about this, so go see H&R Block or get hold of IRS Publication 564, Mutual Fund Distributions, if you need to know more about calculating your adjusted cost basis or you're suffering from insomnia.

Other Investments

Investment real estate is pretty tricky—beyond the scope of this book. There's a 25% capital gain tax on real estate investments, so it can cost not to know all the ins and outs. If you invest in real estate, you'll probably need some help, so at least be sure to get IRS Publication 544.

Interest and dividend payments from stocks, bonds, or mutual funds are taxed as ordinary income at whatever your tax bracket is. It all shows up on your 1099 dividend and interest form from the companies that hold the securities. If you lose one of these forms and forget to declare the income, rest assured the IRS will find you!

Government bond income from direct U.S. treasury securities gives you an edge with state taxes, because the income is tax-exempt, depending on your state income tax laws. This also includes a number of government agency securities, like the Federal Farm Credit Banks (FFCB), the Tennessee Valley Authority (TVA), the Federal Home Loan Bank System, and the Student Loan Marketing Association (Sallie Mae).

Tax-free municipal bonds are pretty much self-explanatory. The interest that they pay, usually every six months, the federal government does not tax. If you buy a municipal bond from your home state, interest will be exempt from state taxes as well. If you're in a 31% federal bracket and a 5% state bracket, a 5% yield with no taxes due is like 7.8% taxable equivalent.

Here's the formula for comparing yields:

rate of tax-free return ÷ (1 - your tax bracket)

So, if you're in the 28% federal tax bracket, a taxable security would have to yield at least 8.3% to match or beat a 6% yield on a municipal security (.06 ÷ .72 [1-.28]). If you're in the 31% bracket, a taxable security would have to yield at least 8.7% (.06 ÷ .69 [1-.31]) before it would be preferable to that tax-exempt yield of 6%.

One more thing to keep in mind here. As you play around with the figures, just be aware that some bonds are subject to the AMT.

AMT—the **alternative minimum tax**—is a whopper if you earn a lot of money and have a lot of items that the government wants to get you for. After you figure out all your taxes, the government says, "Wait just one minute, we want you to calculate them another way and see if we can squeeze more out of you." It looks at things like capital gains, lots of tax-free income, a lot of expenses, a high state tax liability, or a bunch of stock options. The tax is meant to hit higher-earning taxpayers but it can kick in if your income is as low as $22,500. Get a good tax advisor if the AMT applies to you.

Tax-deferred annuities are just investments sponsored by insurance companies that allow you—yeah, you guessed it!—to defer taxes. These are not to be confused with certain qualified annuities that are really retirement plans that allow you to put pre-tax money into them. These non-qualified annuities are for money you've already paid income tax on. Years ago the smart and strong insurance companies lobbied to allow people to put money away tax-deferred so they could have a supplement to their retirement in case their pension plans never kicked in. The government says that if you put your money into one of these contracts, then all the earnings will be tax-deferred. You've got your choice of flavors: **fixed** annuity (fixed dollar payments to the annuitant for the term of the contract) and **variable** annuity (payments to the annuitant depend on the performance of the managed portfolio.) If you take the money out before age 59½, there's a 10% penalty on the earnings. After that age, all the dollars coming out will be taxed as ordinary income: you won't benefit from lower capital gains rates. The original principal is not taxed, so if you put in $50,000 and it grew to $100,000, when you cashed it in you would pay taxes on $50,000 of appreciation.

Life insurance cash values are also tax-deferred and can pay a fixed or variable rate. You can even borrow the money out to use. If you decided to cash in, you would pay taxes on your withdrawals of everything above the premiums you paid over the life of the policy. If you put in $10,000 over the years in premium payments and the cash value was worth $15,000, then if you cashed in you would pay taxes on $5,000 at ordinary income rates.

Real estate limited partnerships are direct real estate interests where general partners run the show of what real estate to buy and manage and the limited partners are passive investors who put up the cash to buy the real estate. Investors get tax benefits that flow through to a limited partner. Each year you have a **K-1 form** that deciphers the income, capital gains, and basis of the partnership.

Reasons for Records

Taxes are the main reason that people force themselves to keep decent records. It's a pretty good incentive to know that you could go to jail if you were trying to beat the IRS. (Don't forget they put Al Capone away. Think about it: after years of violent crimes, the most notorious gangster in history went to prison for tax evasion.)

Yet the most important record keeping is the performance of your investments. Unfortunately, not many people keep records of this. The standard formula is actually pretty simple. It just factors in your beginning market value (BMV), your ending market value (EMV), your net additions and withdrawals, and some time frame.

$$\frac{\text{EMV} - \text{BMV} - (\text{contributions} - \text{withdrawals})}{\text{BMV} + 1/2\ (\text{contributions} - \text{withdrawals})}$$

(Dividing by 1/2 assumes that you invested and withdrew at the halfway point of whatever time frame you're calculating.)

Try doing this at least once a year on all your investments. If you have an advisor, then force him or her to do it—or find a new one. Then just compare the performance against the benchmarks that your portfolio is most like—things like the Dow Jones Industrial Average (30 actively traded blue chip stocks), the Standard and Poor 500 (the 500 most representative companies of the economy), the Russell 2000 (small companies), the Morgan Stanley EAFE (Europe, Australasia, Far East) index (international), the money market yields (short-term guaranteed investments), or the Lehman Brothers bond index (bonds).

If you do this, you should be able to turn your records into profits through buying and selling investments more wisely. And if your figures are better than the figures chalked up by the folks who do it for a living, there might be a job waiting for you on Wall

Street. And then you can hand your decoding ring and this book to your baby sister.

Epilogue

Truth be told, decoding Wall Street is a lifelong adventure. You can't do it in an hour, or a day, or even a month. In fact, just when you think you've got it figured out, the folks on Wall Street invent a new investment vehicle or coin a new investment term. In fact, as Dave and Bob researched this book, we scrubbed and scoured every investment dictionary and website we could find, including the ever-popular Barron's Dictionary of Finance and Investment Terms. And in that book, among the more than 5,000 terms defined and explained was the following entry: **Bo Derek stock.**

Hmm, we thought. What could that be? A pretty stock, a well-endowed stock, a female stock? Truth be told, we—despite our years in the business—had never heard of the term before, We read on. "Bo Derek Stock: perfect stock with an exemplary record of earnings growth, product quality, and stock price appreciation. These stocks are named after the movie *10* in which Bo Derek was depicted as the perfect woman." Now that movie, which was released in 1979, is perhaps little known by the breed of traders, brokers, and investment bankers who currently work on Wall Street so we doubt anyone uses that term today.

Indeed, today, people on Wall Street are more inclined to talk about the affluent investor, or what in private they refer to as **fat cat**, which *Ticker*, a trade magazine for stockbrokers, defines as "a high net-worth investor who lives off interest and dividends, and receives special treatment from advisors."

So if by chance your broker calls you a "fat cat" next time you're chatting, you'll now know what the heck he's talking about. You've decoded his language, you've climbed the Wall (as in Street), you speak the language. You've decoded Wall Street. Congratulations.

Index

Index

Index

Index

Index

Index

J

K

L

Index

Index

Index

S

Index

Index